Reference Service

Reference Service

An Annotated Bibliographic Guide

Marjorie E. Murfin

Lubomyr R. Wynar

1977

Libraries Unlimited, Inc.
Littleton, Colo.

LIBRARIES UNLIMITED, INC.
P.O. Box 263
Littleton, Colorado 80160

Library of Congress Cataloging in Publication Data

Murfin, Marjorie E   1930-
    Reference service.

    Includes index.
    1. Reference services (Libraries)—Bibliography.
I. Wynar, Lubomyr Roman, 1932-   joint author.
II. Title.
Z711.M86   016.0255'2   76-54879
ISBN 0-87287-132-0

TABLE OF CONTENTS

INTRODUCTION

One hundred years ago Samuel Swett Green (1837-1918), then librarian of the Free Public Library of Worcester, published an article in the first issue of *Library Journal* (November 1876) entitled "Personal Relations between Librarians and Readers." This article was based on the report Green had presented to the participants of the founding convention of the American Library Association held in Philadelphia in 1876. In it Green advocated the importance of personal service and guidance to the library patron. Green's service-oriented philosophy of the library served as the foundation for the development of the theory and practice of reference librarianship in following years. Thus, 1876 is to be regarded as a crucial date in the historical development of American librarianship; it was in this year that Dewey and others founded the American Library Association and that Green laid the solid foundation for reference service in American libraries. Since that year, a number of distinguished librarians and library educators have contributed to the development of sound reference concepts and theories that have been applied to daily operations in academic, public, school, and special libraries in this country. Such names as Otis Robinson, Justin Winsor, Melvil Dewey, John Cotton Dana, James I. Wyer, Jesse H. Shera, and Samuel Rothstein are just a few of the many who contributed directly to the dynamic concept of reference librarianship. Today, reference services constitute the major function within any library, and the whole library operation is considered as part of the information reference network.

This annotated bibliographical guide to reference service and the reference process constitutes the first of its kind in this field. Aimed at reference librarians, library administrators, information specialists, library educators, and students, it was compiled with the hope that it will assist them in gathering information, facts and sources, and also in evaluation, planning, decision-making, solving daily problems, and expanding reference services in their libraries. Most importantly, it is hoped that this attempt to gather together in one place the record of the profession's accumulated knowledge may help to stimulate needed research directed toward the improvement of present reference services and the development of new services. It should also serve library school faculty as a working tool for designing new courses.

It is felt that this bibliographical work will prove to be an essential guide in professional library literature and will also serve as a permanent tribute to the 100th anniversary of the American Library Association and the development of reference services in American libraries.

SCOPE

This guide consists of 14 separate chapters covering the multidimensional aspects of reference service and the reference process. Chapter 1 covers the historical development of reference services, including a section on bibliographical and general works. Chapter 2, which deals with the theory and philosophy of reference librarianship, includes general works as well as publications related to information theory, communication theory, and reference process theory. Chapter 3 covers teaching of reference courses, and Chapter 4 includes works on reference librarians and their qualities and characteristics. Chapter 5, dedicated to reference service, has separate sections on the administration of reference services, subject specialists and generalists, centralized and decentralized reference service, in-service training, nonprofessional personnel and their duties, and other relevant topics. Chapter 6 covers reference service in academic, public, school, and special libraries, and Chapter 7 treats special types of reference service (telephone, mail, current awareness services, etc.). Chapter 8 lists works on basic services to special groups, including the handicapped. Chapter 9 covers the reference process, emphasizing communication and the reference interface, typology of reference questions, various aspects of search strategy, and library users. Chapter 10 treats sources of information, with separate sections on the organization and administration of reference collections, evaluation and selection of reference materials, the card catalog, and human resources in reference service. Chapter 11 covers general research, and measurement and evaluation of reference related to all types of libraries, and Chapter 12 deals with cooperative reference services. Chapter 13 treats information centers and services, and Chapter 14 covers information science and information retrieval on a highly selective basis.

It should be stressed that this guide is limited to comprehensive coverage of direct reference service and the reference process. The present-day reference librarian has acquired a vast number of areas of concern and participates in a wide variety of activities and supportive services. The literature on these supportive or auxiliary reference services is distinct and voluminous in its own right. Adequate bibliographies exist in many of these areas, so these topics are not covered in the present bibliography. Thus, interlibrary loan and translation services have been omitted.

Bibliography has not been treated as a separate subject area but is included as it relates to reference librarianship or reference service. Library instruction, as a separate program, has been omitted; it is included, however, when it is related to direct reference service. Abstracting and indexing, as a separate subject, has been omitted but is included when it is related to reference librarianship or reference service. In all, there are 1,258 citations.

TIME COVERAGE

The time span covered begins with Samuel Swett Green's article in 1876 and continues through 1975.

COMPREHENSIVENESS

The authors have attempted to make this work as comprehensive as possible for direct reference service and the reference process. Few works that relate directly to these subject areas have been omitted, with the exceptions noted in the paragraph below.

Selectivity has been exercised in the section on "Information Retrieval," because of the voluminous literature published. Items of most value to reference service have been included. The same selectivity has been exercised in the sections "Current Awareness Service," "Users," "The Card Catalog," "Cooperative Reference Service," and "Information Centers and Services." Introductions to each section provide brief scope notes in regard to subject coverage and selectivity.

SOURCES CONSULTED

Library Literature has been consulted from 1921 through 1975 under all topics relevant to those listed in the table of contents. The same procedure has been followed in *Library Science Abstracts*, later *Library and Information Science Abstracts*, 1950 through 1975, and *Research in Education* (ERIC), now *Resources in Education*, 1966 through 1975. A computerized search of the ERIC data base has also been done under "library reference services." For location of theses and dissertations, *Library Literature* has been consulted from 1921 through 1975 under "library schools—theses." Also consulted were *Dissertation Abstracts International*, 1972 through 1975, and Gail Schlacter and Dennis Thomison's *Library Science Dissertations, 1925-1972* (Littleton, Colorado, Libraries Unlimited, 1974).

In addition, the following periodicals have been examined: *RQ*, 1966-1975; *Library Quarterly*, 1930-1975; *Wilson Library Bulletin*, 1940-1975; *Library Trends*, 1960-1975; *Journal of Education for Librarianship*, 1960-1975; *ALA Bulletin*, later *American Libraries*, 1960-1975; and *Library Journal*, 1965-1975.

Major bibliographical surveys and reference textbooks were also useful in locating relevant citations. It is not possible to list all of them here, with all the additional bibliographical sources that were consulted. However, a record of these sources can be found in the introduction to each subject section, where the most helpful bibliographical sources for that particular area are listed.

ANNOTATIONS

Annotations, which are descriptive and informative, attempt to include the following information whenever possible: 1) purpose of the work; 2) topics covered; 3) key concepts and ideas; 4) key information, facts, statistics, results, findings, etc.; 5) author's viewpoint; 6) conclusions. In the majority of cases, materials listed were personally examined. In cases where this was not possible, existing information was drawn on for preparation of annotations. Also included are a very few relevant citations for which it was not possible to prepare annotations. In a few cases, works were considered to be of equal importance in several subject areas and are therefore listed and annotated under more than one topic.

ACKNOWLEDGMENTS

We would like to express our gratitude to Mary Smith of the Kent State University Libraries Reference Department for her help in locating and forwarding materials. Also of help have been the reference staffs of both Kent State University Libraries and Ohio State University Libraries.

M.E.M.
L.R.W.

June 1976

CHAPTER 1

THE EARLY HISTORY
OF REFERENCE SERVICE THROUGH 1920

See also: Chapter 2, Theory and Philosophy of Reference Service
Chapter 5, Reference Service

For purposes of this bibliography, the historical period of reference service is defined as extending to 1920. Works covered here are those of any publication date whose subject is reference work of this period. Also included are materials written through 1920 on the subject of reference work.

Most helpful in this area is Samuel Rothstein's *The Development of Reference Services Through Academic Traditions, Public Library Practice, and Special Librarianship* (Association of College and Research Libraries, 1955), which includes an extensive bibliography. The bibliography is divided into sections covering 1) definitions: research, research libraries, and reference service; 2) nineteenth century American scholarship and the rise of research; 3) the development of research libraries in the nineteenth century; 4) the genesis of reference service; 5) reference service in general research libraries before World War I: theories of reference service; 6) reference service in the general research library before World War I: organization and practice; 7) special libraries and the concept of amplified reference service; 8) legislative and municipal reference; 9) the development of industrial research in the twentieth century; 10) reference service for industrial research personnel; 11) reference service in the general research libraries, 1917-1940; 12) research service in the general libraries before World War II; 13) reference and research since 1940. Many annual reports, surveys, letters, and other unpublished materials are also included.

Bibliographical coverage of the history of reference work is also provided in Bohdan Wynar, *Introduction to Bibliography and Reference Work* (Rochester, N.Y., Libraries Unlimited, 1967).

BIBLIOGRAPHIES

1.   Cannons, H. G. T. **Bibliography of Library Economy**. Chicago, American Library Association, 1927. 680p.
"A classified index to the professional periodical literature in the English language relating to library economy, printing, methods of publishing, copyright, bibliography, etc., from 1876 to 1920." Section T, on the reference department, includes management, information desk, assisting readers, access to reference shelves, and college and

university reference libraries, relative functions, coordination, etc., of reference and lending departments. Articles are arranged within this section chronologically by year. Unannotated.

2. Harris, Michael F. **A Guide to Research in American Library History**. 2nd ed. Metuchen, N.J.: Scarecrow, 1974. 275p.

The first part of this book consists of three chapters discussing the state of the art in American library history, philosophy and methodology for research, and sources of information. The second part is an annotated bibliography of graduate research in American library history.

3. **Library and Information Science Abstracts**. London, The Library Association, 1950– . Bi-monthly.

An index arranged in classified order covering literature on library and information science in approximatey 280 U.S. and foreign periodicals in library science and related areas. Some of these periodicals are fully indexed, except for one-page articles, news items, and letters to the editor, while others are selectively indexed. Gives full bibliographical citations and abstracts for periodical articles and conference papers, but does not include books, theses and dissertations, or other materials. Includes author index and alphabetical subject index.

4. **Library Literature**. New York, Wilson, 1921– . Quarterly.

An author and subject index to the literature on library and information science in approximately 218 U.S. and foreign library science periodicals. These periodicals are fully indexed, and certain other periodicals covered by other Wilson indexes are scanned selectively for articles. In addition to periodical articles, it lists books, book reviews, conference papers, theses and dissertations, pamphlets, audiovisual materials, and occasional unpublished materials. Gives full bibliographical information. No annotations.

GENERAL WORKS

5. Adams, E. M., Jr. "A Study of Reference Librarianship in the American College: 1876-1955." Unpublished Master's thesis, East Texas State, 1956. 61p.

6. Ahern, Mary E., and others. "Reference Work with the General Public," *Public Libraries* 9:55-65 (February 1904).

Fifteen short articles from the early days of reference service discussing reference work in both college and public libraries. Covers such topics as qualities that reference librarians should possess, arrangement of the reference collection, and the educational function of the library. Also included are a number of criticisms and suggestions concerning reference work made by librarians and drawn from their own experiences.

7.   Bacon, Corrine. "Reference Work from the Librarian's Point of View,"
       Library Journal 27:927-932 (November 1902).
The author discusses the importance of reference work and gives the following
pointers on service: 1) be approachable, 2) be knowledgeable on a wide variety of
subjects, 3) be tactful, 4) be patient, 5) read newspapers regularly, 6) be accurate,
7) know your tools, 8) know your town and home area, 9) keep a sense of humor.
Describes three types of patrons—those who know what they want and are able to
express it, those who are timid and apologetic, and those who want you to do their
work for them.

8.   Bishop, William W. "The Amount of Help to Be Given to Readers,"
       Bulletin of the American Library Association 2:327-332 (September
       1908).
Discusses the wide differences in ability to use the library between different groups
of readers. Advocates the need for open shelves to bring users closer to books and
permit browsing. Most students know little about library use and professors fail to
teach these skills in class. Reference librarians should strive to educate readers in use
of the library. In regard to assistance to scholars, no limits should be set except
those of time and money. It would be desirable for more money and staff to be
provided for this purpose.

9.   Bishop, W. W. "The Theory of Reference Work," *ALA Bulletin* 9:134-139
       (June 1915).
The author argues that major aspects of a total philosophy of reference should
include 1) the library's attitude, 2) qualifications of reference librarians, 3) discussion
of the nature of reference service, 4) tools, and 5) quarters. He also discusses the
problem of specialist versus generalist. He advances the philosophy that the reference
librarian is the interpreter of the library whose function is not to locate information
for patrons but to assist them in locating information for themselves. Thus, it follows
that knowledge of the "machinery" is more important than knowledge of the topic.

10.   Briggs, Walter B. "Reference Work in Public and College Libraries: A
       Comparison and a Contrast," *Library Journal* 32:492-495 (November 1907).
Based on the author's experiences in both university and public libraries. Comparisons
are made of reference collections, readers, characteristics of questions asked, and
administration and functions of reference departments.

11.   Brindley, John. "The Legislative Reference Movement," *Iowa Journal of
       History and Politics* 7:132-141 (January 1909).
A scholarly study of the legislative reference movement, emphasizing the role of
Dr. Charles McCarthy of the Legislative Reference Department of Wisconsin.

12.   Child, William B. "Reference Work at the Columbia College Library,"
       Library Journal 16:298 (October 1891).
The author, speaking before the New York Library Club, defines reference as "the
assistance given by a librarian to readers in acquainting them with the intricacies of
the catalog, in answering questions, and, in short, doing anything and everything in
his power to facilitate access to the resources of the library in his charge."

13. Clapp, Verner W. "Three Ages of Reference Work," *Special Libraries* 57:379-384 (July-August 1966).

Reference work is reviewed in historical perspective, beginning with Spofford, Librarian of Congress, who, lacking tools available today, relied on his own personal knowledge of the Library's collection. Progress came with the continued production of new reference books. Computerization is now used to produce such tools as concordances and indexes. Computerized transmission promises to make materials readily available, whatever their location. This suggests the possibility of creating one reference library for large areas.

14. Clatworthy, L. M. "Reference Work," *Library Journal* 21:263-264 (June 1906).

The author considers the entire collection as the reference collection and the librarian as guide. Classification and cataloging are the foundations of reference work. Also stressed are the importance of educating patrons in the use of the library and in knowing the types of patrons who ask questions.

15. Crunden, Frederick. "Reports on Aids and Guides, August '83 to June '85," *Library Journal* 11:309-330 (August-September 1886).

The author, in his report to the American Library Association, describes a survey of 108 libraries where he found 53 giving "personal help." Reference service included assisting readers to the best books and to sources of information.

16. Cutter, C. A. "Proceedings of the Conference of Librarians, London, October, 1877, Sixth Sitting," *Library Journal* 2:278 (November-December 1877).

During this discussion Samuel Swett Green recommended that all readers should receive personal assistance. Cutter suggested that readers should be provided with annotated lists of new accessions to save librarians' time in advising of books of interest.

17. Dana, John Cotton. "Misdirection of Effort in Reference Work," *Public Libraries* 16:108-109 (March 1911).

This early article on reference suggests that the primary purpose of the reference librarian is to instruct rather than to provide answers to questions. Stresses that time should be spent on worthwhile questions rather than frivolous ones. The importance of questions can be judged by the following hierarchy: 1) promotion of new knowledge, 2) promotion of professional knowledge (business, the arts, etc.), 3) instruction of groups, 4) instruction of individuals, 5) quest for culture, 6) recreation, 7) frivolous.

18. Dudgeon, M. S. "The Scope and Purposes of Special Libraries," *Special Libraries* 3:129-133 (June 1912).

Considers the way in which the special library differs from the general reference library. The role of the special librarian includes collecting, summarizing, analyzing, grouping, and presenting data. Discusses special knowledge, techniques, and methods needed by special librarians.

19.   Fletcher, W. I. "Short Talk on the ABC of Reference Work," *Library Journal* 26:396-397 (July 1901).

The letters ABC represent the importance of the following elements in reference work: attendants, bibliographies, and classification and cataloging. Those readers with questions should come first to the attendant rather than being sent to the catalog. Bibliographies, or well-made lists of books and papers on a subject, are more effective than the subject catalog. Classification is also to be preferred to the subject catalog. The subject catalog is of little value; rather than trying to improve it, we should attempt to develop the bibliographical apparatus and guide readers in its use. The well-equipped, conscientious and devoted attendant is of first importance in this.

20.   Foster, William E. "Assistance to Readers," *Library Journal* 18:257 (July 1893).

Foster discusses five requirements needed for effective reference service and relates these to the Providence Public Library, emphasizing a carefully-chosen collection, classified and cataloged. Also stressed are open shelves and an experienced person at the information desk.

21.   Foster, William E. "Report on Aids and Guides to Readers, 1883," *Library Journal* 8:233-245 (September-October 1883).

Part of a series of reports submitted to the American Library Association describing reference tools such as lists, bulletins, and guides. Also discusses personal assistance to readers, noting with satisfaction that this service has increased in libraries all over the country.

22.   Freeman, Marilla. "Scientific Management and the Reference Department as a Bureau of Information," *ALA Bulletin* 7:331-336 (July 1913).

Discusses techniques for effective reference work in a smaller public library in light of the author's experience at the Goodwyn Institute Library. Advocates relying on the pamphlet file and newspaper clippings for current materials and mentions other sources of current information available at that time. Describes publicity for the reference department placed in street cars. Presents the philosophy that the public library should serve as an information and referral center.

23.   Green, Samuel Swett. "Libraries as Bureaus of Information," *Library Journal* 21:324-326 (July 1896).

Green discusses the ideal library where everyone with questions is helped to find answers. Use of interlibrary loan to find information is considered; the author advocates a philosophy of liberal service where every attempt is made to help the patron find answers. Examples are given to illustrate this kind of service.

24.   Green, Samuel Swett. "Personal Relations Between Librarians and Readers," *Library Journal* 1:74-81 (October 1876).

This article, one of the first advocating reference service, was based on a paper read by the author before a library conference in 1876. He suggested that friendly personal service be given to patrons of public libraries who need assistance in selecting, finding, and using materials. Some examples of reference assistance are given, and the author observes that reference service can increase library popularity and public support.

25.   Green, Samuel Swett. **The Public Library Movement in the United States, 1853-1893**. Boston, Boston Book Co., 1913. 336p.

Much is included here on the historical background of personal assistance to readers drawn from the author's own experience. Biographical sketches are given of early librarians such as Justin Winsor and William F. Poole.

26.   Hazeltine, Mary E. "Fundamentals of Reference Service," *Wisconsin Library Bulletin* 15:85-90 (April 1919).

This early work discusses the significance of reference service and its role in the library. The reference librarian must be familiar with both sources of information and the community. Practical suggestions are given for improved service.

27.   Kaplan, Louis. "The Early History of Reference Service in the United States," *Library Review* 83:286-290 (Autumn 1947).

Progress made in reference service from 1875 to 1900 is described. Kaplan remarks that the key librarians of this period were all men, and he discusses their part in the development of reference. He suggests reasons for the growth of reference service, such as the production of reference aids and the introduction of the Dewey system of cataloging and classification.

28.   Kaplan, Louis. **The Growth of Reference Service in the United States from 1876 to 1893**. Chicago, Publications Committee of the Association of College and Reference Libraries, 1952. 12p. (ACRL Monograph, No. 2).

This study considers in detail the progress of reference service from the time of its birth, beginning with the publication of Samuel Swett Green's paper, to the World Library Congress in 1893. He describes the library's change from a storehouse to a working institution and attributes growth of reference service to 1) staff assigned to reference work, 2) open shelves, 3) publication of guides and reference tools, 4) economic and intellectual changes in America.

29.   Kaplan, Louis. "Reference Services in University and Special Libraries Since 1900," *College and Research Libraries* 19:217-220 (May 1958).

This article considers how the concept of the reference librarian's function has changed during the twentieth century. In 1920 it began to be recognized that undergraduates needed reference assistance, and in 1930 Wyer advanced the desirability of subject specialization and the concept of the scholar-librarian. The Carnegie Corporation stressed the need for research librarians to assist scholars. Subject specialization was criticized by some as creating glorified research assistants or resulting in scholars rather than librarians. Kaplan advances the idea that it is most important to be first a librarian and then a scholar.

30.   Kitahara, Kunihiko. "The Early Development of Reference Work in Japanese Libraries, 1868-1920," *Library and Information Science* 8:17-49 (1970).

Describes how students returning from the United States in the late nineteenth century introduced reference methods. The Japanese library journal, begun in 1907, has contributed greatly to the development of reference. The Imperial Library made personal assistance available in the late nineteenth century, and other Japanese libraries now giving reference assistance are described.

31. Lapp, John A. "The Growth of a Big Idea," *Special Libraries* 9:157-159 (June 1918).

The author sees the emergence of a new concept of reference librarianship in special libraries, described as "the librarian-specialist, whose function is to gather information, condense and combine it, and interpret the results to the man on the spot."

32. McBride, M. "Reference Service for Congress before 1915." Unpublished Master's thesis, Drexel Institute of Technology, 1955. 76p.

33. Mudge, Isadore G. "History of the Columbia University Reference Department." Unpublished manuscript, New York, Columbia University, 1941.

Together with general historical development, this work gives descriptions of early techniques in reference work. Describes detailed procedures to be followed in locating different kinds of information, such as quotations, and locating specific materials, such as manuscripts.

34. Phelps, Rose B. "Reference Services in Public Libraries—The Last Quarter Century," *Wilson Library Bulletin* 32:281-285 (December 1957).

The last quarter century is surveyed and high points and landmarks, such as the Public Library Inquiry, are considered. There is discussion of the development of public library standards such as the Post-War Standards, with particular attention to reference service. A survey of reference librarians in public libraries should reveal the most important trends of this period. Cooperative reference service, interlibrary loan, and other improvements are considered. Publicity is helpful in bringing reference service to non-users who need it.

35. Poole, William F. "Conference of Librarians, Cincinnati, Ohio, May, 1882, 4th Session: Libraries and the Public," *Library Journal* 8:201 (July-August, 1882).

Samuel Swett Green advocates reference service for cultured and uncultured. Cutter, on the other hand, is still reluctant to give reference service but allows his assistants to do so for a fee. Poole expresses his pleasure in giving reference service but admits it is usually only given to privileged members of the community.

36. Powell, Walter. "The Reference Library," *Library Association Record* 2:77-86 (June 1924).

Discusses early principles for the development of reference service formulated by the Birmingham Committee. The reference library should be able to supply authoritative information on all subjects and answer all questions. Also considered are reference sources, subject classification, interlibrary loan, and subject sections.

37. Ranganathan, S. R. "Reference Service Through Four Centuries," *Library Herald* 9:87-93 (July-October 1966).

Considers reference service to be the supreme and ultimate purpose of a library and relates reference to the five laws of library science. Describes the beginning of reference service and the emergence of the concept of promoting the use of libraries. Covers the later developments of ready reference and reader's advisory service in public libraries. Discusses the latest developments in sophisticated techniques of documentation, particularly in relation to India.

38. "Reference Work in Libraries," *Library Journal* 16:297-300 (October 1891).

The first article specifically referring to reference work in the title. Includes papers on reference work at the Brooklyn Library, Pratt Institute Library, and Columbia College Library. All have open-shelf collections to give more time for staff to provide reader assistance, and all agree that aid should be given according to the degree of help required by the type of patron and question.

39. Richardson, E. C. **The Reference Department**. Chicago, American Library Association, 1911. 9p. (American Library Association Manual of Library Economy).

Covered here are definition of reference work, selection, activities and administration, systematic instruction in use of reference books, interlibrary reference and bibliography.

40. Rosenberg, Ida L. "Problems of a Reference Librarian," *Library Journal* 29: 120-123 (March 1904).

Considers difficulties facing reference librarians of the time. Supports the ideas of John Cotton Dana and notes that the paramount duty of the reference librarian is library instruction.

41. Rothstein, Samuel. "Development of Reference Services in American Research Libraries." Unpublished Master's thesis, University of Illinois, 1954. 281p.

42. Rothstein, Samuel. **The Development of Reference Services through Academic Traditions, Public Library Practice and Special Librarianship**. Chicago, Association of College and Reference Libraries, 1955. 124p. (ACRL Monographs, No. 14).

A lengthy study covering the development of reference service from 1875 to 1955. Considers definitions of reference work and covers such topics as the rise of research libraries, growth and organization of reference service, policies, practices, and patterns of service over the years. Covers academic, public, and special libraries. Relates the development of reference to social, political, cultural, economic, and technological factors and discusses these in the light of reference theory. A final chapter considers trends since 1940, including developments in documentation. Bibliography.

43.   Rothstein, Samuel. "The Development of the Concept of Reference
        Service in American Libraries, 1850-1900," *Library Quarterly* 23:1-15
        (January 1953).
The first section of this paper shows how personal assistance to the reader developed
from the stage where it was only a felt need to the point where it became a recognized part of library service. The second section traces the development of reference
service in the Providence Public Library.

44.   Spofford, Ainsworth R. **A Book for All Readers**. New York, G. P. Putnam's
        Sons, 1900. 509p.
A wide variety of aspects of library work are considered in 27 chapters by an early
librarian of Congress. Of particular interest is the chapter on "Aids to Readers,"
which considers the librarian as the "interpreter of the intellectual stores of the
library. It is a good and safe rule to let no opportunity of aiding a reader escape."
Emphasizes the intellectual stimulation of searching for information and the
benefits derived by the librarian from performing reference work. Discusses types
of information asked for by readers of this time and gives sample reference questions.
Describes how to locate answers in available reference books.

45.   Thompson, Madeline C. "History of the Reference Department of the
        University of Illinois Library." Unpublished Master's thesis, University of
        Illinois, 1942. 175p.
Describes how "personal assistance" built up to become a department on its own.
The formal organization of the Reference Department, in this case, followed three
years after the appointment of the first staff member.

46.   U. S. Bureau of Education. **Public Libraries in the United States of
        America: Their History, Condition and Management, Special Report,
        Part I**. Washington, D.C., U.S. Government Printing Office, 1876.
Three essays of importance to reference work are included here. In one essay,
Ainsworth Spofford lists important reference works and suggests that they should
be placed on open shelves. In another, Melvil Dewey presents his decimal classification and subject index. Another, by Charles Ammi Cutter, speaks out in favor of
the dictionary ctalog for quick reference.

47.   Van Valkenburg, Agnes. "How Far Should We Help the Public in Reference
        Work?" *Massachusetts Library Club Bulletin* 5:102-108 (July-October 1915).
The author speaks out for more generous aid to the reader on genuinely important
questions. Notes that due to shortage of personnel and heavy work loads, it would
not be possible to give "too much" help.

48.   Vitz, Carl. "Cleveland Experience with Departmentalized Reference
        Work," *Bulletin of the American Library Association* 9:169-174 (July
        1915).
The advantages and disadvantages of the newly organized subject departments are
discussed. Disadvantages were 1) subject librarians failed to use valuable general
sources no longer easily available, 2) interdisciplinary users were inconvenienced,

3) costs were increased. However, it was felt that service was, on the whole, much improved because it provided more research help to the "continuous worker in some special field."

49. Winsor, Justin. "Library Questions and Answers," *Library Journal* 3:159 (June 1878).

Techniques of answering readers' questions are discussed. The author feels that teaching is the primary function of reference work and that readers should be directed to books where they may find answers themselves.

CHAPTER 2

THEORY AND PHILOSOPHY
OF REFERENCE SERVICE

See also: Chapter 1, The Early History of Reference Service Through 1920
            Chapter 9, The Reference Process (Communication and the Reference
              Interface)
            Chapter 14, Information Retrieval (Information Retrieval and
              Reference Service); Search Strategies and the Subject Approach
              to Information; User Interaction)

Included in this chapter, "Theory and Philosophy of Reference Service," are
those works which discuss aspects of both theory and philosophy of reference
service. The section on information theory convers general theories of information science, including such aspects as information flow and transfer. The section
on communication and reference process theory covers general communication
theory and communication theory as related to the reference process, as well
as related theories and formulations of the reference process.

One of the most extensive bibliographies covering the broad area of theory and
philosophy is that found in Bernard Vavrek's *Communications and the Reference
Interface* (Pittsburgh, University of Pittsburgh Book Center, 1971). Other bibli-
ographies emphasizing communication theory can be found in Patrick Penland's
listed works. Overviews of reference theory and philosophy can be found in
William Katz's *Introduction to Reference Work*, 2nd ed.,Vol. 1 (New York,
McGraw-Hill, 1974) and Bohdan Wynar's *Introduction to Bibliography and
Reference Work* (Rochester, N.Y., Libraries Unlimited, 1967). Selected list-
ings on information theory are to be found in "Theory [of Information;
Information Retrieval; and Systems]" in *Bibliography of Research Relating to
the Communication of Scientific and Technical Information* (New Brunswick,
N.J., Rutgers University Press, Bureau of Information Science Research, Graduate
School of Library Science, 1967), pp. 49-57.

GENERAL WORKS

50.   Asp, William. "Search for Tomorrow; or Facing New Information Needs
        without Tears," *Minnesota Libraries* 23:316-322 (Autumn 1972).
The author discusses reference service in the future based on his own ideas and
experiences. Major areas covered are accessibility of reference and information
service, accountability of reference librarians, and the significance of new technology in the provision of information.

51.   Baily, F. W. "How Much Personal Assistance Should a Reference Librarian
      Give to Patrons?" *Wilson Library Bulletin* 4:11-14 (September 1929).
A number of aspects of level of service are discussed, but emphasis is given to type
of patron. The busiest person will need the most assistance and the most liberal
service, while groups such as students and housewives should be encouraged toward
self-help. Education of readers is stressed.

52.   Barnett, Abraham. "The University Student and the Reference Librarian,"
      College and Research Libraries 20:321-324 (July 1959).
The author stresses the importance of the educational function, by which he means
"sympathetic intellectual guidance," as a part of reference service. The immature
student needs self-confidence and motivation. "We should conduct a genuine search
on behalf of the student—but keep before us the educational value of the method of
search. . . . Reference searches are opportunities to acquaint students with various
forms of information." Other related sources can also be pointed out during this
process. Bibliographies should be prepared for graduate students in connection with
their classes. Educational functions such as these make the library a scene of successful learning for students.

53.   Bay, J. Christian. "Sources of Reference Work," *Bulletin of the Medical
      Library Association* 14:10-15 (July 1924).
The author criticizes the conservative theory of reference service and advocates that
mere "guidance" is inadequate. "Critically sifted" information is important and
reference librarians should not "merely indicate a mass of literature but illumine
it."

54.   Blake, Fay, and Edith Perlmutter. "Libraries in the Marketplace: Informa-
      tion Emporium or People's University?" *Library Journal* 99:108-111
      (January 15, 1974).
The author criticizes recent recommendations that libraries become "fee-based
supermarkets" by charging patrons rather than supporting themselves from tax
funds. Proponents of this view argue that this would increase productivity and
economic efficiency, convince users of the library's value, and ease competition
for public funds. The author considers that these views have no foundation either
socially or economically. Instead, we should try to improve service by utilizing
resources now available. New services are suggested that could be substituted for
traditional services in order to reach non-users.

55.   Brough, Kenneth J. "Personal Assistance to Readers." In *Scholar's
      Workshop*. Urbana, University of Illinois Press, 1953. pp. 142-159.
      (University of Illinois Contributions to Librarianship).
Traces library development from a storehouse to a working institution and relates
this to the development of reference. The nature and importance of reference work
are discussed. Personal assistance is considered in terms of its educational function.
The author believes that "bibliographical work on a straight service basis lies outside the field of reference work." Reference work should emphasize teaching and
there should be organized instruction in use of the library.

56.   Collison, R. L. W. "A National Reference Library Service." In Library
      Association, Public Libraries Conference, Harrogate, 1966. *Proceedings*.
      pp. 3-11.
Reference is discussed as a process that is carried out in all parts of the library.
Failure to realize this can often result in ineffectual and uneven service. A national
reference service would guarantee certain basic services at each public library service
point. Basic training should be given to all staff since they will encounter reference
problems throughout the library. An appendix includes a list of basic reference books
with prices.

57.   Craig, Florence S. "Care and Feeding of the Discriminating Reader," *Iowa
      Library Quarterly* 16:225-231 (October 1952).
The author advocates an active philosophy of reference service in which the reference
librarian helps the reader to preserve an open mind, to recognize distortions and
misinformation in mass media, and to look at all sides of controversial issues. The
reader must be encouraged to communicate his knowledge to others. An important
role of the librarian is to reinforce education. Librarians should go out into the
community and actively promote books and reading and encourage others to do this
also.

58.   Dana, John Cotton. "Misdirection of Effort in Reference Work," *Public
      Libraries* 16:108-109 (March 1911).
The author, who advocated the conservative theory of reference service, considered
that the duty of public librarians was to instruct patrons in the use of the library
rather than to find answers for them.

59.   Eatough, Judy. "Whither Reference?" *RQ* 11:206-208 (Spring 1972).
The functions of reference work are discussed and related to the *Minimum Standards for Public Library Systems, 1966*. Philosophies of minimum and maximum
service are considered and the reference librarian's role is related to the three vital
functions of the library.

60.   Emery, Richard. "Steps in Reference Theory," *Library Association Record*
      72:88-90 (March 1970).
Emery reviews philosophies based on amount and type of service, method, functions,
and various combinations of the above. He concludes that a philosophy of reference
should be based on past and present functions and methods and empirical evidence
should be drawn from the best current practice. This philosophical framework would
supply guidelines for immediate action and for future development.

61.   Freeman, Marilla. "Ideals in Reference Service," *Wilson Library Bulletin*
      7:244-245 (December 1932).
The author expresses a belief in liberal reference service and recommends that there
should be no negatives when giving reference service. Suggests that if an answer can't
be found, further suggestions should be provided. Often patrons can be given material
to look at while the reference librarian explores other sources.

62. Freides, Thelma. "Will the Real Reference Problem Please Stand Up?" *Library Journal* 91:2008-2012 (April 15, 1966).

The author discusses the opposing attitudes of Wallace Bonk's "title-centered" approach and Thomas Galvin's "reference interview" approach. Both Bonk's identification of basic sources and Galvin's "little socio-dramas" and "fake experiences" miss the true purpose of reference work, which is to interpret the total communication network to the user. This approach, which has been suggested by Shera and Egan, begins with the realization that comprehension of the problem is the first step toward finding an answer.

63. Galvin, Thomas. "Education of the New Reference Librarian," *Library Journal* 100:727-730 (April 15, 1975).

Observes that very few public, academic, or school libraries have developed their services to the point where the potential demands of the public are fully supplied. The new bibliographic tools and technologies have not resulted in correspondingly improved reference service. Efforts toward measurement and evaluation have not advanced. The library and reference education both remain materials-oriented rather than people-oriented. We must set new goals appropriate to enhanced capabilities of our present and future technologies. This should be the foundation for a "massive up-grading" of reference and information service. With the more stringent financial climate and demands for accountability, we can't continue to provide "more of the same" minimal service. We must set our goals higher even though we cannot yet provide higher-level service to everyone at the present time. Bibliographical, physical, and intellectual access are all important. Reference should not consist of handing a bibliographical reference to someone, but should include seeing that he locates the information and is able to utilize it. Libraries should be evaluated by quality of service statistics, as well as circulation statistics. Library school students must have a clear vision of the potential of full information delivery systems.

64. Horn, Roger. "Some Questions About Service," *RQ* 9:27-29 (Fall 1969).

The author raises the following questions central to a philosophy of reference service. "Do we have a moral obligation in reference service? Should we give people what they need or what they want? How do we know what people want? How can we tell their wants and needs apart? Shall we serve only those who ask?" He suggests we should be concerned about the substance of what we provide for our public. The library has various aims; it provides (as does, for example, a restaurant or the church) for both temporary wants and long-range needs.

65. King, Jack B., Herbert F. Johnson, and Anne Mavor. "What Future, Reference Librarian?" *RQ* 10:243-247 (Spring 1971).

The author suggests that reference librarians spend a large part of their time in the field working with library clientele. This concept is explained in terms of the Hamline Project and is illustrated by the case of a small businessman seeking information. It often takes a great deal of time for the user to go through the information-seeking process whereby he identifies his need, defines it, consults friends and tries other solutions, goes to the library, tries self-help, and finally consults the reference librarian. Solutions suggested by the Hamline Project are to move the reference librarians out into the college campus and to broaden the information base of the library. Description is given of how this can be done. Librarians in the field are in a position to help patrons identify information needs and to provide materials at a much earlier date than with traditional library service.

66.　Langley, Geoff. "A Reference Service for the Seventies," *Assistant Librarian* 63:5-6, 8, 10 (January 1970).
This article stresses the need for a National Information Service in Great Britain. Problems with local reference service are shortage of staff and the present Public Library Ladder career structure. In addition, to increase reference usefulness, the service must be publicized; but on the other hand, there are not sufficient facilities for increased use. A National Information Service might provide the solution for these problems.

67.　Learned, W. S. **The American Public Library and the Diffusion of Knowledge**. New York, Harcourt, 1924. 89p.
Dr. Learned, an early proponent of liberal reference service, stresses that all the library's resources should be used to render full service to each patron.

68.　McClure, Charles. "A Reference Theory of Specific Information Retrieval," *RQ* 13:207-212 (Spring 1974).
Reference theory, instead of being drawn from current practice, should be based on the answer to the following question: "What is the role of the library in the community and how can the reference librarian best fulfill this role?" The author advances that this role is dissemination of all types of information to the specific extent requested to all persons, using any and all sources of information retrieval. He discusses the background of reference theory, particularly in regard to the instruction versus information controversy. He argues that "for many patrons, instructional reference service is synonymous with confusion, wasted time and minimal results," and that all who desire information, regardless of level of culture and education, should receive it.

69.　McCombs, Charles F. **The Reference Department**. Chicago, American Library Association, 1929. 42p. (Manual of Library Economy, No. 22).
The author represents the moderate philosophy of reference service advocating a compromise between guidance and full information service. The moderate viewpoint recognizes the desirability of fulfilling requests related to worthy endeavors, but, on the other hand, realizes that librarians will not always have the time and resources to do so.

70.　Masuda, Minoru. [On Bishop's Theory of Reference Work] . (In Japanese). *Toshokan-Kai* 23:105-109 (September 1971).
Discusses W. Bishop's article, "Theory of Reference Work," with its advocacy of minimum reference service in its historical perspective. Notes that it seems old fashioned today when librarians must be specialists with a knowledge of the collections of other libraries.

71. Mesthene, Emmanuel. "Using Accumulated Knowledge." In Linderman, W., ed., *The Present Status and Future Prospects of Reference/Information Service*. Chicago, American Library Association, 1967. pp. 157-164.

Discusses the need for information centers which "sift through large masses of data, collect relevant data, review a field and distill information in a manner that goes to the heart of a technical situation." These people collect, assimilate, and transform information for new uses. The author comments that computers cannot perform pre-linguistic functions of managers such as perception, intuition, sensitivity, and courage. The starting point for any project is thinking or finding questions, while research is concerned with finding answers. It is here the new role of information specialist can be defined as one who is "collater, reviewer, compiler, abstracter, bibliographer, sifter, and distiller who collects, prepares, and cooks into acceptable food for thought." Followed by comments by Grieg Aspnes and discussion.

72. Petrof, Barbara. "Theory: The X Factor in Librarianship," *College and Research Libraries* 26:316-317 (July 1965).

Stresses the importance of research in developing a theoretical framework for librarianship. However, most research at the present time is practical and oriented toward the problems of one particular library rather than theoretical in nature. Thus, the development of theory through research may come from library educators rather than from those in the profession.

73. Pierce, P. A. "A Study of the Philosophy of Librarianship: A Review of the Relevant Literature, 1930-1950." Unpublished Master's thesis, Drexel Institute of Technology, 1951. 46p.

74. **Programming for Reference Service: Working Paper No. 8.** Detroit, Mich., Wayne State University Libraries, 1973. 32p. ERIC document ED077532.

Presents a perspective or philosophy of reference service which can be used to plan a reference service on a consistent basis throughout a library system. This philosophy proposes that the reference librarian has two responsibilities: 1) in all cases, to explain the organization of the library and/or the literature; 2) in some cases, to provide the user with the answer, if this can be done within the user's problem-solving time frame and is cost beneficial, as judged from the user's time for both the user and the reference librarian. The number of correct or incorrect answers is not important because the obligation is to reveal an organization, not an answer. Reference service can be planned consistently because it is not based on the complexity of the organization of the literature, but on the methodology of using the organization. The user has a defined responsibility to learn for himself if the librarian can't respond within the user's problem-solving time frame. A protocol is recommended for estimating work load according to the above philosophy of reference service.

75. Rahman, Abdul. "Philosophy of Reference Service," *Annals of Library Science* 8:150-156 (December 1961).

Considers Dr. Ranganathan's book *Reference Service*. Examines the purpose-complex of a library system and gives a detailed description of reference service. Examines the subject in regard to the "five laws" of library science and uses a funnel diagram to explain the relationship of ready reference and long-range reference service. Examines some library techniques from a holistic viewpoint and concludes with a mystic view of reference service.

76. Ranganathan, S. R. "Reference Service and Humanism." In Rowland, Arthur. *Reference Services*. Hamden, Conn., Shoe String, 1964. pp. 31-34. (Contributions to Library Literature, No. 5).

Discusses the conflict between social or group interests, and human interests. Human interests are those by which the individual progresses from helpless infancy to self-governing maturity. Considers library development in relation to this type of humanism. Libraries and books must be humanized, and reference service answers this need. Cataloging and classification need not be limited by the abilities of library users and can achieve greater perfection as long as reference service is available to guide and assist patrons.

77. Rawski, Conrad, ed. **Toward a Theory of Librarianship; Papers in Honor of Jesse Hauk Shera**. Metuchen, N.J., Scarecrow, 1973. 564p.

A collection of essays by notable British and American librarians. Includes essays on the research and writing of library history, information retrieval, library education, and other basic issues. Also includes a bibliography of nearly 400 books and other literature written by Jesse Shera.

78. Rees, Alan M. "Broadening the Spectrum." In Linderman, W., ed. *The Present Status and Future Prospects of Reference/Information Service*. Chicago, American Library Association, 1967. pp. 57-65.

Defines reference service, reference sources, and reference work. Defines the reference process as incorporating the sum total of variables involved in the performance of reference work by an intermediary designated as reference librarian. Provides a diagram of this process. Discusses the inability of users to formulate questions and also considers relevance judgments, describing work being done at Western Reserve University. Considers broadening of information sources by networks and a national library system. Greater depth of reference service is discussed in terms of information analysis centers and information services based on evaluation and critical judgment of subject content of materials. In comments on the future of reference/information service, the author focuses on whether the reference librarian is really necessary as an intermediary. Points out that elimination of the intermediary represents a return to the historical concept that the librarian's only function is to assist patrons in using the library. He observes that, unless research is done by the library profession on this subject, the trend toward elimination of the intermediary will continue. Comments by Frances Henne follow.

79. Robbins, Jane. "Reference Librarian: A Street-Level Bureaucrat?" *Library Journal* 97:1389-1392 (April 15, 1972).

Michael Lipsky's article, "Toward a Theory of Street-Level Bureaucracy," is used as the basis for this criticism of reference work, particularly in urban libraries. Reference work meets the definition of "street-level bureaucracy" in that there is constant interaction, independence on the job, and an important impact on citizens. The environment is typical in that resources are inadequate, job expectations are ambiguous and contradictory with unattainable goals. Some specific criticisms are routines and regulations that interfere with interaction with users, time limits on finding answers, jobs which make the reference librarian look busy or devices that shield him or her from the public. Includes recommendations for reform.

80.   Rugh, Archie. "Toward a Science of Reference Work: Basic Concepts," *RQ* 14:293-299 (Summer 1975).

The basic concept underlying reference work is that expressed by the generic term "book." The author defines concepts in reference work, including "book," "literary" and "practical" form, "concrete entities," "sources of information," "bibliographic tools" and "non-bibliographic tools," "reference book," "reference collection," and "direct" and "indirect" reference service. These concepts, as defined, may serve as a guide in reference study and practice and as a foundation for the development of reference theory. The author criticizes the Reference and Adult Services Division's "Commitment to Information Services" for including formal library instruction in direct services and including "access to informational sources through cooperation with other libraries" in indirect services, and also because collection building is omitted altogether but should be included in indirect services.

81.   Schiller, Anita. "Reference Service: Instruction or Information." *Library Quarterly* 35:52-60 (January 1965).

In this article, the author considers two opposing philosophies of service: one is that the basic function of reference service is to educate the patron to find information for himself, and the other considers that direct assistance should be given in finding the desired information. A definition of basic function is necessary before measurement and evaluation can be attempted. The educational concept developed from lack of resources and belief in the teaching obligation and in the desirability of self-improvement. Growing needs, resources, and specialization have encouraged direct information service. The author stresses that the primary function of reference service should be to provide the best quality of information to all, with the instructional function as secondary.

82.   Sharr, F. A. "Silent upon a Peak in Darien; Presidential Address to the Library Association of Australia, 1969," *Australian Library Journal* 18:303-315 (October 1969).

There is a need for an organized body of scientific principles to serve as a foundation for the study of librarianship. Theories should be developed from a study of people and ideas. Librarianship has a creative function in generating new ideas, increasing understanding, and developing wisdom. Professional subject study is vital. Considers how librarianship meets the definition of a profession.

83.   Shera, Jesse H. "Foundations of a Theory of Reference Service." In *Reference, Research, and Regionalism; Selected Papers from the 53rd Conference of the Texas Library Association, Austin, Texas, March 24-26, 1966.* The Association, 1966. pp. 50-62.

The author notes that reference work is increasingly directed toward giving professional help in a literature search for a relatively complex or esoteric problem. This involves time, effort, and ability to communicate and to understand the patron's needs. He discusses the educational and informational functions of reference. Theory should be developed to guide reference service, as well as standards of measurement to judge its quality. Mechanized information work has helped to define the complex relationships between people and information. The revised version of this article was published in J. H. Shera, *Knowing Books and Men; Knowing Computers Too* (Littleton, Colo., Libraries Unlimited, 1973), pp. 196-206.

84.   Shera, Jesse. **Libraries and the Organization of Knowledge**. Hamden, Conn., Archon Books, 1966. 224p.

Included here is a collection of essays on problems in librarianship. Some topics covered are the intellectual processes of society, social utility of graphic records, and the management of knowledge. Librarianship is interdisciplinary in that it orders, structures, and relates all knowledge. Its purpose is the storage and retrieval of information to aid man's progress toward a better society.

85.   Shores, Louis. "Basic Reference: An Information Theory," *RQ* 13:199-205 (Spring 1974).

In this article, the author recapitulates some of the elements of basic reference theory in order to help to reconcile "reference art" and "information science," two groups who have mutually underestimated each other. There is need for a balance between humanistic culture and science culture in formulating reference theory, and some truths are not subject to scientific determination. Details his own efforts in emphasizing the importance of reference book reviewing in the literature and asserts that great reference books should be studied for unique suggestions for information retrieval.

86.   Shores, Louis. "Books: Continuous Communicability," *Saturday Review* 41:26 (March 22, 1958).

In this article, the author introduces the concept of the "generic book," which can be defined as the "sum total of man's communication possibilities."

87.   Shores, Louis. "British Reference: The Process of Free Inquiry Necessary to Education and Research," *ALA Bulletin* 50:288-291 (May 1956).

Reference is defined by Shores as the "process of free inquiry." The importance of this concept has been reinforced by wartime and other experiences with totalitarian powers. British reference service tends to the liberal philosophy, as evidenced by the Civic Information Service and Personal Inquiry Service. Librari.ns participate in research projects, and cooperative reference and rural reference services are well developed.

88.   Shores, Louis. "A Frame of Reference," *Library Journal* 78:88-93 (January 15, 1953).

Discusses the ideological conflict between the East and West and stresses free inquiry as the cornerstone of Western civilization. Free inquiry depends upon availability and accessibility of material. He describes progress in the *British National Bibliography*, union catalogs, and other cooperative efforts. Considers the "loaded information" of the Russian system in contrast to our policy of making all viewpoints available. Public clearinghouses are needed to gather information.

89.   Shores, Louis. "The Future of Reference in American Society," *Wilson Library Bulletin* 32:286-288 (December 1957).
Reference service is defined by Shores as "the process of free inquiry necessary to education and research." He discusses the effects on reference service of trends toward automation and increased intellectual freedom. As a result of these trends he anticipates increased demands on the reference librarian.

90.   Shores, Louis. "Reference Becomes Teaching," *Texas Libraries* 29:41-48 (Spring 1967).
Reference librarianship should be active rather than passive and should assume the initiatory responsibility for the promotion of free inquiry. Promotion of free inquiry involves both active education on public issues, and teaching library use since "half of knowledge is in knowing where to find it." The SDI services offered by some universities and information centers are a step toward active educational programs.

91.   Sinclair, Dorothy. "The Next Ten Years of Reference Service," *ALA Bulletin* 62:57-63 (January 1968).
The Reference Services Division of the American Library Association has been working toward setting up goals for reference service and establishing standards, but progress has been slow. Reference service in the next ten years will be directed toward achieving objectives and improving service and also toward cooperative alliances. Reference librarians must develop and learn new techniques to meet the challenge of competition in the provision of information.

92.   Sklovsky, G. A. "The Information Ecosystem in the Knowledge Environment," *Australian Library Journal* 21:5-11 (February 1972).
The author considers the handling of information in Australia and compares the development of libraries and information systems to the ecosystem model, where a change in any part of the system affects all other parts. The growth of information requires new management procedures and the Australian National Information System is considered in this light. The author concludes that there is need for improvement in information handling in Australia. Bibliography.

93.   Strable, E. G. "Some Questions and Answers about Library Reference/ Information Service," *Idaho Librarian* 18:86-92 (July 1966).
Some important questions must be answered before reference philosophy can be developed. These questions relate to how important the reference function of the library actually is, how well it is now being performed, and what type of information is needed by patrons. The question of instruction versus information must also be resolved.

94.   Taylor, F. R. "Into the Seventies: A Survey of Some Factors Which Could Influence the Future Pattern of Reference Service Provision," *Library World* 71:115-119 (October 1969).
Discusses the effect on reference service in Great Britain of the following: the Library Association, Reference, Special, and Information Section's *Standards for Reference Library Service in Public Libraries*, the Maud Report, the Dainton

Report, and the Saunders Report (*Education and Training for Scientific and Technological Library and Information Work*). A future possibility would be a network of libraries joined in cooperative reference service with telex facilities, speedy loan, photocopy, and research services.

95.   Vavrek, Bernard. "Eliminate the Reference Department," *RQ* 9:33-34
       (Fall 1969).
The reference function should not be limited to a particular department or area. Since the purpose of the library is to bring users together with the information they need, all activities of the library have a reference function.

96.   Vavrek, Bernard. "The Emergence of New Reference?" *Journal of
       Education for Librarianship* 10:109-115 (Fall 1969).
The author calls for a new concept of reference service which would deal with all the variables in the entire library that stand between the patron and the information he needs. Reference service has traditionally been oriented toward reference books. To function in the new role, however, reference librarians must understand more about the role of the library in mass communication, the avenues of communication open to the patron, and how patrons satisfy their information needs without reference help. Finally, they must improve their ability to communicate with the patron by better interviewing techniques.

97.   Vavrek, Bernard. "Is There a Current Crisis in Reference Librarianship?"
       Pennsylvania Library Association Bulletin 29:119-121 (May 1974).
The author asserts that there is a crisis in reference librarianship due to financial pressures and demands for accountability and to the fact that no adequate means of measurement and evaluation have been established.

98.   Vavrek, Bernard. "The Reference Librarian as a Technician," *RQ* 7:5-8
       (Fall 1967).
The development of theory in reference work has been hindered by emphasis on practical techniques, particularly use of resources and dealing with the patron. Technique is only an aspect of reference work. "Professionalism is what gives shape to the process."

99.   Vavrek, Bernard. "Reference Service: Is the Medium the Message?" *RQ*
       8:37-38 (Fall 1968).
Reference service is the "sum total of the variables standing between the reader and the information," and, thus, it involves the entire library. The method of communicating information is as important as the information itself and should include education of the patron so that he becomes less dependent on the librarian.

100.   Vavrek, Bernard. "A Theory of Reference Service," *College and Research
       Libraries* 29:508-510 (November 1968).
The author contends that the basic function of reference service is to guide the flow of information to users as effectively as possible. Based on this, reference comprises all those variables which stand between the patron and the information he needs. Thus, "reference is the library." In the past, more effort has been expended on

discussing philosophies of levels of service rather than on building theories based on the nature of the reference process.

101.   Wyer, James I. **Reference Work: A Textbook for Students of Library Work and Librarians**. Chicago, American Library Association, 1930. 315p.
The chapter "Reference Work—Theory and Objectives" traces the development of reference service beginning in 1871, defines reference work, and discusses its nature and theoretical bases. Considers the issue of "mechanism versus humanism."

102.   Wynar, Bohdan S. "Reference Theory: Situation Hopeless But Not Impossible," *College and Research Libraries* 28:337-342 (September 1967).
Reviews the historical background of reference from 1876 to the present and discusses reference philosophy regarding levels of service. The reference role of the library must be re-examined at the present time. The author reports on his study of 227 articles on reference published from 1954 through 1964. Only two of these articles were concerned with theory. The survey also revealed 1) a general agreement on the nature of reference service, 2) lack of theory of reference, 3) tendency to describe specific operations rather than principles. Librarians must become acquainted with research in information exchange and retrieval. An interdisciplinary approach is necessary in formulating reference theory.

INFORMATION THEORY

103.   Artandi, Susan. "Information Concepts and Their Utility," *Journal of the American Society for Information Science* 24:242-245 (July-August 1973).
The author draws attention to the mathematical theory of communication and semiotics to serve as a framework for development of theory. She considers the applicability of Shannon's theory in situations dealing with information in the semantic and pragmatic sense. She points out the difference between information as a measure of uncertainty and information as a means of removing uncertainty Since natural language is based on a series of signs, the study of semiotics is relevant to the study of information. Aspects of document surrogation are described in this light. More research is needed before a new theory is developed. Vladimir Slamecka and Charles Pearson, at the Georgia Institute of Technology, are studying "semiotic foundations of information" under a National Science Foundation grant.

104.   Brookes, B. C. "Jesse Shera and Theory of Bibliography," *Journal of Librarianship* 5:233-245 (October 1973).
Considered here is the suggestion by Shera made some 20 years ago that a more analytical study of bibliography might help to develop theory for both library and information science. Discusses developments since that time and advances that Shera's concept of "macrobibliography" or social epistomology is important in developing theory and for design of future library and information systems.

105.   Debons, Anthony, ed. **Information Science: Search for Identity**. New York, Dekker, 1974. 491p. (Books in Library and Information Science, Vol. 7).
Presented here are 33 papers that summarize a ten-day meeting on information transfer. Debons, in a final paper, describes the four major areas of concern as the nature of information, technology in relation to human needs, the effects of information technology on man and his institutions, and the needs of institutions that gather and disseminate information.

106.   Egan, Margaret, and Jesse Shera. "Foundations of a Theory of Bibliography," *Library Quarterly* 22:125-137 (April 1952).
Bibliography should be viewed from a "macrocosmic" viewpoint as one of the instrumentalities of communication, which is, in turn, an instrument of social organization and action. Bibliographic services must be viewed in this context and must be carefully planned with consideration of the kinds of situations in which these services will be used.

107.   Foskett, D. J. "Information Science as an Emergent Discipline: Educational Implications," *Journal of Librarianship* 5:161-174 (July 1973).
Considers the nature of information science and its relationship to librarianship. Technology should not be allowed to dictate the direction of education. Services, rather than techniques, should be emphasized in library education. Users and their needs and the social role of information transfer should be studied.

108.   Harmon, G. *Human Memory and Knowledge: A Systems Approach.* Westport, Conn., Greenwood Press, 1973. 159p.
Attempts to "explore the relationships between human memory limitations and the formation of various fields of systematic knowledge." This inquiry compares the formation of a limited number of sub-disciplines, disciplines, and interdisciplinary fields. Special emphasis is given to the rise and development of information science, the focal discipline of the study.

109.   Harmon, Glynn. *Human Memory and Knowledge: A Systems Approach.* Science," *Journal of the American Society for Information Science* 22:235-241 (July-August 1971).
"A potential long range role for information science involves active participation in forming a complete supra-system of knowledge which would unify the arts, sciences, and professions." Reviews some important factors in the history of information science and the reference process.

110.   **Information Theory: An ASTIA Report Bibliography**. Arlington, Va., Armed Services Technical Information Agency, 1962. 52p. AD269800. Supplement, September, 1962, AD447069.
Lists and annotates documents cataloged by ASTIA from 1953 through January 1962. Arranged alphabetically by source within subject area.

111.   Maron, M. E. "Theoretical Librarianship and Information Science,"
        Information: Part 2, 2, No. 4:3-6 (1973).
Theory in librarianship revolves around the problem of intellectual access to stored
information. This involves the field of information science or cybernetics and the
scientific study of both natural and artificial "knowing" systems. Progress in
theoretical development will come as liabrarianship moves toward information
science.

112.   Murdock, John, and David Liston. "A General Model of Information
        Transfer: Theme Papers," *American Documentation* 18:197-208
        (October 1967).
"An item of knowledge becomes an item of information when it is 'set in motion'—
when it enters the active process of being communicated or transferred from one or
more persons, groups or organizations. . . . Many people will argue that knowledge,
as defined here, has no intrinsic value—that only when it is successfully transferred
is its value to be realized. Others go further, arguing that the value of information
cannot be realized until it is actively applied in decision making. Either of these
viewpoints must necessarily concede that value is dependent on transfer." A model
of information transfer is given. Aspects include 1) direct channel, 2) primary
recorded media channel, 3) archival channel, 4) secondary recorded media channel,
5) information center channels, 6) release restrictions.

113.   Redmond, Donald, Michael Sinclair, and Elinore Brown. "University
        Libraries and University Research," *College and Research Libraries*
        33:447-453 (November 1972).
Analyzes the research information cycle in three stages—origin of the message,
informal communication, and formal communication. A circular representation is
given, beginning with personal communication to a colleague, oral group communication (lectures, etc.) producing "primary" literature. This is extracted and compiled,
becomes standard fact, and is, in turn, superseded by new research.

114.   Rosenberg, Victor. "Scientific Premises of Information Science," *Journal
        of the American Society for Information Science* 25:263-269 (July 1974).
The author suggests the possibility that the fundamental premises on which information science is currently based are wrong. He proceeds to attempt "to evaluate
critically the nature of the scientific endeavor to understand information and its
relationship to human beings," and "to explore the pathogenic social and political
consequences of the mechanistic view." The author suggests as an alternative that
information scientists pay attention to the social, cultural, and spiritual aspects
of human communication. The new concentration should be on examining and
developing new concepts as a basis for research.

115.   Simon, H. R., ed. "Introduction: Why Analyze Bibliographies?" *Library
        Trends* 22:3-7 (July 1973).
Discusses approaches to analyzing bibliographies—one from the perspective of
general information theory, and the other from specialized viewpoints. Important
criteria to consider are coverage, recall, precision, and novelty (or notice of items
new to the user). In order to determine information flow in a specialized area, the

following questions may be asked: 1) "Which journals cover the world's literature in this area?" 2) "In what countries are they published?" 3) "In what language?" 4) "How much is written in each subject field, where published, and in what language?" It is also important to determine the factors that are responsible for course and strength of information flow.

116.   "Theory [of Information; Information Retrieval; and Systems] ." In *Bibliography of Research Relating to the Communication of Scientific and Technical Information*. New Brunswick, N.J., Rutgers University Press, Bureau of Information Sciences Research, Graduate School of Library Service, 1967. pp. 49-57.
Includes 67 annotated listings in the area of information theory.

117.   Williams, James G., and Chai Kim. "On Theory Development in Information Science," *Journal of the American Society for Information Science* 26:3-9 (January-February 1975).
Written in response to a paper by Heilprin recently read to the ASIS Special Interest Group, and to an article by Susan Artandi in the July-August issue of the *ASIS Journal*. Information science is a pragmatic discipline which has neglected theory. The papers of Heilprin and Artandi do not make their theoretical notions clear to the author, who suggests that 1) the type of theory (e.g., factor-isolating, factor-relating) be explicitly stated, 3) objectives taken into account should be stated. Heilprin's definition of information science as "the propagation of invariant patterns," provides a new view but needs clarification. The author discusses the nature of scientific theory, functions of theory in science, form of theory presentation, theory validation, and theory and information science. An appendix with a reply by Susan Artandi is included.

COMMUNICATION AND REFERENCE PROCESS THEORY

118.   Applbaum, Ronald, and others. **Fundamental Concepts in Human Communication**. San Francisco, Canfield Press, 1973. 240p.
Focuses on the speech communication process. Chapters cover 1) an introduction to communication, 2) intrapersonal communication, 3) interpersonal communication, 4) small group communication, 5) intercultural communication, 6) non-verbal communication, 7) source variables, source credibility, 8) message variables, 9) variables affecting receiver behavior, 10) theories in communication, 11) communication research. At the conclusion of the book is a section on "definitions of communication," giving 24 different definitions of communication by a variety of scholars. Each definition includes bibliographical information on the source. Bibliography.

119.   Bunge, Charles A. "Charting the Reference Query," *RQ* 8:245-250 (Summer 1969).
Presented here is a flow chart describing the reference process from the initial question to the final resolution. The chart is based on the author's study of seven Midwest libraries where matched pairs of professional and non-professional reference librarians were given the same set of reference questions to answer.

120. Butler, Pierce. "Survey of the Reference Field." In *The Reference Function of the Library. Papers Presented before the Library Institute at the University of Chicago, June 29-July 10, 1942*. Chicago, University of Chicago Press, 1943. pp. 1-15.

This classic essay defines reference as that process by which civilized man is able to obtain specific information at will by use of books that have been organized into a library. He notes that any book can be a reference book, regardless of its content. The processes by which civilization advances are discovery, conservation, and transmission of knowledge. Information is acquired by 1) education, 2) social communication, 3) consultation, and 4) reference.

121. Fairthorne, R. A. "The Theory of Communication," *Aslib Proceedings* 6:255-267 (November 1954).

There is an inexorable relation between the physical processes of communication and what an individual wants to say. If a given proposition or statement is translated into various languages, it loses no semantic content if the translations are reversible. By reversible is meant that the original statement can be reconstructed from the translations without guess-work, by explicit rules.

122. Gardiner, George L. "The Empirical Study of Reference," *College and Research Libraries* 30:130-155 (March 1969).

Four empirical studies of references are considered in the first section. The second section shows how the basic principles behind these studies are deficient, thus invalidating results. The third section discusses the conventional concept of reference as performed only by reference librarians and concludes that this concept is faulty. The fourth section considers that reference is problem-solving behavior, and the final section proposes a new framework for the further empirical study of reference based on this concept.

123. Gardiner, G. L. "On Reference and its Empirical Studies: A Critical Review." Unpublished Master's Thesis, University of Chicago, 1967. 53p.

124. Goffman, William. "A General Theory of Communication." In Saracevic, Tefko, comp. *Introduction to Information Science*. New York, Bowker, 1970. pp. 726-747.

Information science aims to provide a unified approach to the study of various phenomena connected with the notion of information, including all aspects of information flow among any population. The author defines the communication process as the sequence of events resulting in transmission of information from one object to another. It is difficult to formally define or precisely measure this process; thus, the author suggests it be measured in terms of outcomes. Three broad problems relating to outcomes are 1) desired behavioral outcome, 2) representation of information so that it is understood, 3) technical problems in accuracy of transmission. Discusses communication in terms of the epidemic process, whereby ideas spread in the same way as infectious germs. Thus, the epidemic process provides a model by which we can understand the communication process.

125.   Gothberg, Helen M. "Communication Patterns in Library Reference and
        Information Service," *RQ* 13:7-14 (Fall 1973).
The importance of communication in the reference process is stressed. Negotiation
of the reference question and reasons for failure are discussed. The communication
process is considered, including linguistic and kinesic research, information and
transactional theories, interpersonal relationships, and verbal and non-verbal communication. Library communication, in general, is dealt with in the light of library
education and the image and role of librarians. References.

126.   Holler, Frederick. "Toward a Reference Theory," *RQ* 14:301-309 (Summer
        1975).
The author defines reference theory as a "cohesive set of postulates for linking the
user to needed information in documents provided by libraries and other document
centers." The ability of library users to find information without assistance has not
improved over the years, and reference theory must be developed to become a part
of general educational knowledge. Retrieval of information is a full-fledged discipline
and should be taught and practiced within the requirements of a general education.
The author attempts to formulate a general theory of reference by developing postulates concerning information, sources, recipients, channels, information media, data
bases, retrieval structure and tools, transformation, access symbols, time, relevance,
and purpose. Tables and references included.

127.   Jahoda, Gerald, and Paul Olson. "Analyzing the Reference Process," *RQ*
        12:148-156 (Winter 1972).
The author defines the reference process as the sum total of steps taken to answer
the question. Several models of the reference process are shown in diagrams.

128.   Jahoda, Gerald. "Reference Question Analysis and Search Strategy Develop-
        ment by Man and Machine," *Journal of the American Society for Informa-
        tion Science* 25:139-144 (May-June 1974).
Nine steps are outlined in the reference process and then considered in relation to
the possibility of automation. It was concluded that such automation was not feasible.

129.   Lin, Nan. **The Study of Human Communication**. Indianapolis, Bobbs-
        Merrill, 1973. 247p.
Attempts to integrate and bring into focus what is known about human communication. Relates information theory to human communication research. Chapters cover
1) definitions, traditions, review of research, and a conceptual framework, 2)
encounter, 3) flow of human communication, 4) impact of human communication,
5) attitude change, 6) decision and action, 7) organization and adaptation of
communication, 8) theorization. Bibliography.

130.   McFadyen, D. "Psychology of Inquiry: Reference Service and the Concept
        of Information/Experience," *Journal of Librarianship* 7:2-11 (January 1975).
Many needs are reflected in reference inquiries, including the need for information
and for experience. These two needs, while dependent on each other, represent
different types of logic and consciousness. Open-ended question-negotiation and
search strategy techniques should seek the limits of the inquiry rather than an

answer *per se*. Information/experience models and theories are considered. The relationships between information and experience are examined in terms of parallel situations in the sciences and humanities. Two different types of inquiry (information and experiential) require two different types of reference service (information- and reader-oriented).

131.   Neill, S. D. "Problem Solving and the Reference Process," *RQ* 14:310-315 (Summer 1975).

The author believes that present flow charts of the reference process do not adequately represent the thought process of the reference librarian. He has selected Guilford's operational model for problem-solving, which he feels represents the operations that take place in conducting a query negotiation and search. This model represents a communication system with inputs from the environment and from psychological factors within the individual himself. It is structured in terms of 1) the memory storage box (figural, symbolic, semantic, behavioral), 2) "operational" factors (cognition, memory, divergent and/or convergent production, evaluation), 3) product categories (units, classes, relations, systems, transformations, implications). Convergent and divergent production, recall, and other factors are discussed in detail. Personal qualities of those high in problem-solving ability are discussed. References.

132.   Norman, Donald. **Memory, Knowledge, and the Answering of Questions**. La Jolla, Calif., California University, Center for Human Information Processing, 1972. 57p. ERIC Document ED097003.

An examination of theory reveals that the representation of knowledge cannot be separated from its use. The answering of questions is a complex process in the structural framework containing knowledge of the questioner, the question, and the world around. Teaching is an interactive process based on the knowledge the learner possesses or does not possess. A structure for representing semantic information is described and is being tested by simulation on a digital computer.

133.   Penland, Patrick. **Communication for Librarians**. Pittsburgh, Pa., Pittsburgh University, Graduate School of Library and Information Sciences, 1971. 189p.

Designed to help the library profession address significant communication problems. Three major areas are covered: 1) history and theory of communication, communication institutions, communication structures in biological and social organizations; 2) transfer of meaning, processing of messages in different media, analysis of message content and systems; 3) individual behavior, social interaction, attitude formation and change, public opinion, and consequences of exposure to different methods. Extensive bibliography.

134.   Penland, Patrick R. **Communication Research for Librarians**. Pittsburgh, Pa., Graduate School of Library and Information Sciences, University of Pittsburgh, 1972. 132p. ERIC Document ED071729.

Describes research methods in communication in relation to librarianship and covers proposals, theory, measurement design, observational methods, experimental control and extrapolation, search and discovery. Includes study questions, sample proposal outlines and forms, glossary of terms, and bibliography.

135.   Shannon, C. E., and W. Weaver. **The Mathematical Theory of Communication**. Urbana, Ill., University of Illinois Press, 1949. 117p.

In the first part of this book Shannon develops a mathematical theory of communication. In the second part Weaver suggests that there are three levels of problems in general communication. The first is a technical problem—"How accurately can the symbols of communication be transmitted?" The second is a semantic problem—"How precisely do the transmitted symbols convey the desired meaning?" The third problem is one of effectiveness—"How effectively does the received meaning affect conduct in the desired way?" The first level is basically an engineering problem, and the mathematical theory of communication is developed on this level. Weaver considers the significance of this theory on the other two levels.

136.   Shera, Jesse H. "The Challenging Role of the Reference Librarian." In *Reference, Research, and Regionalism; Selected Papers from the 53rd Conference of the Texas Library Association at Austin, Texas, March 24-26, 1966.* The Association, 1966. pp. 34-42.

The author discusses the changing pattern in reference service toward 1) more sophisticated reference research, 2) subject specialization, and 3) the introduction of information retrievel and automation. The reference process is analyzed in terms of Rees's flow chart—"The Operational Structure of the Reference Process." The author then supplies his own flow chart, representing the reference process in more detail from the information need through the response.

137.   Shoshid, Norma J. "Freud, Frug, and Feedback," *Special Libraries* 57:561-563 (October 1966).

Theories of non-verbal communication, if adapted to the reference interview, could lead to improved communication. The author discusses how the reference encounter is affected by verbal and non-verbal communication and by pre-conceived role expectations. Experiments at the University of Southern California are described, which indicate that neither the librarian nor the patron is generally aware of what the other is trying to communicate through non-verbal communication. An awareness of this kind of feedback can greatly enhance communication.

138.   Taylor, Robert S. "Question-Negotiation and Information Seeking in Libraries," *College and Research Libraries* 29:178-194 (May 1968).

The author seeks to illuminate the communication function of the library and focuses on communication problems in the reference encounter, particularly "how one person tries to find out what the other wants to know when the latter cannot describe his need precisely." The inquiry is not a literal command but a question that is "open-ended, negotiable and dynamic." The discussion of the negotiation process is based on interviews with special librarians and information specialists. Describes four levels of needs—visceral, conscious, formalized, and compromised. Five types of information needed are subject, objective and motivation, personal characteristics of inquirer, relationship of inquiry to file organization, and anticipated or acceptable answers. These are discussed in detail. Self-help and possible systems and devices are discussed, particularly in regard to the special library. The inquiry process is vital because here the inquirer begins to understand what he means, resolves his problems, and adjusts his question to available resources.

139.   Vavrek, Bernard. **Communications and the Reference Interface**. Pittsburgh, University of Pittsburgh Book Center, 1971. 130p.

This doctoral dissertation is based on a survey by the author who asked reference librarians at three Pittsburgh area libraries to record reference questions each day from 9:00 A.M. to 9:00 P.M. for a six-month period. For each interaction they were to record both the initial question and the question in its final form. Questions were then analyzed in terms of their content and the search patterns which they represented in terms of Boolean search strategy. The author's hypothesis—"the product of the reference interface is a search strategy which attempts to make the reference inquiry isomorphic with the classification of knowledge in the library"—was shown to be valid.

140.   Vavrek, Bernard. "The Nature of Reference Librarianship," *RQ* 13: 213-217 (Spring 1974).

The author discusses the need for a philosophy of reference based on theories of effective interpersonal communication. He discusses four aspects of communication and constructs an interpersonal communication model as a basis for a theory of the reference process. On the basis of this, he advances that reference courses should stress the human element and interpersonal relationships over information resources and should stimulate enthusiasm. He also relates this theory to evaluation of reference service.

CHAPTER 3

TEACHING OF REFERENCE

Included in this chapter are works on the teaching of reference and bibliography, literature of subject areas, and government documents. Selected representative works on information science education are also included, and reference textbooks and manuals are covered in a special section.

The authors have found no comprehensive bibliography of the teaching of reference. A bibliographical review of the literature of reference teaching is available in Kathryn Oller's "Guide to Library Education, Part 1: Curriculum Reference," *Drexel Library Quarterly* 3:65-71 (January 1967). A bibliography is also included in M. E. Singleton's "Reference Teaching in Pioneer Library Schools, 1883-1903" (Unpublished Master's thesis, 1942). Bibliographical coverage of education for librarianship in general can be found in Carmal E. Carroll, *Professionalization of Education for Librarianship; With Special Reference to the Years 1940-1960* (Metuchen, N.J., Scarecrow, 1970), pp. 344-355.

For bibliographical coverage of the teaching of information science, see Gerald Jahoda, "Education for Information Science," in *Annual Review of Information Science and Technology*, Volume 8 (American Society for Information Science, 1973), pp. 321-344.

GENERAL WORKS

141.   Aiyepeku, W. O. "Ground Rules for the Study and Teaching of Subject Literatures," *Journal of Librarianship* 6:80-90 (April 1974).
Studies of the characteristics of subject literature show there is no common basis for determining what constitutes the literature of a subject. Substantial knowledge exists on the bibliometric and documentation characteristics of many subjects, yet library schools continue to teach essentially basic reference sources in large groups of subject areas. The author suggests four criteria for determining the scope of subject literature. Education for librarianship must reflect both established and controversial knowledge, and a curriculum for literature of geography is proposed to illustrate this.

142.   Allen, Kenneth W. "The Use of Slides for Teaching Reference," *Journal of Education for Librarianship* 6:137-139 (Fall 1965).
Based on a study of the effectiveness of using slides to teach school library materials to future teachers. Two matched groups were given an identical lecture, one without slides and one with slides. A significant difference in learning was found in favor of

the group viewing the slides. The lecture was given to a third group with and without slides, and they expressed a clear preference for the version with slides.

143.   Arlt, Gustave. "Bibliography—An Essential Piece of Equipment," *Library Journal* 86:1539-1541 (April 15, 1961).
Reviews the history and development of bibliography and its function of acquainting scholars with the most valuable publications in every area of learning. Describes how the functions of the bibliographer and librarian are related. Discusses many types of library situations in which sound bibliographical training is essential and relates this to library education.

144.   Baylis, Claire. "The Teaching of Reference Work," *An Leabharlann* 4:174-179 (December 1973).
Discusses the need to provide actual reference experience for students and considers how sound knowledge and techniques may be developed. Sections give suggestions on levels of experience, time-tabling, staff, syllabus, and methods of teaching.

145.   Benge, R. C. **The Study of Reference Material**. 3rd ed. London, The Library Association, London and Home Counties Branch, 1963. 92p.
A basic British text exemplifying the British viewpoint on the teaching of reference materials and methods.

146.   Benge, R. C., and E. P. Dudley. "Study of Reference Material as Part of Library Education," *Library Association Record* 58:420-424 (November 1956).
Describes a systematic approach to subject literature for those taking library examinations. Outlines the bibliographic tools for the survey of any chosen subject field and considers the main kinds of materials and headings for the study of all types of materials.

147.   Bergen, Daniel. "Librarianship and the Social Sciences at Syracuse University," *Journal of Education for Librarianship* 5:248-254 (Spring 1965).
The author describes his methods of teaching a "Literature of the Social Sciences" course. Goals are to develop understanding of the total communication structure of the social sciences, both the formal bibliographic structure and the informal transmission of information. Each student completes a project in an area of the social sciences, comparing the conceptual structure to the formal communication structure. A few key sources in each area are studied thoroughly and related to other tools in the same area.

148.   Bichteler, Julie. "Self-Paced Instruction in Library Science—Second Thoughts," *Journal of Education for Librarianship* 13:188-192 (Winter 1973).
Discusses self-paced and traditional methods in teaching of basic reference in regard to the personalized system of instruction (PSI), as used at the University of Texas at Austin. Considered are the problems that arise when PSI is used concurrently with traditional courses and problems with readiness tests. Also discussed are problems of lack of student interaction. Modifications are proposed to achieve a compromise between traditional and self-paced instruction in teaching basic reference.

149.   Blazek, R. D. "Relevance in Bibliography of the Humanities," *Journal of Education for Librarianship* 15:22-33 (Summer 1974).
The author discusses a course in bibliography of the humanities and suggests five ways to add meaning and relevance to this course.

150.   Bonk, Wallace J. "The Core Curriculum and the Reference and Bibliography Courses," *Journal of Education for Librarianship* 2:28-33 (Summer 1961).
Twenty-five schools of library science were surveyed to determine which books were taught in basic reference classes. There was very little agreement, and the author points out the need for more uniformity. He suggests that the lists he has collected be used as an indication of those most important reference tools which should be included in all basic reference courses.

151.   Bonk, Wallace J. "The Core Reference Course," *Journal of Education for Librarianship* 4:196-208 (Spring 1964).
The author believes that a reference course should be simple and practical, oriented toward teaching students a specific job. Basic principles are useful if related to practical work. Librarianship is, for the most part, applied science rather than pure science. It is more important to study the books themselves than to occupy time with reference philosophy and theory. It is still necessary for students to memorize lists of books. However, less emphasis should be given to details of format and more to the type of information contained in each book.

152.   [Bonk, Wallace]. An Interview: "A Reference Encounter; How Reference Should be Taught," *Library Journal* 90:1818-1824 (April 15, 1965).
Based on an interview by *Library Journal* editors with Wallace Bonk and Thomas Galvin concerning the teaching of reference. Bonk suggests that major emphasis be put on finding information and study of reference resources, while Galvin stresses the importance of the communication process and the reference interview. Galvin advocates role playing as a device in teaching the interview and describes the elements of the reference interview.

153.   Bonk, W. J. **Use of Basic Reference Sources in Libraries**. Washington, D.C., U.S. Office of Education, 1963. 242p. ERIC Document ED003287.
A study concerned with defining the content of the curriculum in basic reference courses. Questionnaires were sent to reference librarians in various types and sizes of libraries asking them to rate the usefulness of selected lists of reference books. Tabulations were made of 1) responses for each reference tool by type and size of library, 2) titles added to the list by respondents, 3) titles not held by responding librarians. Results indicated that the spread of titles found useful varies widely between large and small libraries. Reference courses must aim at the largest area of agreement between all libraries. It is recommended that the minimum list of titles taught in basic reference courses should include the titles rated vital by half or more of the reference librarians of Ph.D. institutions serving enrollments of 20,000 or more.

154. Bonn, George S. "Notes About a Course in Government Publications," *Journal of Education for Librarianship* 6:3-7 (Summer 1965).
The author describes his seminar in governmental publications for advanced students and doctoral candidates. Instead of exams, three projects are given: 1) annotated bibliography of government publications, 2) critical paper on aspects of government data gathering, 3) oral report on content and organization of another library's document collection.

155. Boyd, Anne M. "Personnel and Training for Reference Work," In Butler, Pierce, ed. *The Reference Function of the Library*. Chicago, University of Chicago Press, 1943. pp. 249-267.
Discusses methods of training for reference work, including advanced training. Describes traditional methods and newer ideas. Reader-centered courses, specialization, and second-year training are considered.

156. Bunge, Charles. "Library Education and Reference Performance," *Library Journal* 92:1578-1581 (April 15, 1967).
This article gives preliminary data for a study done by the author comparing professional and non-professional reference personnel in regard to speed and accuracy in finding answers to factual questions. The purpose of the study was to provide objective data on the value of library education for reference work.

157. Carroll, Leontine. "Down With the Lists," *RQ* 6:29-31 (Fall 1966).
Criticizes the title-centered approach to teaching reference. Lists vary from school to school and encourage students to answer questions "the way we've always done it," without the use of imagination. Stressing types of resources might be a better approach. More and better research must be done on the reference process before teaching of reference can improve.

158. Cheney, Frances N. "An Experiment in Teaching Bibliography of the Social Sciences," *RQ* 10:309-312 (Summer 1971).
The "cooperative case" method was used here, with each reference student meeting with a graduate student in one of the social sciences and interviewing them, discovering their needs, educational level, knowledge of the library and special subject needs. The reference student continued to work with them in locating research information to meet their needs. The author concludes that the method, as a whole, may not be the best one for teaching social science literature, but that the interview was very effective in teaching how to explain use of sources and how to overcome communication difficulties.

159. Cheney, Frances N. "The Teaching of Reference in American Library Schools," *Journal of Education for Librarianship* 3:188-198 (Winter 1963).
Gives an overview of the teaching of reference in library schools and remarks on trends toward rapid turnover of personnel and toward male instructors. Advocates a "type" approach to reference rather than a title-centered approach, but warns against superficiality and meaningless generalizations. Syllabi should be prepared by the American Association of Library Schools for basic reference and "literature" of courses.

160.   "Comments on the Cheney Method," *RQ* 11:130-139 (Winter 1971).
A number of articles which comment on Frances Cheney's "An Experiment in
Teaching Bibliography of the Social Sciences." These articles comment on the
effectiveness of teaching reference through actual work with materials as opposed
to the lecture method.

161.   Corvo, Joseph. "How Good is Library Education? Views on Teaching
        Reference," *RQ* 4:1-3, 15 (March 1965).
Three views of teaching reference are given by reference librarians from a large
public library, a medium-sized public library, and a university library. Suggestions
are for reference librarians as teachers, reference courses specialized by type of
library, more field work, a broad background in different types of library work,
knowledge of different types of material, more emphasis on procedure, more on
government documents and foreign materials, more emphasis on individual titles
and types, and on reference attitudes. There was universal agreement that more
practical field experience is needed.

162.   Dale, Doris C. "One Approach to Bibliography," *RQ* 9:240-243
        (Spring 1970).
This advanced seminar in bibliography at Southern Illinois University chose Black
American studies as its topic and subdivided the field into nine areas. Students
prepared annotated bibliographies of 100 items. Class discussions covered bibliographical problems and lectures discussed sources to be used in the literature
searches.

163.   Donohue, Joseph C. "Research on Information-Seeking: Its Place in the
        Teaching of Librarians," *International Library Review* 4:97-101
        (January 1972).
The traditional method of teaching reference is described, and departures from this
method are considered. Four approaches to a study of "library heurology" are
presented: 1) introspective approach, 2) survey method, 3) field study method,
4) the controlled experiment.

164.   Eisenbach, Elizabeth. "No Case Histories, No Papers, No Texts—Only the
        Reference Desk, or Learning by Doing," *RQ* 11:331-335 (Summer 1972).
Describes the UCLA School of Library Science's course on advanced bibliography.
Students were given the option of writing a paper or gaining practical experience
at the UCLA College Library. Required were: 1) one hour at the reference desk and
one hour in other assignments for the reference staff per week, 2) devise questions
and write annotations for a syllabus for undergraduate library instruction, 3) turn
in an evaluation of the experience at the end of the quarter. Student evaluations
were unanimous in regard to the value of reference desk work and less unanimous
concerning off-desk assignments, though they agreed it added perspective. The
author recommends two courses—one a practicum and the other a bibliographical
seminar.

165.   Fetros, John G. "The Value of the Reference Question in Training
        Programs," *California Librarian* 33:164-168 (July 1972).
The author emphasizes the importance of practical work in education for reference
service and believes that the "question" approach should be used rather than a
materials approach. A cross section of reference questions has a universal value,
since patrons in certain types of libraries are essentially interested in the same types
of information. The author gives 14 questions from the Liverpool Public Library in
England and 50 questions from the San Francisco Public Library. He also lists and
describes a number of specific articles and books that contain collections of reference
questions for various types of libraries. In addition, he mentions newsletters, other
sources of questions, and methods whereby collections of questions may be obtained.
Teaching manuals could be developed in three ways: 1) questions with sources of
answers and thought processes, 2) questions with sources of answers, 3) questions
without answers.

166.   Frick, E. "Reference Curriculum," *Cornell University Library Bulletin*
        174:15-16 (January 1972). (Special issue)

167.   Galvin, Thomas J. **The Case Method in Library Education and In-Service
        Training**. Metuchen, N.J., Scarecrow, 1973. 288p.
Discusses the rationale of problem-oriented instruction in professional education.
Considers this approach as it applies to a variety of areas of library work, including
sections covering the problem-oriented approach in teaching general reference and
in teaching the subject literatures. Bibliography.

168.   Galvin, Thomas J. "The Case Technique in Education for Reference
        Service," *Journal of Education for Librarianship* 3:251-263 (Spring 1963).
A case study is defined as a record of a reference encounter in a specific library
situation. Reference interviews are conducted in the classroom, and later students
attempt to locate the information wanted by the patron. There are generally no
correct or incorrect answers. Reference sources are studied, along with the interviews. The author feels this method prepares the student more effectively for the
realities of reference service.

169.   Galvin, Thomas J. "Teaching Reference through the Case Method,"
        Southeastern Librarian 16:232-235 (Winter 1966).
The case method is described as it is used at Simmons College School of Library
Science. This method is used in combination with traditional methods in various
courses, including basic reference. Its advantages are that it develops those aspects
of reference work dependent on human skill and focuses on problem-solving rather
than on memorization of a body of facts.

170.   Galvin, Thomas J. "Teaching Reference with Case Studies: An Interim
        Report," *Journal of Education for Librarianship* 5:234-237 (Spring 1965).
The author describes the case study method used in teaching basic reference at
Simmons College School of Library Science. He notes that the title-centered approach
neglects the most important aspects of reference work. Students study 125 titles in
connection with the course; however, the case studies often lead to use of secondary

sources. This method is effective in that it teaches understanding of reference methodology, after which students can master titles on their own.

171.   Gilluly, Maureen. "A Student Sounds Off," *RQ* 11:208-210 (Spring 1970).
A student notes the defects in teaching reference without actual practical experience. Suggests "roving experience" where a student would gain experience in different types of libraries.

172.   Grotzinger, Laurel. "One Road through the Wood," *Journal of Education for Librarianship* 9:24-34 (Summer 1968).
Four major approaches to reference are discussed: 1) list-centered lecture, 2) bibliographic types rather than titles, 3) case study method, 4) information science approach. John Dewey's five steps characteristic of reflective thinking are related to the reference process. Concludes that if methods of scientific inquiry are followed, the four approaches above can be combined for improved teaching of reference.

173.   Gull, C. D. "The Challenges of Teaching the Information Sciences," *Journal of Education for Librarianship* 6:61-64 (Summer 1965).
Difficulties in teaching information science are related to the following lacks in student background: 1) lack of training in mathematics and logic, 2) poor foreign language ability, 3) little science background, 4) limited general experience. Instructors also often have these same deficiencies of background. Other difficulties include lack of suitable textbooks and periodical literature. Most information science courses probably should be taught on the doctoral level.

174.   Gwinup, Thomas. "The Reference Course: Theory, Method, and Motivation," *Journal of Education for Librarianship* 11:231-242 (Winter 1971).
The author criticizes the title-centered approach to reference teaching with its memorization of details on scope and format of each source. He notes that this separates study of reference sources from the reality of answering actual reference questions. Instead, he suggests the "types of material" approach, role playing, guided research questions, and case studies. Reference theory should be related to the practical aspects of reference work.

175.   Harbeson, E. L. "Teaching Reference and Bibliography: The Pathfinder Approach," *Journal of Education for Librarianship* 13:111-115 (Fall 1972).
Describes use of "pathfinders" in teaching reference and bibliography. Pathfinders are defined as brief guides to specific subjects which suggest a wide variety of sources. They provide the kind of guidance needed by persons working on their own and unfamiliar with the subject. Reference students prepare pathfinders on topics relevant to their course work and subject interests.

176.   Harris, Katharine G. "Reference Service Today and Tomorrow: Objectives, Practices, Needs, and Trends," *Journal of Education for Librarianship* 3:175-187 (Winter 1963).
Considers trends in reference service toward departmentalization, increased telephone service and demands by students and businessmen, and a greater reluctance to answer time-consuming questions. Failures in teaching reference are given as: 1) too much

theoretical and too little practical information provided, 2) not enough field work, 3) not enough actual reference problems employed.

177.   Hart, Patricia. "Library Education and the Reference Librarian," *Ontario Library Review* 49: 178-181 (November 1965).

Training for reference work should be a cooperative effort between library school and library. Reference work is one of the most important professional functions in public libraries, and there is some question whether library schools are providing the needed reference librarians. Considered in respect to reference education are library schools, in-service training, utilization of professionally trained staff, and continuing education.

178.   Held, Ray E. "Teaching Reference and Bibliography," *Journal of Education for Librarianship* 5:228-233 (Spring 1965).

This basic reference course is taught by the title-centered lecture approach. Suggestions made are that the number of sources taught should equal four times the number of class meetings, one should present the harder bibliographical tools first, and there should be frequent review. Problems are assigned in which the students use the sources, and tests are given often. It is preferable to deal with the books by type rather than by subject.

179.   Hernon, Peter. " 'Pathfinders'/Bibliographic Essays and the Teaching of Subject Bibliography," *RQ* 13:235-238 (Spring 1974).

"Pathfinders" are brief guides to specific subjects which include topic definitions, subject headings, classification numbers, introductory sources, reference sources, documents, and any other relevant sources of information. This article describes how they are used in teaching reference work in subject areas.

180.   Hershfield, A. F., and R. S. Taylor. **Effecting Change in Library Education. Curriculum Design for Library and Information Science**. Syracuse, N.Y., Syracuse University, School of Library Science, 1973. 87p.

In these two papers, the authors stress the importance of multimedia in information dissemination and the need for change in library education. Presented are findings of research studies and innovative curriculum developments concerned with people, information, and technology at the Syracuse University School of Information Studies.

181.   Horn, Andrew. "Planning the Course in Reference and Bibliography," *Library Journal* 86:1537-1539 (April 15, 1961).

The author describes how he planned and organized the courses in reference and bibliography for the new graduate library school at UCLA. Describes the courses that were established in method and theory of bibliography, and a required one-year course in reference service and materials covering reference history, functions, selection, evaluation, national and trade bibliographies, materials by type, reference work in history, geography, government publications, humanities, social sciences, and physical and life sciences.

182. Houk, Wallace E. "A Subject-Interest Method for Teaching Reference,"
    Journal of Education for Librarianship 11:148-155 (Fall 1970).
In this reference course taught at Kansas State Teacher's College, the student selects
a subject that interests him and prepares a paper or an oral report, relating the
sources studied to this subject. This approach is too time-consuming to use for all
sources studied, but it is effective in that the students examine sources more thought-
fully and understand more about them.

183. Jahoda, Gerald. "Education for Information Science," In *Annual Review
    of Information Science and Technology*, Volume 8, 1973. Washington,
    D.C., American Society for Information Science, 1973. pp. 321-344.
Surveys educational programs and discusses types of programs, curriculum design,
program content, teaching methods and materials, environment of academic programs, desirable student characteristics, manpower requirements, and accreditation.
Extensive bibliography.

184. Jordan, Helen. "Team Teaching Library Science and Subject Fields,"
    Southeastern Librarian 20:190-192 (Fall 1970).
Describes a study done in the Department of Library Science and the Department
of English at Columbia College, South Carolina. A reference librarian and an English
professor prepared a course, including both bibliographical knowledge and literary
content. Details are given describing and evaluating the course.

185. Kilgour, Frederick G. "Implications for the Future of Reference/Information
    Service." In Linderman, W., ed. *The Present Status and Future Prospects of
    Reference/Information Service*. Chicago, American Library Association,
    1967. pp. 172-183.
The author discusses the impact upon libraries of three major developments: 1) the
expansion of the knowledge industry; 2) the invention of the computer, 3) the
introduction of systems concepts into libraries. These trends will lead eventually to
the development of new areas of library interests and new intellectual efforts.
Studies of users and their needs will also be made easier by data provided by
computerization.

186. Kinney, Mary. "Teaching the Use of Government Publications at Simmons
    College," *Journal of Education for Librarianship* 1:87-93 (Fall 1960).
This article reviews the teaching of government documents in basic reference and
"literature" courses. Teaching is by "types" such as guides to foreign countries and
coastal charts. The more complicated sources are taught by use of transparencies
and other audiovisual methods. Problems are given where students must consult
actual sources.

187. Knightly, John, and John L. Sayre. "Self-Paced Instruction in Library
    Science," *Journal of Education for Librarianship* 12:193-197 (Winter 1972).
The personalized system of instruction (PSI) is described as it is used in basic reference courses at the University of Texas. The background of PSI is reviewed and
instruction is given on how to apply it to the basic reference course. Student responses
were favorable, with 39 percent saying that this was one of their best courses and 54
percent saying it was "above average."

188. Larsen, John C. "Titles Currently Studied in Humanities Courses," *Journal of Education for Librarianship* 10:120-128 (Fall 1969).

This survey attempted to determine the titles studied in humanities courses at accredited library schools. The number of titles studied varied from 87 to 740. For each subject within the humanities, 92 percent of all titles were listed by less than half the schools. Greater uniformity, but not necessarily standardization, is suggested.

189. Lilley, D. B. "Graduate Education Needed by Information Specialists and the Extent to Which It Is Offered in Accredited Library Schools." Unpublished Ph.D. dissertation, Columbia University, 1969. 250p.

190. Logsdon, Richard. "Critique and Synthesis," *Journal of Education for Librarianship* 3:199-203 (Winter 1963).

Defines reference service as personalized service to the reader. Discusses the following changes that need to be made in reference teaching: more subject specialization should be encouraged and more theory discussed. Every library school course should be considered as a reference course and curriculum should provide more challenge for high ability students.

191. Lynch, Mary Jo, and George Whitbeck. "Work Experience and Observation in a General Reference Course—More on Theory vs. Practice," *Journal of Education for Librarianship* 15:271-280 (Spring 1975).

192. Martin, Miles. "The Community Information Specialist at the University of Toledo," *RQ* 12:361-363 (Summer 1973).

The Chairman of the Department of Library and Information Science at the University of Toledo describes the background of the Community Information Specialist program. Discusses selection of students, curriculum, teaching methods, field work and internship, and the writing of a thesis. Describes types of jobs obtained by graduates and organizations with whom the program works.

193. Mignon, Edmond. "Information Science in the Teaching of Traditional Reference Service." In North, Jeanne, ed. *Communication for Decision Makers: Proceedings of the 34th Annual Meeting of the American Society for Information Science, Denver, November, 1971*. Vol. 8. Westport, Conn., Greenwood Press, 1971. pp. 143-146.

Information science is seen as a way of thinking about information. This way of thinking, which may be adapted to conventional library education, is characterized by emphasis on process rather than materials and on analysis rather than description of common phenomena. At the University of California at Berkeley, the REFSEARCH language is used in training future reference librarians. Students convert natural language reference questions into a set of search specifications, which are matched by the system to stored profiles of the properties of standard reference books.

194. Moore, Everett T. "Reference and Bibliography are Basic in UCLA School," *Library Journal* 86:1536-1537 (April 15, 1961).

Discusses the formation of reference curriculum prior to opening of the School of Library Service at UCLA. This was done by consultation with key reference

librarians who were heads of branch libraries. Emphasis was put on sound bibliographic instruction and a strong laboratory collection to avoid pressure on the
library's reference collection.

195.　Needham, Christopher, ed. **The Study of Subject Bibliography with Special
　　　　Reference to the Social Sciences**. University of Maryland, School of
　　　　Library and Information Science, 1970. 221 p.
The author describes a course taught at the University of Maryland in the Literature
of the Social Sciences which combined the sociological and bibliographical aspects of
the social sciences.

196.　Oller, Kathryn. "Guide to Library Education, Part 1: Curriculum:
　　　　Reference," *Drexel Library Quarterly* 3:65-71 (January 1967).
Reviews the literature on teaching of reference. A survey revealed that a substantial
portion of the library school curriculum deals with reference. There is little agreement in titles studied. Useful supplements are courses on abstracting and indexing,
search strategy, and documentation. Book or problem-oriented methods of teaching, as advocated by Shores and Galvin, are discussed. Audiovisual techniques, flow
charts, class visits, guest lectures, and use of books during class periods are discussed.
Criticism about reference teaching is given by reference librarians.

197.　Orgren, C. F. "Differences in Learning under Two Strategies of Computer-
　　　　Assisted Instruction for a Basic Reference Course in Library School."
　　　　Unpublished Ph.D. dissertation, University of Michigan, 1971. 139 p.

198.　Parker, E. B. "Information Science Education," *Information; Part 2*:
　　　　2, No. 4:7-10 (1973).
Some possible objectives of information science education are 1) professional training to operate existing communication systems, 2) training to develop new systems,
3) training scientists to understand general information processes. The information
scientist needs 1) an understanding of computer hardware, 2) knowledge of user
needs and behavior, 3) understanding of communication science as an interdisciplinary study. Describes the Ph.D. program in information science at Stanford
University's Communication Department, which emphasizes scholarly development
in areas of behavioral sciences, computer science, and analysis of social institutions.

199.　Pierson, Robert M. "The Teaching of Reference Librarianship," *Journal
　　　　of Education for Librarianship* 9:351-361 (Spring 1969).
Comments on reference teaching in general. The method used is not as important as
the quality of the teaching. A moderate position should be taken in the theory versus
practice controversy. Teachers should emphasize their particular subject strengths
and allow for their weaknesses in arranging course content. Instead of giving large
workloads, give thought provoking assignments. Study of titles should emphasize
patron needs. An outline of a suggested course is given.

200.   Rapoza, Rita S. "Teaching Communication Skills," *RQ* 10:218-220
        (Spring 1971).
Reference courses at Mankato State College in Minnesota feature a program to teach communication skills which includes six 50-minute periods studying and practicing the reference interview.

201.   Rees, Alan M., and Tefko Saracevic. "Teaching Documentation at Western
        Reserve University," *Journal of Education for Librarianship* 6:8-13
        (Summer 1965).
Three of the ten courses offered in the Documentation Program at Western Reserve University are described here. They cover the area between the core program and the more specialized courses. Documentation covers recording and organizing materials, and indexing and abstracting. Information Retrieval Systems analyzes various retrieval systems. Information Systems II is a laboratory course which gives practical experience with the total operation of a system.

202.   "Reference Course," (Letters), *RQ* 4:6 (July 1965).
Mother Mary Dennis, of the Department of Library Science at Villanova University, describes her method of teaching reference. New approaches were tried in order to get away from the "lists and memorize" method. The author suggests assignments that simulate actual job situations. Course assignments include reading a reference article each week and showing how it could be applied in a particular type of library. Students also plan a reference service and reference collections for use in their particular type of library.

203.   Rogers, A. Robert. "Shock of Recognition: An Experiment with Video-
        tape," *OLA Bulletin* 41:10-12 (April 1971).
Describes an experiment done with the author's class in Literature of the Humanities at Kent State University. Students prepared skits on problems in humanities reference service, which were then videotaped.

204.   Shera, Jesse H. **The Foundations of Education for Librarianship**. New York,
        Becker and Hayes, 1972. 511p.
The purpose of this book is to present a thorough study of library education. Considered are the role of library and its contributions to society. The meaning and requirements of this role are examined in regard to graduate library education. The origin of libraries and the history of library education are reviewed. Against this background the author critically examines existing library education and makes suggestions for improvement.

205.   Shera, Jesse H. **Knowing Books and Men; Knowing Computers Too**.
        Littleton, Colo., Libraries Unlimited, 1973. 363p.
This volume consists of 29 of Shera's essays, written between 1931 and 1973. One section covers library education ("Of Library Education," pp. 322-359).

206.   Shores, Louis. "We Who Teach Reference," *Journal of Education for Librarianship* 5:238-247 (Spring 1965).
The author believes the approach to reference teaching should be balanced between study of titles and on-the-job situations. An outline of his course is given, based on his book *Basic Reference Sources*. He describes his personal methods, use of audiovisuals, and the way in which he relates reference to information retrieval, censorship, and comparative bibliography.

207.   Shoshid, Norma. "Reality in Reference Teaching," *Journal of Education for Librarianship* 9:35-41 (Summer 1968).
Role-playing is an effective supplement to add reality to reference teaching. The problem used should be clear and should have a possible solution. Techniques are acting out different solutions, role reversal, and substitution of participants. Role-playing should be followed by class discussion. Illustrates this technique with sample encounters and presents a teaching outline for role-playing.

208.   Singleton, M. E. "Reference Teaching in Pioneer Library Schools, 1883-1903." Unpublished Master's thesis, Columbia University, 1942. 195p.
Early reference teaching placed heavy emphasis on a number of selected reference books, usually taken from Alice Kroeger's *Guide to the Study and Use of Reference Books*. Reference work was considered to consist primarily of skill in the use of reference books.

209.   Slavens, Thomas. "Computer-Assisted Instruction for Reference Librarians," *Journal of Education for Librarianship* 10:116-119 (Fall 1969).
Problems that can be alleviated by the use of computer-assisted instruction are lack of faculty, lack of individual instruction for students at different levels, inadequate teaching methods, and lack of self-instructional materials. It can also be used for diagnostic tests, to develop programmed learning, and to simulate reference situations.

210.   Slavens, Thomas P. **The Development and Testing of Materials for Computer-Assisted Instruction in the Education of Reference Librarians.** Ann Arbor, Mich., University of Michigan, School of Library Science, 1970. 182p.
This study represents an attempt to solve three problems: 1) unsatisfactory teaching methods, 2) variation in education and skill of students, 3) lack of self-instructional materials. Computer-assisted instruction makes available: 1) simulated reference situations, 2) instructional period to evaluate discrimination and performance, 3) easily revised self-instructional materials. One hundred sixty-seven reference works were annotated and 850 questions were devised to deal with these sources, and these were incorporated into a linear program. Real reference interviews were recorded and simulated in the program. Results of the study indicated that the group of students using the computerized program scored higher than those not using the program.

211. Slavens, Thomas. "Teaching Reference Work: Some Current Approaches," *Library Journal* 93:1591-1593 (April 15, 1968).
Accredited library schools were surveyed to determine the ways in which they taught reference work, and instructors wrote resumes and evaluations of their methods. Some techniques described are case studies, projects, audiovisual aids, visits, and field work.

212. Starks, David D., Barbara Horn, and Thomas Slavens. "Two Modes of Computer-Assisted Instruction in a Library Reference Course," *Journal of the American Society for Information Science* 23:271-277 (July-August 1972).
Described here is an experimental program of computer-assisted instruction in teaching reference at the University of Michigan. Details are given on how the experimental program was planned and carried out, and its effectiveness is evaluated.

213. Stych, F. S. "Teaching Reference Work: The Flow Chart Method," *RQ* 5:14-17 (Summer 1966).
In humanities courses at the University of Sheffield Postgraduate School of Librarianship, the flow chart method is used to study the search strategy and decision-making process of reference librarians. This aids students in visualizing actual reference encounters.

214. "Success Story: Students Run Teletype Reference Center," *Library Journal* 97:2028 (June 1, 1972).
Describes how students in advanced reference classes at the University of Iowa operate a teletype service utilized by libraries throughout the state. Results of the program are discussed and financial information is given.

215. Taylor, Margaret. "A Self-Study Approach to Reference Sources," *Journal of Education for Librarianship* 12:240-246 (Spring 1972).
The author describes a self-study approach to reference used at the University of Hawaii. A self-study manual served to introduce the student to basic reference sources on his own, thus freeing class time for other purposes. Basic reference was taught to two comparable groups of graduate students, one using the manual and skipping part of the scheduled class sessions, and the other meeting for regular periods but not using the manual. The group using the manual showed higher scores on a final test and much enthusiasm was shown by students for the manual and the advantages of self-study.

216. "Teaching Reference Work," *Library Journal* 86:1536-1541 (April 15, 1961).
Three librarians discuss the teaching of reference at the University of Southern California. The organization of reference and bibliography courses is described. These contributions were prompted by a U.S. Field Seminar on Library Reference Services for Japanese Librarians. For individual contributions, see Everett Moore, Andrew Horn, and Gustave Arlt.

217. Thomas, Sarah M. "Reference Work in Library and Information Science Curricula." In *Reference Work: Background and Implications.* Israel Society of Special Libraries and Information, Centers, Tel Aviv, 1971. (Contributions to Information Science 5; Clarissa Gadiel Memorial Issue). pp. 11-16. ERIC Document ED056714.

Reviews different methods of reference teaching. Observes that reference courses should not be isolated in the educational program just as reference service cannot be separated from other library activities. Emphasizes the interrelationships among all library activities and notes that all activities should be directed toward the user and his requirements.

218. Whittaker, Kenneth. "Teaching Reference: The Changing British Scene," *Journal of Education for Librarianship* 13:116-122 (February 1972).

Teaching reference and bibliography has changed in Great Britain in the last decade in both content and method. This is due to the following: 1) the British Library Association has revised its syllabi and methods of examination, 2) undergraduate courses have been set up at non-university schools, 3) teachers of reference have become professional.

219. Whitten, Benjamin, Jr. "Social Sciences Bibliography Course: A Client-Oriented Approach," *Journal of Education for Librarianship* 16:25-32 (Summer 1975).

The author describes an experiment in teaching social sciences bibliography conducted at the University of Southern California School of Library Science. Social sciences faculty were told that library science students would provide bibliographical assistance in connection with faculty research projects. The faculty member would, in turn, provide guidance and advice to the student working with him or her. Sixty faculty responded and were interviewed by students. Class time was spent in surveying social science disciplines, historical developments, research methodologies, and examining reference tools.

220. Wieman, C. D. "School Library Reference Work: An Investigation into Educational Objectives Relevant to School Librarianship for a General Undergraduate Reference Course." Unpublished Master's thesis, University of Wisconsin, 1969. 72p.

221. Wilson, T. D. "Teaching Subject Bibliography," *Journal of Education for Librarianship* 9:338-344 (Spring 1969).

Given here is a description of the teaching of reference and bibliography in the United Kingdom. The project method is discussed, in which papers are assigned on various bibliographic materials. Illustrations are projects on indexing and abstracting and citation counts in a year's issue of a journal. Students also prepare a bibliography and a literature survey. Appendices include an outline of the study program for subject bibliography courses.

222. Wood, Raymund, F. "Bibliography and the Seminar," *Journal of Education for Librarianship* 9:18-24 (Summer 1968).

The small seminar of about eight students is well suited to the teaching of bibliography. The professor should assign topics and sub-topics limited enough so that the end result will be a comprehensive scholarly bibliography.

223. Ziskind, Sylvia. "An Introduction to Reference," *Journal of Education for Librarianship* 9:41-44 (Summer 1968).

Basic reference is described as taught at Immaculate Heart College in Los Angeles. Ten units are taught by comparison of information from handouts and from Winchell and Barton. Each student must prepare a report on a reference book and a test is given at the end of every two units. Search questions are given weekly.

REFERENCE TEXTBOOKS AND MANUALS

Included in this section are general reference texts intended for use in educating and training professional and/or non-professional reference personnel. General reference texts designed to teach reference service in subject areas (humanities, social sciences, sciences, and government documents) are also included in this section. Reference texts are considered as those that do not merely serve as guides to reference materials, but present other aspects of reference work as well. Also in this section are guides (manuals) that, in the author's opinion, qualify as general guides to reference materials.

224. Asheim, Lester, and associates. **The Humanities and the Library: Problems in the Interpretation, Evaluation, and Use of Library Materials**. Chicago, American Library Association, 1957. 278p.

Discusses humanities literature in the areas of religion, philosophy, fine arts, music, and literature. Considers the major characteristics of these fields and criteria for evaluating the contents of books in these areas, reference work, and major reference sources.

225. Bloomberg, Marty. **Introduction to Public Services for Library Technicians.** 2nd ed. Littleton, Colo., Libraries Unlimited, 1976. (Library Science Text Series). 251p.

Covered are circulation services, reference services, use of the catalog, library classification, and working with bibliographic citations. Reference sources are covered in chapters on almanacs, yearbooks, dictionaries, encyclopedias, biographical reference works, bibliographies, atlases and gazetteers, directories and handbooks, indexes, and reference sources in humanities, social sciences, and science and technology. Also covered are non-book materials, government documents, interlibrary loan, and special materials and services. Designed to be used in library technicians' courses and as an in-service guide for non-professionals in medium-sized and small libraries.

226.   Cavanagh, Gladys, and Dora Osterheld. **Reference Syllabus for Use in Advanced Reference Classes**. Madison, Wisc. Wisconsin University, Library School, 1965. 273p.

Designed as a workbook for study of reference materials, to be used in conjunction with Shores and Winchell. Arrangement follows Shores, and citations are given to Winchell annotations. "Full bibliographical information is omitted in the syllabus for titles appearing in Winchell." Questions for discussion are included in each unit.

227.   Cheney, Frances N. **Fundamental Reference Sources**. Chicago, American Library Association, 1971. 318p.

Intended as a text for students in basic reference courses. Begins with an introduction to reference service and covers guides to reference materials, reviewing and evaluating of reference books. Chapters cover bibliographic information, biographical information, sources on words, encyclopedias, sources of statistics, and sources of geographical information. Each chapter has an introduction, followed by major individual sources. Each title is described in terms of scope and arrangement, and bibliographical data are included. Citations to Winchell are also given. An appendix includes detailed guidelines for reviewing various types of reference materials. A list of readings is given.

228.   Collison, Robert L. W. **Library Assistance to Readers**. 5th ed. New York, Philosophical Library, 1965. 159p.

In this book, the library's physical facilities and collections are examined from the viewpoint of patron use. Advisory work with readers and types of materials and services available are discussed with readers' needs in mind.

229.   Cowley, John D. **The Use of Reference Material**. London, Grafton and Co., 1937. 158p.

This general textbook was prepared to assist students in preparing for the University of London diploma examination in librarianship. Covered are the inquiry, search routines, types of materials, and reference tools.

230.   Freides, Thelma. **Literature and Bibliography of the Social Sciences: A Guide to Search and Retrieval**. Los Angeles, Melville, 1973. 284p. (Information Science Series).

Analysis of scholarly social science literature. Coverage is limited to communication among social scientists, excluding general data sources and popular sources. Many types of publications are evaluated in terms of structure, function, evolution, and prospects for improvement. Each aspect of social science literature is illustrated by annotated lists of reference works. Literature searching techniques are discussed.

231.   Galvin, Thomas J. **Current Problems in Reference Service**. New York, Bowker, 1971. 162p.

A collection of 35 problems of current concern to reference service. Studies relate to location of information in reference sources, use of bibliographies and indexes. Others are dependent on knowledge of types of reference sources, such as biographical or geographical sources, dictionaries, encyclopedias, and handbooks.

232.　Galvin, Thomas J. **Problems in Reference Service—Case Studies in Method and Policy**. New York, Bowker, 1965. 177p.

The author has prepared 30 case studies for use in graduate library instruction. The problem situations dealt with include the reference interview, relating the inquiry to source materials, and formulation and interpretation of policy.

233.　Grogan, Denis J. **Case Studies in Reference Work**. Hamden, Conn., Shoe String Press, 1967. 166p.

A collection of 156 case studies that follow reference inquiries through the steps of the reference process. The questions require use of sources such as encyclopedias, yearbooks, directories, bibliographies, and dictionaries. Chapter II discusses the elements of the reference process and the importance of the reference interview in determining patron needs.

234.　Grogan, Denis J. **More Case Studies in Reference Work**. Hamden, Conn., Linnet Books, 1972. 293p.

This collection of 189 case studies continues Grogan's previous collection (*Case Studies in Reference Work*, 1967) and follows the same format. Difficult reference inquiries are followed, and search strategy and sources used are described. While older books mainly concentrated on encyclopedias, bibliographies, and dictionaries, *More Case Studies* includes books of quotations, gazetteers, and biographical sources.

235.　Henne, Frances, and Dorothy Cole. **Course Outline: Reference and Bibliography**. Chicago, University of Chicago, Graduate School of Library Science, 1945. 100p.

This course outline includes objectives, relation of the course to the curriculum, sources of materials, displays, and guest lectures. It defines reference work and gives descriptions and types of questions. Reference work in subject areas and use of bibliographies are outlined.

236.　Hilliard, James M. **Where to Find What: A Handbook to Reference Service**. Metuchen, N.J., Scarecrow, 1975. 265p.

A brief subject guide to reference sources intended to help reference librarians locate quick answers to unfamiliar questions. An annotated list of reference books and some textbooks are arranged under 450 broad and specific subjects. This book is based on the author's reference teaching and in-service training experience. No title or author index.

237.　Hutchins, Margaret. **Introduction to Reference Work**. Chicago, American Library Association, 1944. 214p.

This classic work discusses the nature and purpose of reference work and defines it as "direct personal aid within a library to persons in search of information for whatever purpose, and also various library activities aimed at making information as easily available as possible." Covered are reference questions, the reference interview, search strategy, and questions relating to bibliography, biography, history, geography, current information, and statistics. Selection of reference materials covers principles, reference works and aids, circulation, periodicals, newspapers, pamphlets, audiovisual materials, and government publications. Organization of reference materials covers the reference area, non-book materials, special collections and aids. Organization and administration covers staff, coordination of services, and administration as affected by clientele. Other common functions discussed are reader's advisory service, library instruction, literature searching, interlibrary loan, and public relations. Concludes with discussion of evaluation and reporting of reference work. While this text is dated, it is still valuable for a general discussion of the nature of reference service.

238.   Katz, William A. **Introduction to Reference Work**. New York, McGraw-Hill, 1974. 2 vols. (McGraw-Hill Series in Library Education).
Volume I, *Basic Information Sources*, begins with a section on the reference process covering reference service and the public, reference service and the library, information sources, reference forms, and evaluating reference sources. Part 2, "Control and Access to Information," covers bibliographies, national library catalogs, trade bibliographies, and indexing and abstracting services. Part 3, "Sources of Information," has sections on 1) encyclopedias, 2) almanacs, yearbooks, current sources, and statistics, 3) subject almanacs, yearbooks, handbooks, manuals, and directories, 4) biographical reference sources, 5) dictionaries, 6) geographical sources, 7) government documents. Volume II, *Reference Services and Reference Processes*, begins with coverage of the reference process, channels of communication, the user and non-user of reference service. The second section, on the interview and search process, also includes a section on diagramming of the reference process. The third section covers "Pamphlets to Reports," non-print materials, and readers' advisory aids. The final section covers the library and the computer, and evaluation of reference sources and services.

239.   Malinowsky, H. Robert, Richard A. Gray, and Dorothy A. Gray. **Science and Engineering Literature: A Guide to Reference Sources**. 2nd ed. Littleton, Colo., Libraries Unlimited, 1976. 300p.
Updates and augments sources listed in the 1967 edition. Examines the structure and organization of scientific literature, its forms and basic documents. Chapters are included on the various disciplines in science and engineering, with stress on the interdependence of reference tools in these fields. Types of materials covered are bibliographies, reviews, histories, dictionaries, encyclopedias, handbooks, directories, standards, and periodicals. New chapters are included on the history of science and information retrieval.

240.   Matarazzo, J. M. **Library Problems in Science and Technology**. New York, Bowker, 1971. 167p.
Thirty-five case studies are presented involving problems in reference work with scientific and technical literature. In addition, information is provided in the appendix on the use of the library pathfinder as a teaching tool to complement the case method.

241.   Morehead, Joe. **Introduction to United States Public Documents**.
        Littleton, Colo., Libraries Unlimited, 1975. 289p. (Library Science
        Text Series).
Designed to be used in library schools as a textbook in government documents
courses. Covers the Superintendent of Documents, the Government Printing Office,
the depository library system, administration of the collection, guides to government publications, and types of government agencies and their publications.

242.   Mudge, Isadore Gilbert. **Guide to Reference Books**. 6th ed. Chicago,
        American Library Association, 1936. 504p.
The purpose of this guide is to provide a "textbook" and "reference manual."
Works are selected with a view toward usefulness in a general library. Reference
works are arranged according to subject, with sections on essays and general literature, periodicals, debates, dissertations, societies, museums, encyclopedias, and
dictionaries. This old edition is valuable for its textual introductions.
See also entry 883.

243.   Mukherjee, A. K. **Reference Work and its Tools**. Calcutta, World Press
        Private Ltd., 1964. 335p.
The author discusses philosophy, concepts, principles, nature, techniques, and
organization of reference service. Fourteen categories of work are discussed, including such areas as answering inquiries, preparing bibliographies, assisting readers in
use of the library, interlibrary loan, maintaining indexing and abstracting services,
translation services, collecting information on library resources, and cooperating
with bibliographical centers and union catalogs. Documentation and reference work
in different types of libraries are discussed. Other sections discuss organization of
reference service, selection and evaluation of reference tools, qualifications of
reference librarians, and organization of materials. Some 643 Western reference
sources are listed alphabetically by title. Annotations are given in a separate section. Appended are lists of Indian reference tools, one of "conventional sources,"
and the other "ideological source materials."

244.   **Reference Tools and Services**. Santa Monica, Calif., Systems Development
        Corporation, Research and Development Division, 1969. ERIC Documents
        ED070496, ED070497, ED070498, ED070499, ED070500.
This combination workbook and instruction manual is designed for non-professional
library personnel in science and technology work. It provides an introduction to
basic reference and bibliographic tools in this area. Instructional packages cover
1) use of reference and bibliographic tools, 2) general technical encyclopedias and
engineering handbooks, 3) directories, 4) indexing and abstracting services, 5) trans-
literation of Russian to English.

245.   Roberts, A. D. **Introduction to Reference Books**. 3rd rev. ed. London, Library
        Association, 1956. 237p.
An introductory chapter is followed by discussion of encyclopedias, dictionaries,
newspapers and yearbooks, directories, bibliographies, serials, indexing and abstracting services, current bibliographies, directories and societies and institutions,

government publications, biography, and geography. Another short chapter covers literature of special subjects with a list of recent guides to the literature in those areas. Also covered are reference philosophy and other significant concepts, as well as such topics as subscription books, reproduction processes, and microtexts.

246. Rogers, A. Robert. **The Humanities: A Selective Guide to Information Sources**. Littleton, Colo., Libraries Unlimited, 1974. 400p.

Covers all major areas of the humanities, each area beginning with narrative discussion in terms of trends and accessing information. Following this is an annotated listing of principal information sources. Intended as a guidebook to information sources in the humanities.

247. Sager, Donald. **Reference: A Programmed Instruction**. 1st rev. Columbus, Ohio, Ohio Library Foundation, 1971. 147p.

This instructional manual was prepared for Ohio reference workshops for nonprofessional library personnel. Questions are based on major reference sources and are set up in programmed format. Each possible answer is explained in terms of its adequacy.

248. Shores, Louis. **Basic Reference Sources: An Introduction to Materials and Methods**. Chicago, American Library Association, 1954. 378p.

Arranged in three sections, this book begins by discussing the function of reference service. Thirteen chapters are given to a description of general reference works, and five chapters deal with reference sources in subject fields. Introductory discussions are given for each field, with detailed descriptions of specific works. Outdated, but still important in the context of the historical development of library science curriculum.

249. Stevens, Rolland E. **Reference Books in the Social Sciences and Humanities**. 3rd ed. Champaign, University of Illinois, Illini Union Bookstore, 1971. 188p.

Written as an aid in teaching reference service. Arranged in sections covering general works, education, psychology, sociology and social work, anthropology, economics and business, political science and law, history, philosophy, religion, literature, music, fine arts, theatre, and dance. Most references are annotated. Each chapter includes sample reference questions.

250. Taylor, Margaret. **Basic Reference Sources. A Self Study Manual: Preliminary Edition**. Metuchen, N.J., Scarecrow, 1973. 297p.

Designed to supplement reference class sessions. Arranged by type of work, with each unit containing questions designed to emphasize the important features of each particular tool.

251. Wyer, James. **Reference Work: A Textbook for Students of Library Work and Librarians**. Chicago, American Library Association, 1930. 315p.

The first section, on materials, covers reference theory, selection and evaluation of reference materials, groups and characteristics of types of publications (such as periodicals, newspapers, government documents, and learned society publications) and organization of the collection, and interlibrary loan. The second section, on methods, covers handling reference questions, finding facts and materials, doing research, and reference methods in subject areas and in types of libraries. The third section, on administration, covers the reference librarian, reference department, inter-departmental comity, training the public, and rooms and furniture. Chapters include bibliography and thought questions.

252.   Wynar, Bohdan S. **Introduction to Bibliography and Reference Work: A Guide to Materials and Sources**. 4th ed. Rochester, New York, Libraries Unlimited, 1967. 310p.

Designed to be used as a text for basic reference and bibliography. The first unit covers all aspects of reference work and includes an outline, extensive readings, and a list of guides to reference materials. Other units cover bibliographies, indexes, encyclopedias, dictionaries, biography, and government documents. Each of these units includes a thorough introduction, outlines, readings, analytical discussion of individual works, and references to published reviews.

253.   Ziskind, Sylvia. **Reference Readings: A Manual for Librarians and Students**. Hamden, Conn., Shoe String, 1971. 310p.

Arranged in sections covering 1) dictionaries, 2) encyclopedias, 3) yearbooks and annuals, 4) handbooks and manuals, 5) indexes, serials, and directories, 6) bibliographies, 7) biographical dictionaries, 8) government publications, 9) atlases, gazetteers, and guidebooks, and 10) audiovisual materials. Evaluative discussion of titles and citations to reviews. An appendix gives examples of quizzes and search questions.

CHAPTER 4

REFERENCE LIBRARIANS

See also: Chapter 1, The Early History of Reference Service
Chapter 2, Theory and Philosophy of Reference Service
(General Works)
Chapter 3, Teaching of Reference
Chapter 6, Reference Service in Types of Libraries
Chapter 7, Special Types of Reference Service

Materials included in this section are those pertaining to the educational, personal, intellectual, professional, and any other characteristics and qualifications of reference librarians. Also included are biographical and anecdotal works about particular reference librarians. The broader subject of the role of reference librarians is not covered here but is treated in Chapter 2, Theory and Philosophy, in Chapter 5, Reference Service (General Works), and in Chapter 6, Reference Service in Types of Libraries. *See also* Chapter 3, Teaching of Reference, for material on educational and other qualifications.

A brief bibliography on reference librarians is given in James Wyer, *Reference Work* (Chicago, American Library Association, 1930).

Bibliographical coverage of the background, characteristics, and qualifications of librarians in general can be found in the following sources: Anita Schiller, and others, *Characteristics of Professional Personnel in College and University Libraries* (Springfield, Illinois State Library, 1969), pp. 105-113; Howard Clayton, *Investigation of Personality Characteristics Among Library Students at One Midwestern University* (U.S. Office of Education, 1968), pp. 11-25, 100-103; Elizabeth Stone, *Factors Related to Professional Development of Librarians* (Metuchen, N.J., Scarecrow, 1969), pp. 230-254; Perry Morrison, *Career of the Academic Librarian: A Study of Social Origins, Educational Attainments, Vocational Experiences, and Personality Characteristics of a Group of American Academic Librarians* (Chicago, American Library Association, 1969; ACRL Monographs, No. 29), pp. 152-165.

254.   Bryan, Alice. **The Public Librarian: A Report of the Public Library Inquiry**.
New York, Columbia University Press, 1952. 474p.
This classic study is valuable for the picture it provides of the librarian. It includes information on personal characteristics, educational status, economic status, and development of library careers. Also covered are in-service training, communication, and the education of librarians.

255.   Bundy, Mary Lee, and Paul Wasserman. "Professionalism Reconsidered," *College and Research Libraries* 29:5-26 (January 1968).

The authors point out specific ways in which librarians fall short of the professional model. These criticisms are particularly applicable to reference librarianship. Criticisms are that librarians 1) balk at offering judgments on quality or relevancy of materials, 2) are geared only to printed sources of information, 3) are medium- rather than client-oriented, 4) emphasize collection building rather than rapid access of information, 5) are often without special subject training, so they do not utilize non-conventional sources or pursue substantive information in depth.

256.   Cox, Carl T. "Return to the Basic Guides," *Tennessee Librarian* 18:127-131 (Summer 1966).

The author examines the problems facing reference librarianship in regard to the knowledge explosion. He advocates a return to the "basic guides," the guides of omniscience, humility, persistence, and professionalism.

257.   Donovan, William. "The Reference Librarian and the Whole Truth," *RQ* 8:196-198 (Spring 1969).

Argues that reference librarians have too little confidence and are fearful of discussing subjects with patrons, contributing knowledge, and expressing opinions. There should be realistic person-to-person communication, freely expressed remarks and opinions, more discussion with the patron of his areas of interest.

258.   Durkee, Douglas W. "We Can't Always Be Right," *RQ* 9:110-111 (Winter 1969).

Particular faults of reference librarians are outlined as 1) a dislike for new technology, 2) lack of sales resistance, 3) inadequate at weeding collections, 4) poor at providing attractive displays, 5) status conscious, 6) insufficient use of interlibrary loan, 7) unimaginative in answering reference questions, 8) reluctant to work evening hours.

259.   Foskett, D. J. "The Changing Role of the Librarian," *Times Literary Supplement* 70:63-64 (January 15, 1971).

The author discusses the status of the reference librarian and observes that this status has increased in the last years. The reference librarian has, in many cases, become an important member of the research team. Information science and computerization could result in a lowered status as the reference librarian becomes a "keeper of the machines" as he was formerly a "keeper of the books."

260.   Holleman, W. Roy. "The Reference Librarian," *Special Libraries* 52:314 (July 1961).

The personal qualities and attitudes of the reference librarian are discussed as they play a role in library public relations. Desirable qualities for reference librarians are considered.

261. Mearns, David. "Master of Materials: Random Reflections on Reference Librarianship." In Rowland, Arthur. *Reference Services*. Hamden, Conn., Shoe String, 1964. pp. 177-183. (Contributions to Library Literature, No. 5).
Describes faults and undesirable attitudes of reference librarians. Considers that qualities important for reference librarianship are literacy, intuition, ability to understand and transmit information, imagination and resourcefulness, enthusiasm, persistence, knowledge of the collection, humility, and love of serving people.

262. Mittal, R. L. "Split-Mind and Reference Service," *Indian Librarian* 14:70-72 (September 1959).
The quality of "split mind" is described as the alert and associative mind which retains problem questions of one patron while helping another. If these unanswered problems are retained in the mind, the reference librarian will recognize solutions when these are found during the process of helping other patrons and then provide these answers to the original patrons. Suggested by the author is a psychological test to measure this quality.

263. Owen, G. A. "Creative Reference Work," *Wilson Bulletin* 7:26-29 (September 1932).
In addition to skill, three other qualities are needed in reference work. These are ability to communicate with the patron, broad subject background, and a mind open to new ideas.

264. Reed, Janet. "The Reference Mystique, Part 2," *Cornell University Libraries Bulletin* 183:6-7 (May 1973).
Observes that library school classes in reference do not prepare students for actual reference work. Abilities of a good reference librarian include a good memory, detective ability, tactfulness, and the ability to handle a number of questions at once.

265. Reed, Sarah Rebecca. "Reference Librarian," *Library Journal* 81:21-23 (January 1, 1956).
The qualities and characteristics of a good reference librarian are described. Some of the problems of reference service are discussed. Considered essential to superior service is the relationship between the reference librarians and the administration.

266. Schiller, Anita R. **Characteristics of Professional Personnel in College and University Libraries**. Urbana, Illinois University, Library Research Center, 1968. 129p.
This survey, financed by the U.S. Office of Education, covered professional librarians employed in higher educational institutions of varying types, sizes, and means of control in 1966-1967.

267. Smith, Anne Marie. "Qualifications for an Ideal Reference Librarian," *Canadian Library Association Bulletin* 13:216 (April 1957).
Described here are both the academic and the personal qualifications necessary for successful performance of reference work.

268.   Spicer, Caroline. "The Reference Mystique," *Cornell University Libraries Bulletin* 183:4-5 (May 1973).
The way in which reference questions are answered often seems like "magic" to the patron. The author describes this process as one of analysis, search, and interpretation. Qualities required for successful completion of this process are patience, perceptiveness, and flexibility.

269.   Waddell, J. N. "Career of Isadore G. Mudge; a Chapter in the History of Reference Librarianship." Unpublished Ph.D. dissertation, Columbia University, 1973. 344p.

270.   Whyte, E. A. "Constance M. Winchell, Reference Librarian." Unpublished Research Paper, Long Island University, 1971. 70p.

271.   Wyer, James I. **Reference Work: A Textbook for Students of Library Work and Librarians**. Chicago, American Library Association, 1930. 315p.
The chapter entitled "The Reference Librarian" discusses educational, personal, and staff qualifications. In addition, traits and trait actions of a reference librarian are given, along with a rating scale.

CHAPTER 5

REFERENCE SERVICE

See also: Chapter 1, The Early History of Reference Service
Chapter 2, Theory and Philosophy of Reference Service
Chapter 3, Teaching of Reference
Chapter 6, Reference Service in Types of Libraries
Chapter 11, Research in Reference (Measurement and Evaluation)

      Included in this section are works dealing with reference service in general, covering such topics as administration, structure of the department, subject specialists and generalists, in-service training, and other aspects of reference service. Works concerning reference services in different types of libraries are not included here, but will be found under type of the library. Works on reference service that are intended to be used in teaching are included in Chapter 3, "Teaching of Reference."
      An annotated bibliography of reference service in general can be found in Gertrude Schutze, *Information and Library Science Source Book* (Metuchen, N.J., Scarecrow, 1972). Bibliographical coverage of reference service in general can also be found in Harold Smith, "Reference Services," in *Five Years Work in Librarianship, 1951-1955* (London, Library Association, 1958); James Wyer, *Reference Work* (Chicago, American Library Association, 1930); William Katz, *Introduction to Reference Work* (New York, McGraw-Hill, 1974); Bohdan Wynar, *Introduction to Bibliography and Reference Work* (Rochester, N.Y., Libraries Unlimited, 1967); and Frances N. Cheney, *Fundamental Reference Sources* (Chicago, American Library Association, 1971).

GENERAL WORKS

272.   "As Attractive as Buddhism? A Report on a Reference and Information Services Conference, Columbia University, March 30-April 1," *Library Journal* 91:2423-2430 (May 15, 1966).
Describes papers that were read and gives detailed descriptions of comments, reactions, and discussion following each paper. Each paper is critically evaluated, reactions of the audience are noted, and comments, pro and con, are presented. A valuable critical comment that adds dimension to the conference papers.

273.   Blanchard, J. R. "Postwar Reference Service," *Wilson Library Bulletin* 21:614 (April 1947).
Reference service declined during the war years. In order to build service up again it is necessary for reference librarians to be pleasant, to follow through on questions, and to provide a liberal level of service.

274. Bostick, Christina, ed. "Reference Service," *Cornell University Library Bulletin* (May 1973). (whole issue)
This issue is devoted to reference service and contains the following articles:
1) Caroline Spicer, "The Reference Mystique"; 2) Janet Reed, "The Reference Mystique, Part 2"; 3) Martha Hsu, "Olin's Experiment"; 4) Josephine Thorpe, "Pioneering in the Pre-Olin Days"; 5) Fran Lauman "Chimes and Quicksand."

275. Brandes, Julian. "Recent Trends in Library Reference Services," *School and Society* 70:193-195 (September 1949).
Discusses trends toward subject divisional reference service and subject specialization. Also discussed is McDiarmid's organizational plan of four years of service: 1) fact-finding and information, 2) education and advisory service overseeing subject divisions, 3) recreational reading, 4) research. Considers the trend in reference education toward correlating the concepts, principal schools of thought, and bibliography of a field in "literature of subjects" courses. Trends toward programs of in-service education, increased service to researchers, and special industrial research services such as literature searching and translation for fees.

276. Butler, Pierce, ed. **The Reference Function of the Library. Papers Presented before the Library Institute at the University of Chicago, June 29-July 10, 1942.** Chicago, University of Chicago Press, 1943. 366p.
This collection of 17 essays by different authors includes a survey of the reference field and the reference functions in various sizes and types of libraries. Also covered are special subject reference work, administration, personnel, book selection, wartime reference functions, and special collections.

277. Clapp, Verner. "Some Thoughts on the Present Status and Future Prospects of Reference Work." In Linderman, W., ed. *The Present Status and Future Prospects of Reference/Information Work*. Chicago, American Library Association, 1967. pp. 1-11.
Describes the rewarding aspects of reference service. Raises questions as to why the catalog is not useful in answering many reference questions, how library instruction can be made more successful, how we can study the factors that dictate the kind of reference service needed by the public in different types of libraries, and how reference books and reference work are related. Discusses the growth of information retrieval. Advocates an active and dynamic reference service that takes initiative in supplying information (such as SDI) rather than a passive or conservative service. Suggests that reference services should be publicized. Looks forward to an eventual national reference system. Group discussion follows this address.

278. Collison, Robert L. W. "Reference Libraries: The Turning Point," *Librarian and Book World* 45:81-83 (May-June 1956).
The author makes an appeal for a uniform standard of reference service throughout Great Britain. Cooperation between reference libraries is discussed. Microcard and microprint may be the means by which even the smaller branch libraries can provide effective reference service.

279. "Conference Report," [Present Status and Future Prospects of Reference Information Service] , *Wilson Library Bulletin* 40:909 (June 1966).
Describes highlights of the Conference on the Present Status and Future Prospects of Reference/Information Service held at Columbia University. Major considerations were changes in reference service due to automation and improvement of traditional service.

280. Day, A. E. "For Their Unfailing Helpfulness . . . ," *New Library World* 74:247-248 (November 1973).
Discusses humorously the acknowledgments and lack of acknowledgments given to reference librarians by authors whom they have helped in their research.

281. Freeman, C. B. "Introduction to Reference Work." In Rowland, Arthur. *Reference Services.* Hamden, Conn., Shoe String, 1964. pp. 156-166. (Contributions to Library Literature, No. 5).
Discusses a number of aspects of reference service from the British point of view. Considered are categories of reference books, qualities of reference librarians, and types of materials, including books, periodicals, trade publications, information indexes, cuttings and illustrations, and local collections and materials. Also discusses the reference interview and search strategy.

282. Ganapathy, K. P. "Reference Service: An Essential Process in Libraries in India," *Indian Librarian* 20:12-21 (June 1965).
An important function of the reference librarian in India is to liberate the multitudes who are frightened by books and ideas. Indian libraries have not yet established adequate reference and readers' advisory services. Thus, it can be seen that the task facing reference librarians in India is formidable.

283. Gellatly, Peter. "Reference, Anyone?" *RQ* 6:62-65 (Winter 1966).
Reference work, in theory, is exciting and challenging. However, in fact, it is boring, with much time spent in busy work. The great majority of questions are intellectually undemanding and routine. These views, as presented by the author in *RQ*, resulted in many replies in the Spring and Summer 1967 issues of *RQ*.

284. Harris, Katharine G. "Reference Service Today and Tomorrow: Objectives, Practices, Needs, and Trends," *Journal of Education for Librarianship* 3:175-187 (Winter 1963).
Present trends in reference service include an increase in departmentalization, telephone service, and demands by patrons, resulting in reluctance to deal with time-consuming questions. Solutions to a number of reference problems are suggested. Reference teaching is criticized because theory is emphasized at the expense of practical information. More on-the-job training and practical reference problems should be utilized.

285. Henn, Shirley. "Reference: A Summary," *Virginia Librarian* 16:20-21 (Summer 1969).
Talks presented by a panel of Virginia librarians are summarized. Discussed are trends in automation, interlibrary loan, service to students, and problems in reference service.

286. Jain, Sushil K. "The 3 R's of Library Service," *RQ* 11:51-53 (Fall 1971).
A library provides three main services: reference, research, and reading. Reference or referral services are repetitive in nature, and reference librarians should instead perform professional services that involve consultation, judgment, and individual attention.

287. Khandwala, V. K. "Role of Reference Service in a Library," *Indian Librarian* 20:85-88 (September 1965).
Discusses organization and patterns of reference service. Also considers theories of reference.

288. Kumar, Suseela. **The Changing Concepts of Reference Service.**
Delhi, India, Vikas, 1974. 327p.
Based on lectures given at the Documentation Research and Training Centre by the author, who is Regional Librarian of the British Council Library in Madras, India. Case studies and anecdotes of reference work are given, drawn from the author's experiences with reference work and reference librarianship in India.

289. Laythe, Rosamund. "Who Are We?" *Learning Today* 6:16-17 (Winter 1973).
Discusses trends in reference service, including expanded service, service for individual needs, and media and vertical file materials playing a larger role. The author also anticipates that service will become more "aggressive," utilizing "floating librarians" who are not tied to a desk.

290. Library Association. Reference, Special and Information Section. Mort, G., ed. *Proceedings of the 18th Annual Conference and Study Group, York, April 3-6, 1970.* London, the Section, 1971. 50p.
These four papers deal with 1) restructuring library and information systems, 2) the open university, 3) cooperation between public and university libraries, 4) developments in official economic statistics.

291. Linderman, Winifred, ed. **The Present Status and Future Prospects of Reference/Information Service.** Chicago, American Library Association, 1967. 186p.
This conference report includes papers on the following topics: 1) "Users and Their Needs," by Helen Focke; 2) "Areas of Need," by Marian Allen; 3) "Community Resource Centers," by Leonard Freiser; 4) "Relevance Judgments," by Alan Rees; 5) "State and Regional Service," by John Lorenz; 6) "National Information System," by Foster Mohrhardt; 7) "Reference Tools," by Katharine Harris; 8) "Machine-Generated Tools," by Pauline Atherton; 9) "Economics of Reference Work Publishing," by Edwin Colburn; 10) "Applications of Automation," by Joseph Becker; 11) "Information Storage and Retrieval," by Emmanuel Mesthene; and 12) "Indexing," by Grieg Aspnes. One purpose of this collection of papers is to overcome the reluctance in the profession to discuss change in reference/information systems.

292.   Morris, Richard B. "Adventures in the Reference Room," *Wilson Library Bulletin* 41:492-501 (January 1967).
Compares reference service in the 1920s with the future automated reference service. Also discusses the problems of bibliographical control of unpublished materials.

293.   Murray, Florence B. "Reference and Cataloguing in the Last Quarter Century," In Rowland, Arthur, ed. *Reference Services*. Hamden, Conn., Shoe String, 1964. pp. 23-30. (Contributions to Library Literature, No. 5).
Considered here are the effects of specialization on reference service, problems of dealing with non-book materials, the improvement of bibliographical control, the introduction of documentation and mechanization, and the growth of special, regional, and national libraries.

294.   Nagasawa, M. "Reference Function of the Modern Library," *Library Science*, No. 2:173-187 (1964).
Discusses the purpose and function of reference service in linking the user to library resources. Stresses the importance of understanding the information-gathering habits of library users. Considers the place of mechanized techniques in reference service.

295.   Poole, Mary E. "What is Reference Work?" *Library Journal* 85:1522-1524 (April 15, 1960).
This article is based on a lecture given to a reference workshop of the Nevada State Library. Definitions of reference work are discussed. The author divides reference questions into three categories—information, reference, and research. The responsibilities and qualifications of reference librarians are briefly discussed.

296.   **Preconference Seminar on Reference Service in Texas Libraries**. San Antonio, Texas, Texas Library Association, 1968.
Discussed in this report are different types of reference service in Texas, covering the State Library, university libraries, public and other types of libraries. Specific projects in different libraries are described. Plans, programs, and statistics are included.

297.   **Reference Work: Background and Implications**. Tel Aviv, Israel Society of Special Libraries and Information Centers, 1971. (Contributions to Information Science 5; Clarissa Gadiel Memorial Issue). 34p. ERIC Document ED056714.
Papers in honor of Clarissa Gadiel by her colleagues. Includes "Information Education at the Grass Roots," by Hans Wellisch; "Reference Work in Library and Information Science Curricula," by Sarah M. Thomas; "Dealing with Journals in Special Libraries," by Susal Weil; "The One Man Show Reference Business: The Satiric Approach," by Esther Amiel.

298. Rothstein, Samuel. "Reference Service—The New Dimension in Librarian- ship," *College and Research Libraries* 22:11-18 (January 1961). Also, *Wilson Library Bulletin* 37:411-416 (January 1963).

This article is based on a paper given to the Reference Services Division of the American Library Association in 1960. Discusses the lack of adequate reference service and defines reference as "personal assistance given by the librarian to indi- vidual readers in pursuit of information." This requires recognition by the library and a specific organization. Reference service functions are instruction, guidance in choice of books, and information service. Philosophies of level of service are discussed. Advocates larger library and reference budgets, use of technology, foundation grants for expanded reference service projects on a demonstration basis.

299. Rowland, Arthur R., ed. **Reference Services**. Hamden, Conn., Shoe String Press, 1964. 259p. (Contributions to Library Literature, No. 5).

This collection includes 31 essays by well-known library figures. Topics covered are the past, present, and future of reference service, organization and administration, and the reference librarian and his or her work.

300. Sayers, William. "Organization of Information for the General Public." In Rowland, Arthur, ed., *Reference Services*. Hamden, Conn., Shoe String Press, 1964. pp. 71-77. (Contributions to Library Literature, No. 5).

Describes the development of information service in British public libraries, begin- ning about 40 years ago. Discusses materials, staff needed, and organization of the collection. Notes that questions which seem trivial or unimportant on the surface may actually be vital to the patron's interests.

301. Sharp, Henry A. "An Impression of American Reference Work," *Library World* 38:159 (January 1936).

Among other impressions, the author, an English librarian, notes the growing emphasis on subject specialization.

302. Sinclair, Dorothy. "Meanwhile Back at the Reference Desk," *RQ* 5:10-12 (Fall 1965).

Points out that reference librarians are caught between the traditional perfectionist standards of the past, the economics and belt-tightening of the present, and the automated systems of the future. She suggests the following ways to improve ref- erence work during this trying interim period: 1) more effective and thorough reference interviews to save wasted time, 2) faster and more efficient ways of searching a large number of indexes, 3) cooperation in production and use of home-made indexes.

303. Smith, Harold. "Reference Services." In Sewell, P. H. *Five Years Work in Librarianship, 1951-1955*. London, The Library Association, 1958. pp. 245-252.

Reviews developments in reference service during the period 1951-1955, primarily in Great Britain, with some coverage of the United States. Considers cooperative reference and interlibrary loan services in detail. Discusses trends toward subject specialization and departmentalization in Great Britain and the United States. Reviews the literature on reference work. Concludes by noting five significant trends in reference service. Bibliography.

304. Soule, Byron. "Frozen Assets." In Rowland, Arthur, ed. *Reference Services*. Hamden, Conn., Shoe String Press, 1964. pp. 108-111. (Contributions to Library Literature, No. 5).

A professor of chemistry describes the ideas in books as "frozen assets" if they can't be located when needed. Discusses problems of classification and making books available. Considers that reference experts provide needed services and often save much money to business and industry by providing vital information.

305. Stevens, R. E. ed. "The Library: Its Reference Function," *Journal of Higher Education* 40:323-326 (April 1969).

Discusses two significant trends in reference service. The first is the trend toward full information provision, in which reference librarians compile bibliographies, undertake literature searches, and locate specific information for patrons rather than referring them to sources of information. The second trend is toward the "referral center," where patrons are referred to agencies or persons as sources of information.

306. Stewart, James D., ed. **The Reference Librarian in University, Municipal and Specialized Libraries**. London, Grafton and Co., 1951. 288p.

An account of practice and procedures in various types of reference libraries. Chapters, written by experts, cover reference work in 1) university libraries; 2) municipal, commercial and technical libraries; 3) scientific and technical research libraries; 4) medical libraries; and 5) newspaper reference libraries. An annotated list of "Essential Books for the Reference Library," by A. J. Walford is included.

307. Sumner, Ellen L. "The Reference Librarian and Reference Service: A Stocktaking and Meditation," *West Virginia Libraries* 18:1-10 (June 1965).

The author considers reference librarianship as a profession and comments on its public image. Also discussed are reference work, continuing education of reference librarians, the breed of information scientists, and interlibrary cooperation.

308. Texas Library Association. **Reference, Research and Regionalism. Selected Papers from the 53rd Conference, Austin, Texas, March, 1966**. Austin, Tex., The Association, 1966. 60p.

Papers included are "The Dilemma of Subject Analysis for Modern Library Service," by C. J. Frarey; "The Systems Approach to Reference Service," by J. L. Connor; "Foundations of a Theory of Reference Service," and "The Challenging Role of the Reference Librarian," by Jesse Shera; and "Reference Needs and Services for a Special Collection," by E. Hinkle.

309.   Thaxton, Mary L. "The Dispensation," *Virginia Librarian* 16:22-26
        (Fall 1969).
This article is written in the form of a humorous dialogue between a reference
librarian, professor, instructor, students, and various other library users. It highlights the status of the reference librarian and the conditions of change within
the library.

310.   Thirsk, J. W. "Reference Libraries," *Librarian and Book World* 45:83-85
        (May-June, 1956).
Analyzes the types of users of reference libraries and the improvements needed to
upgrade service. The advantages of microfilm for little-used materials are noted
and the need for more money to improve service is stressed.

311.   Usher, Robert J. "Some Needs in Reference Work," *Library Journal*
        51:761-766 (September 15, 1926).
Points out the need to be familiar with many reference sources and the need for
more printed guides. Discusses use of the library by business. Also comments on
fields of knowledge poorly covered by reference sources of the time.

312.   Vavrek, Bernard. "Reference Service—Back to Basics," *Catholic Library
        World* 47:64-67 (September 1975).
The author discusses problems in library financing and notes that the solution to
financial problems must come from a change in priorities rather than from budgetary increases. He stresses the importance of local information and of library
instruction so that patrons will be able to utilize the full resources of the library.

313.   Wheeler, Joseph L. "Bettering Reference Service," *RQ* 6:99-114
        (Spring 1967).
The author discusses the present status of reference service, administration and
policy, staffing, physical facilities, reference materials, and subject departmentalization. Improvements are suggested that might apply to all types of libraries. In
regard to computerization, he points out that information retrieval, as yet, covers
only limited subject areas and is most suitable for larger libraries. Experimental
programs of information retrieval should be better coordinated. More printed
indexes should be available for use of average patrons.

ADMINISTRATION OF REFERENCE SERVICE

See also: Chapter 5, Reference Service (General Works)
               Chapter 6, Reference Service in Types of Libraries
               Chapter 11, Research in Reference (Measurement and Evaluation)

        This section includes works pertaining to administration of reference
service in general and in particular types of libraries. Also included are some
works concerned with more specific aspects of administration that are not
classifiable elsewhere. Certain areas related to administration of reference
are treated in separate sections following this section: Subject Specialists

and/or Generalists, Subject Departments and/or Centralized Service, In-Service Training, Non-Professional Personnel and Duties, and Special Aids and Devices and Information Desks. Material related to administration of reference is also included in the section "Measurement and Evaluation." Material on the administration of information centers can be found in Chapter 13, Information Centers and Services. Works on administration of computerized reference and information retrieval services will be found in Chapter 14, Information Retrieval.

Bibliographical coverage of administration of reference work for college and research libraries can be found in Guy Lyle's *Administration of the College Library* (New York, Wilson, 1974) and for public libraries in Joseph Wheeler, and Herbert Goldhor, *Practical Administration of Public Libraries* (New York, Harper, 1962). Other bibliographical coverage can be found in William Katz, *Introduction to Reference Work* (New York, McGraw-Hill, 1974) and Bohdan Wynar, *Introduction to Bibliography and Reference Work* (Rochester, N.Y., Libraries Unlimited, 1967). A brief bibliography of historical interest on administration of reference services may be found in James Wyer, *Reference Work* (Chicago, American Library Association, 1930).

314.   Asheim, Lester. "Publicity for a University Library's Reference Department," *Library Journal* 66:206-207 (March 1, 1941).
The author discusses the way in which publicity can stimulate use of reference materials and service.

315.   Barton, Mary N. "Administrative Problems in Reference Work." In Butler, Pierce, ed. *The Reference Function of the Library*. Chicago, University of Chicago Press, 1943. pp. 218-249.
This chapter considers the problem of administrative relationships, cooperation, physical facilities, services, and personnel management.

316.   Blakely, Florence. "Perceiving Patterns of Reference Service: A Survey," *RQ* 11:30-38 (Fall 1971).
Report of a survey by the author of patterns of reference service in large academic libraries. Discusses the following: 1) organization, staffing, and coverage of service points; 2) reference collection; 3) responsibilities and activities; 4) maintenance of special files; 5) publications; 6) library instruction; 7) campus coordination; 8) direct service to patrons; 9) measurement and evaluation. The author notes that reference departments need to overcome their communication gap with the faculty and to participate more fully in the educational process.

317.   Bozone, Billie. "Staff Manuals for Reference Departments in College and University Libraries," *College and Research Libraries* 22:19-20, 34 (January 1961).
Staff manuals are valuable in that they provide self-evaluation, standardize work procedures, and interpret the reference department to faculty and staff. An outline is given to be used in preparation of a staff manual.

318.   Chapman, Ronald F. "Scheduling of Reference Librarians," *RQ* 9:24-26
       (Fall 1969).
This telephone survey of 21 large academic libraries was conducted by the Library
of Congress. Questions were asked concerning scheduling on evening and weekend
hours. Staffing patterns were shown to vary according to the budget and local
demand.

319.   Durkan, Michael J. "Reference Service Patterns in Academic Libraries,"
       Connecticut Libraries 12:25-27 (Fall 1970).
Selected academic libraries were surveyed to determine hours during which reference
service was available. Daytime service from 9:00 A.M. through 5:00 P.M. was universal, with the majority having Saturday morning hours. Only about half of the
libraries provided service on Saturday afternoons or Sunday.

320.   Enoch Pratt Free Library, Baltimore, Maryland. **General Reference
       Department Staff Manual**. Baltimore, Maryland, Enoch Pratt Free
       Library, 1950. 230p.
An introduction to this manual describes its purpose and plan, and the function of
the reference department, its organization and resources and referral policies.
Covered also are the scope and development of the department, physical facilities,
policies, procedures, and materials.

321.   Fenton, F. H., ed. **Reference Library Staffs: An Enquiry into the Staffing
       of Reference Services in the Rate-Supported Libraries of Great Britain
       and Northern Ireland**. London, Library Association, Reference, Special
       and Information Section, 1962. 68p.
A detailed survey made in Great Britain to see what effect the *Memorandum on
the Status and Training of Reference Librarians, 1960*, had had on staffing. Gives
a detailed picture of reference staffing. Includes, for example, the finding that only
200 of 580 library authorities had separately staffed reference libraries. Gives
statistics covering number of reference staff in proportion to population, grading
and status, responsibilities and training. Comments made by reference librarians
on questionnaires are included.

322.   Gwinup, Thomas. "Participation in Decisions: Reference, the Library,
       and the Larger Question," *California Librarian* 36:56-62 (April 1975).
This paper was delivered by the author at a conference of the California Library
Association. Discusses how the Reference and Instructional Services Department
modified its hierarchical structure and now elects a chairman for a specified term.
Promotion and chairmanship are both completely disassociated from rank under
the new system.

323.   Harrison, E. C. "Current Reference Practices in Four University Libraries
       in North Carolina." Master's thesis, University of North Carolina, 1960.
       121p. (ACRL Microcard Series 140).

324.   Heenan, Thomas G. "On Cracking Egg Shells," *RQ* 10:216-217 (Spring
        1971).
Reference should be conceived of as a service rather than a place. Following this
concept, reference books should be placed in the stacks in their subject areas and
reference librarians should be stationed there also. Directional and general information questions could then be handled at a Reader's Service Desk.

325.   Hoehn, Phil, and Jean Hudson. "Who is at the Reference Desk? Academic
        Library Staffing Patterns," *RQ* 8:242-244 (Summer 1969).
Reference staffing patterns were surveyed by the University Federation of Librarians, University of California at Berkeley, in 54 of the largest academic libraries in
the United States. Results of the survey are given and the conclusion is reached
that non-professionals should be used to back up professionals at the reference desk,
freeing the latter for more in-depth service.

326.   Illinois State Library. "Reference Policy," *Illinois Libraries* 53:252-253
        (March 1971).
A copy of the reference policy of the Illinois State Library is presented here. Sections cover services and materials, procedures, and policy. Policy toward school,
public, academic, and special libraries is also given.

327.   King, Jack. "Barriers to Reference Work," *RQ* 7:27-29 (Fall 1967).
Discussed here is the problem of poor communication between reference and technical services staff which can seriously interfere with good service. The author
suggests research by the reference staff to compile statistical profiles of patrons
and cost analyses of various services. This information could be communicated
to the technical services staff for better understanding of the nature of reference
service to the library's patrons and the most practical and effective ways of
providing it.

328.   Knox, Margaret E. "The Development of a Staff for Reference Work." In
        Illinois University. Graduate School of Library Science. *The Library as a
        Community Information Center*. Champaign, Illini Union Bookstore,
        1959. pp. 137-151.
Basic skills needed by the reference librarian are technical knowledge of the library's
resources, human relations skills, and the ability to think creatively. In-service training is necessary to improve skills. Suggestions are job rotation, interlibrary exchange
of personnel, or staff meetings. Whatever form it takes it should be carefully prepared and suited to the individual librarian.

329.   Library Association. Council. "The Status and Training of Reference
        Librarians: Memorandum Approved by the Library Association Council
        in January, 1960," *Library Association Record* 62:259-260 (August 1960).
A memorandum on the function and staffing of the reference library in Great
Britain which stresses the importance of this department. It deals with the number
of staff required and proposes one reference librarian per 20,000 population. Also
discusses qualifications, responsibility, relative status, and training.

330. Lindner, A. L. "Administration of the Reference Activities in Public Libraries." Unpublished Master's thesis, University of Illinois, 1954. 41p.

331. Lyle, Guy. **The Administration of the College Library**. 4th ed. New York, Wilson, 1974. 320p.
The chapter on "Reference Services," pages 90-105, covers objectives, organization, qualifications of reference staff, selection of reference materials, work with students, and interlibrary loan.

332. Lynch, Mary Jo. "Academic Library Reference Policy Statements: Toward a Definition of Service," *RQ* 11:222-226 (Spring 1972).
In order to formulate a reference policy at the University of Massachusetts, a survey was done of reference policy in 76 academic libraries. Results show that most reference departments operate informally, adjusting their service to changes in patron needs. The author believes that service would improve if more thought were given to priorities and specific objectives and policies were formulated. A draft outline of Massachusetts University's reference service policy manual is given.

333. McColvin, Lionel R. "Organization of Reference Services," *Library Association Record* 56:152-159 (May 1954).
The author considers the functions of reference service and the way in which it should be organized. Describes the ways in which information service differs from reference service.

334. Phelps, Rose B. "The Effect of Organizational Patterns on the Adequacy and Efficiency of Reference Service in the Large American Public Library," *Library Quarterly* 17:281-295 (October 1947).
The organization of reference service in the Los Angeles, Boston, and St. Louis Public Libraries was studied. Positive and negative effects of organizational patterns on reference service are noted. The author concludes that subject departmentalization gives more efficient service.

335. Shaffer, Dale E. **Library Job Descriptions: Examples Covering Major Work Areas**. Salem, Ohio, Dale Shaffer, 1973. 42p. ERIC Document ED087485.
Includes a job description of reference work which would apply to public, college, university, and special libraries. Covers qualifications, responsibilities and duties, and length of contracts.

336. Spencer, Carol. "How to Allocate Personnel Costs of Reference." Paper presented at the 93rd American Library Association Annual Conference, New York, July 7-13, 1974. ERIC Document ED094702.
The seminar on reference measurement, held during the 1974 ALA Convention, determined that work sampling and random time sampling were the best method of allocating personnel costs at the Library of the College of Physicians in Philadelphia. Need for cost information was discussed and alternative methods were studied for advantages and disadvantages. The diary and cost accounting

methods were rejected. The sampling method is reliable, low cost, does not interfere with service, and there is little distortion in data. It eliminates the need to keep masses of data and can be carried out by library managers.

337.   Talmadge, Robert L. "Practices and Policies of the Reference Departments of Large University Libraries Concerning the Preparation of Bibliographies." Unpublished Master's thesis, University of Illinois, 1951. 64p.
Results of this study indicated that compilation of bibliographies was an "extra" which should not and did not receive high priority. Almost one-fourth believed this should not be done for any category of patron and nearly all imposed restrictions on bibliographical service.

338.   Werner, P. A. "Organization of Reference Service in the Small College Library." Unpublished Master's thesis, Drexel Institute of Technology, 1953. 34p.

339.   Wheeler, Joseph L., and Herbert Goldhor. **Practical Administration of Public Libraries**. New York, Harper and Row, 1962. 571p.
A chapter titled "Administration of Reference Services" describes the current status of reference service and defines the reference function. Covers organization, departmental relations, staffing, service, building, collections, service to readers, and publicity. Discusses standards, measurement of service, and evaluation based on self-survey.

SUBJECT SPECIALISTS AND/OR GENERALISTS

See also: Chapter 5, Reference Service (Subject Departments and/or Centralized Service)
Chapter 6, Reference Service in Types of Libraries (Academic Libraries; Special Libraries)

Included in this section are works concerned with reference librarians who function as subject specialists or generalists. Subject departments and/or centralization will be treated separately in the following section.
Bibliographical coverage of subject specialization will be found in J. Periam Danton, "Subject Specialists in National and University Libraries with Special Reference to Book Selection," *Libri* 17:29-41 (1967); Selby Gration, "Reference Bibliographers in the College Library," *College and Research Libraries* 35:28-34 (January 1974); Charles Crossley, "The Subject Specialist in an Academic Library," *Aslib Proceedings* 26:236-249 (June 1974).

340.   Byrd, C. K. "Subject Specialist in a University Library," *College and Research Libraries* 27:191-193 (May 1966).
Describes the role of subject specialists at the Indiana University Library. Subject specialist librarians in humanities, social sciences, and area studies work with both faculty and graduate students. Responsibilities include library instruction, bibliographical assistance, and liaison with academic departments.

341.　Cole, G. L. "Subject Reference Librarian and the Academic Departments:
　　　A Cooperative Venture," *Special Libraries* 65:259-262 (July 1974).
Discusses the role of the subject specialist in regard to academic departments. Subject specialists should participate in faculty activities and keep the department well
informed of library developments. They should visit classes and give lectures for
both graduates and undergraduates, prepare bibliographies, and build the library's
collection in this subject area. In addition, they should evaluate the collection
and plan programs to fill gaps and should know other resources available in the
region.

342.　Crossley, Charles. "The Subject Specialist Librarian in an Academic
　　　Library: His Role and Place," *Aslib Proceedings* 26:236-249 (June 1974).
Briefly reviews the background of subject specialization and gives definitions of
functions, personal characteristics of subject specialists, and objectives. Describes
in detail the subject specialist functions of book selection, reference assistance,
library instruction, liaison with academic departments, current awareness and
information service, compilation of bibliographies, and cataloging and classification. Considers the administrative aspects of subject specialization, such as self-
responsibilities and scheduling, number and types of specialists needed, staff
management, participation in library activities, job satisfaction, pay, and career
prospects. Discusses factors that affect the subject specialist's satisfaction in his
work.

343.　Danton, J. Periam. "Subject Specialists in National and University
　　　Libraries with Special Reference to Book Selection," *Libri* 17:42-58
　　　(1967).
Discusses difference between continental and Anglo-American subject specialists.
Continental subject specialists are more likely to hold academic subject qualifications than library degrees, while the reverse is true for Anglo-American subject
specialists. The Anglo-American subject specialist spends more time on processing
and reference work and less on book selection, while the Continental specialist
spends more time on processing and book selection and less on reference. Librarians should play a more important role in building the collection and exert a
stronger influence on selection of materials.

344.　Gration, Selby, and Arthur P. Young. "Reference-Bibliographers in the
　　　College Library," *College and Research Libraries* 35:28-34 (January 1974).
The authors advocate the use of reference bibliographers whom they describe as
having broad subject competence, familiarity with terminology, bibliographic
tools, and major literature of several related disciplines. These specialists provide
reference service and library instruction, serve as representatives to academic
departments, and build and interpret the collection. As they both build and interpret the collection, they improve the quality of service substantially. Historical
background of the reference bibliographer is given and the authors describe their
experiences with a staff of subject specialists at SUNY, Cortland, New York.

345. Hernon, Peter. "The Academic Reference Librarian as Documents Specialist and Promoter," *Pennsylvania Library Association Bulletin* 30:27-28 (March 1975).

Describes the importance of knowledge of documents on the part of reference librarians. They must have familiarity with documents reference sources, knowledge of publishing practices, government organizations, and problems of bibliographical control. Discusses the reference value of different kinds of government publications and their use in reference service. Considers the relationship between reference and documents departments. Suggests outreach programs to familiarize students with government publications.

346. Humphreys, K. "The Subject Specialist in National and University Libraries," *Libri* 17:29-41 (1967).

The subject specialist is of value in both centralized and decentralized libraries. Discusses responsibilities of book selection, reference service, and maintaining contact with academic departments. Considers qualifications needed by specialists in subject fields.

347. Hunt, Donald R. "Where is the General Reference Librarian and Bread-and-Butter Service?" *College and Research Libraries* 26:307-310, 326 (July 1965).

The rise of subject specialization has been helpful in providing research services in more depth in subject areas. The author is concerned, however, that this emphasis will result in the decrease of general reference librarians. General reference service combines public relations and instruction with reference service. Even in divisional libraries the general reference librarian is needed to help less sophisticated users, handle general questions, refer, and fill in when subject specialists are off duty. The general reference area should be located near the main entrance, catalog, and general reference collection.

348. Hurt, Peyton. "Staff Specialization: A Possible Substitute for Departmentalization," *ALA Bulletin* 29:417-421 (July 1935).

The author describes how subject specialization can be accomplished by individual librarians in a general collection. Prevailing opinion at this time equated subject specialization with departmentalization.

349. Reino, Cecilia. "Conversation with Hendrik Edelman," *Cornell University Library Bulletin* 182:4-7 (March 1973).

The Assistant Director for the Development of the Collection describes his experiences at the reference desk and relates them to collection development. Discusses the relationship between reference questions asked and the nature of the collection and whether reference staff can make recommendations for substantially improving the collection.

350. Stueart, Robert D. **The Area Specialist Bibliographer: An Inquiry Into His Role**. Metuchen, N.J., Scarecrow, 1972. 152p.

Discusses the role and responsibilities of area specialist bibliographers in the university library. This person is involved in collection building, preparation of bibliographies, and sometimes in advanced reference service.

SUBJECT DEPARTMENTS AND/OR CENTRALIZED SERVICE

See also: Chapter 5, Reference Service (Subject Specialists and/or Generalists)
Chapter 6, Reference Service in Types of Libraries (Academic
Libraries; Public Libraries)

Included here are works concerned with the role and function of reference service in the departmentalized and/or centralized library structure in any type of library system, as well as selected works dealing with departmentalized or centralized library systems in general.

Bibliographical coverage in this area is provided in Michael Overington, *The Subject Departmentalized Public Library* (London, Library Association, 1969).

351.   Brock, Clifton. "Reference Service in the Divisional Plan Library: Some Tentative Questions," *College and Research Libraries* 22:449-456 (November 1961).

Recommends staffing subject divisions by specialists with graduate degrees in both library science and the appropriate subject area. It would be desirable for these specialists to select and catalog reference tools for their department. They must also be active in giving research assistance, since researchers have difficulty in keeping up with the growth in published knowledge.

352.   Lundy, Frank A. "Library Service to Undergraduate College Students in the Divisional Plan Library," *College and Research Libraries* 17:143-148 (March 1956).

Describes the decentralizing and regrouping of library functions at the University of Nebraska Library. Discusses how this plan has worked successfully in the case of a relatively "uncomplicated" university. This plan has resulted in a broadening of the responsibilities of both reference and technical processing personnel.

353.   Metcalf, Keyes. "Departmental Organization in Libraries." In Joeckel, Carlton, ed. *Current Issues in Library Administration*. Chicago, University of Chicago Press, 1938. pp. 90-110.

Considers the general principles underlying formation of subject departments and the functions of these departments. Problems concerned with departmentalization are discussed. Such problems can generally be solved more easily in actual library practice than in theory.

354.   Overington, Michael A. **The Subject Departmentalized Public Library**. London, The Library Association, 1969. 167p.

All collections, reference and circulating, should be grouped under broad subject areas. Included in this book are discussions of principles, organization and administration, staffing, materials, and branches. Also covered are the economic aspects and the particular problems of this type of library.

355. Peterson, Harry N. "Subject Departments: How to Avoid Giving the Reader the Run Around," *Wilson Library Bulletin* 30:375-379 (January 1956).

Problems dealt with in this article include: 1) personnel lack of knowledge of materials in other departments, 2) handling interdisciplinary reference questions, 3) coordination of subject department activities, 4) departments may assume self-sufficient attitudes and will not use related materials elsewhere, 5) referring of readers from department to department on difficult questions. Recommendations include separate divisional catalogs, graphic division symbols, duplication of needed materials, a general reference division to coordinate divisions, and close cooperation among the staff.

356. Ranganathan, S. R. "Specialist Library Versus Generalist Library: Reference Service," *Library Science with a Slant to Documentation* 7:80-95 (March 1970).

Report of discussions between students and professors at the Documentation Research and Training Center in 1967. Notable features of specialist service are more long-range reference service and teamwork. Also covered in the discussion are facet analysis of questions, classification schemes, and cataloging rules.

357. Warren, Althea. "Department Organization by Subject." In Joeckel, Carlton. *Current Issues in Library Administration.* Chicago, University of Chicago Press, 1938. pp. 111-134.

The history of subject departmentalization is reviewed and public libraries having subject departments are discussed. Arguments are advanced for the subject departmental plan. Concludes that the feasibility of departmentalization is determined by the size of the library and the amount of its support.

358. Winslow, Amy. "Experience in Departmentalization," *ALA Bulletin* 27:684-687 (December 15, 1933).

Discusses the advantages and disadvantages of subject departmentalization. Personnel problems and greater costs of departmentalization are considered. The author concludes that departmentalization is desirable and is in line with trends toward subject specialization.

NON-PROFESSIONAL PERSONNEL AND DUTIES

See also: Chapter 3, Teaching of Reference
Chapter 11, Research in Reference (Measurement and Evaluation)

This section contains works on two closely related aspects of reference service. The first is the use in reference work of non-professional personnel, defined as those not possessing the master's degree in library science and including all types of persons (from lower educational levels through the Ph.D.) who have been or might be utilized in reference service. The second aspect covered is the professional and/or clerical nature of work done by reference librarians in the performance of their duties. Additional relevant material will be found in Chapter 11, Research in Reference (Measurement and Evaluation).

Some bibliographical coverage of the use of non-professional personnel in reference work may be found in Charles Bunge, *Professional Education and Reference Efficiency* (Springfield, Illinois State Library, 1967). For bibliographical coverage of the use of non-professional personnel in library work in general, see: Alice E. Wright, *Library Clerical Workers and Pages* Hamden, Conn., Shoe String, 1973), pp. 81-83; H. R. Wheeler, "Technician Level of Library Staffing: A Bibliography," *Special Libraries* 60:527-534 (October 1969); J. E. Munro, "Library Technicians: A Selected Bibliography," *Ontario Library Review* 53:101-108 (June 1969); Joanne Boelke, *Library Technicians: A Survey of Current Developments* (Washington, D.C., ERIC Clearinghouse for Library and Information Sciences, 1968); Edwin Strohecker, ed., *Library Technical Assistant: A Report of the Orientation Institute on the Library Technician, July 14-25, 1969* (Louisville, Ky., Spalding College, Department of Library Science, 1970) pp. 44-47.

359. Alsmeyer, Henry L., Jr., and Joseph Grimes. "Graduate Administrative Assistants," *RQ* 9:149-150 (Winter 1969).
Describes successful experiments at Ohio State University and Texas A and M University, where doctoral candidates were assigned to the Reference Department. They contributed effectively by collection building and compilation of bibliographies in their subject field, as well as by work at the reference desk.

360. Anderson, Frank J. "The Literature Searcher," *Special Libraries* 51:557-558 (December 1960).
Describes the job of the literature searcher, which fills the gap between the reference librarian and the researcher. The literature searcher "takes up where the reference librarian is forced to leave off yet stops short of intruding into the areas of basic or applied research." Describes the qualifications needed and methods and procedures.

361. Astbury, Effie C. "Library Technicians and the Reference Service," *Canadian Library Journal* 26:54-57 (January-February 1969).
This article notes that the ALA's *Descriptive List of Professional and Non-Professional Duties in Libraries* lists only one non-professional task under reference work—that of locating simple bibliographical information. Increasing attention is being given to the use of non-professionals in reference work. The author points out some difficulties, which include the need for supervision and the fact that reference work requires a high level of education.

362. Bjorgo, Maynard. "Technicians in Reference Service—Another View," *Canadian Library Journal* 26:58-60 (January-February 1969).
The author teaches reference to library technicians and believes that the reference potential is as great for these students as for those in four-year institutions. A technician can locate simple bibliographical information and use indexes, as well as suggest approaches to information under the guidance of reference librarians. Questions can be handled during busy periods if a report-back procedure is followed.

363. Bloomberg, Marty. "Reference Services." In *Introduction to Public Services for Library Technicians*. 2nd ed. Littleton, Colo., Libraries Unlimited, 1976. pp. 85-93.

Discusses types of reference service, the purposes of reference work, and the role of the library technician in a reference department. Also considers the limits on reference service, reference techniques, question analysis and search, and organization of reference collections.

364. Boyer, Laura, and William Theimer, Jr. "The Use and Training of Non-Professional Personnel at Reference Desks in Selected College and University Libraries," *College and Research Libraries* 36:193-199 (May 1975).

The authors review opinions pro and con concerning the use of non-professionals in reference service. One of the first questions to be answered in regard to this controversy is to what extent non-professionals are presently being used in reference service. One hundred and forty-one libraries at four-year accredited colleges and universities were surveyed. It was found that over two-thirds of the libraries utilized non-professionals in reference service. About 33 percent of total reference desk hours of all the respondents were staffed by non-professionals. Educational level of non-professionals was as follows: three-fifths with a B.A., one-fifth with junior college education, and one-fifth with no college at all. Eighty percent of respondents indicated that there was no formal in-service training program for these assistants.

365. Clark, Alice S., and Howard Pepple. "The Use of Graduate Assistants: Academic Subject Reference Service," *RQ* 8:240-241 (Summer 1969).

Describes an experimental program at Ohio State University Libraries, where five graduate assistantships have been created in subject reference areas. These assistants will receive a stipend in return for 18 hours of work per week. Their duties will include preparing guides to the literature and bibliographic aids. Benefits might include increased cooperation between the library and academic departments, and possible recruitment of subject specialists for librarianship.

366. Corth, Annette. "Corth's Commandments [on reference]," *Special Libraries* 65:473 (October-November 1974).

Twelve pointers given by the author to reference technicians are described here.

367. Evrard, Connie, and C. C. Waddington. "Undergraduate Survey: Its Role in Changing Patterns of Reference Service," *Drexel Library Quarterly* 7:351-356 (July-October 1971).

In an effort to accelerate in-depth use of its libraries by undergraduates, Brown University has designed a plan of bringing advanced graduate students, veterans of intensive summer training in reference work, into contact with the undergraduate users.

368. Goodrich, Susan. "No, I'm Not a Librarian, but May I Help You?" *Michigan Librarian* 38: 24-25 (Winter 1972).

The author is one of the student reference assistants who are used at the reference desk at Central Michigan University; she describes and evaluates her experiences. The only requirement for these assistants is a basic library class.

369. Grazier, Robert T. "Graduate Assistant Program at the University of Florida," *College and Research Libraries* 16:360-364 (October 1955).

Describes and evaluates the graduate assistant program begun in 1948 at the University of Florida, where practicing librarians or library school students were offered graduate assistantships to work in the library compiling bibliographies and conducting needed surveys and studies. The program did not attain its objectives; there was a shortage of interested applicants, and, after obtaining the subject degree, the librarians tended to leave the library profession and switch to that subject field.

370. Hsu, Martha. "Olin's Experiment: Information vs. Reference," *Cornell University Libraries Bulletin* 8:8-12 (May 1973).

An information desk was established at Cornell Olin Library, staffed by highly trained assistants who handled directional and simple information questions and also acted as a filter, referring the more difficult questions to reference librarians. The author concludes that the assistant was able to handle successfully a large number of questions of different types; thus freeing the reference librarian for more specialized service.

371. Marcy, Henry O. "Would You Believe One Reference Instructor?," *RQ* 6:180-183 (Summer 1967).

Observes that most questions that come to the reference desk could be handled by non-professionals. Suggests that professional reference librarians be specialists with several degrees and be reserved for bibliographic work and consultation on difficult questions.

372. Mathis, Harold. "Professional or Clerical: A Cross-Validation Study," *College and Research Libraries* 26:525-526, 531 (November 1965).

A number of Michigan librarians were studied to determine the nature of the various jobs they performed. It was then considered whether these duties were of clerical or professional nature.

373. Palmer, Roger C. "Resident Reference," *RQ* 11:339-340 (Summer 1972).

Suggests that reference service be expanded to the stacks, where service would be offered by graduate and advanced undergraduate students. These students would provide service in stack areas related to their major subject and would be given brief training in bibliographic tools of that area.

374. Perkins, John W. **Library Information Service**. Inglewood Public Library, Inglewood, California, 1974. 27p. ERIC Document ED094796.

Describes the paraprofessional information service at the Inglewood Public Library. Reference assistants staff an information desk and answer the telephone, orient patrons to the library, screen information requests, and provide ready reference service. Reference assistants are classified as Senior Library Clerks under the Reference Department. This work is intended as a reference assistant manual and as information for library planners.

375. Searson, Marilyn. "Extent of Selected Professional and Non-Professional Duties among Academic Reference Librarians in North Carolina, South Carolina, and Georgia: A Survey," *South Carolina Librarian* 18:17-18 (Fall 1974).

Discusses the results of a survey conducted in North Carolina, South Carolina, and Georgia. Academic reference librarians in these areas were sent questionnaires to determine the extent of professional and non-professional duties. It was found that in the largest libraries, only 18 percent, 37 percent, and 22 percent of librarians devoted time to professional activities, respectively. The percentages for small colleges were 48 percent, 76 percent, and 48 percent, respectively.

376. Tebbets, Diane R., and Hugh Pritchard. "Undergraduate Reference Aids," *RQ* 12:275-276 (Spring 1973).

Undergraduate student assistants were used at the University of New Hampshire to give aid in stack areas. They give simple information and directions and help students locate books. When reference questions are asked, they refer students to the reference desk, assuring them they will receive sympathetic help.

377. Young, Arthur P. "A Report and a Challenge: Student Assistants," *RQ* 9:295-297 (Summer 1970).

It was hypothesized that upper-level college students could perform reference work in an undergraduate library with a qualified professional librarian available for difficult questions. After intensive instruction in reference work, the students worked at the desk, thus freeing professional librarians for other reference activities. Benefits were said to be less cost for direct service, recruitment opportunities, and more time for other professional reference activities.

IN-SERVICE TRAINING

See also: Chapter 3, Teaching of Reference

This section includes works pertaining to on-the-job education and development of both professional and non-professional reference personnel. However, training manuals, educational materials, and textbooks on teaching reference are included in Chapter 3, Teaching of Reference.

378. Fitch, V. E. "In-Service Training in Public Libraries." Unpublished Master's thesis, University of Southern California, 1957. 72p.

379. Isaacs, Julian M. "In-Service Training for Reference Work," *Library Association Record* 71:301-302 (October 1969).

This program of in-service training is used in the commerce and technical department of a public library in Great Britain. Involved in this method are personal supervision and assessment. "Question papers" are prepared dealing with different types of reference questions.

380. Knox, Margaret E. "For Every Reference Librarian—A Development Program," *Southeastern Librarian* 11:303-310, 320 (Winter 1961).
The author discusses the need for a post-professional training program for reference librarians. She describes how such a program can be planned and includes principles and suggested activities.

381. Library Association. Reference, Special and Information Section. *In-Service Training. Proceedings of the 12th Annual Conference, Nottingham, March 20-23, 1964.* Edited by Amy Mason. London, Library Association, 1964. 47p.
A conference devoted to in-service training over the whole field of public and special libraries. "Training in reference work at present seemed to be either a matter of 'being thrown in at the deep end' or of working along with another member of the staff." Among suggestions put forward were that senior members of the reference staff devote time regularly to teaching reference students.

382. Orton, N. E. "Orientation and In-Service Education for Professional Librarians at the Enoch Pratt Free Library." Unpublished Master's thesis, University of Texas, 1966. 68p.

383. "Staff Enrichment Project Launched in Illinois," *Library Journal* 98:1537 (May 15, 1973).
Briefly reported here is a project funded by the Illinois State Library to upgrade reference personnel. The program is explained, including funding goals and basic plans. Some libraries have rejected this program, and reasons for this are given.

SPECIAL AIDS AND DEVICES AND INFORMATION DESKS

See also: Chapter 5, Reference Service (Non-Professional Personnel and Duties)
Chapter 6, Reference Service in Types of Libraries (Academic Libraries)
Chapter 7, Special Types of Reference Service (Innovations)
Chapter 11, Research in Reference (Measurement and Evaluation)
Chapter 13, Information Centers and Services (Public Libraries)

Included here are works that give ideas and suggestions for special files, and other aids and devices that lead to more efficient performance of reference work. Also included are works pertaining to information desks established in libraries for the purpose of answering directional questions and giving simple catalog help and library instruction.

384. Babcock, H. "Reference Question File," *Medical Library Association Bulletin* 25:240-241 (May 1937).
Describes the file in use at the Medical Library of the New York State Library.

385. Fetros, John G. "Information Files of Old Chestnuts and Chestnut Nags," *Wilson Library Bulletin* 48:329-331 (December 1973).
Describes how an information file can aid reference service in providing quick answers to questions that are time-consuming to research. The author uses the example of locating the name of a horse named after a famous person.

386. Harrelson, Larry. "Large Libraries and Information Desks," *College and Research Libraries* 35:21-27 (January 1974).
Large academic and public libraries were surveyed to determine the presence of an information desk, its function, staffing patterns, and times of service. Fifty-three percent of academic libraries and 36 percent of public libraries did not have an information desk, and in these cases the function is performed by the reference department. A centralized reference service is usually able to assume the information desk function, while a decentralized service has more need for a separate information desk. This study expands Kleiner's 1967 study.

387. Kleiner, Jane P. "The Information Desk: The Library's Gateway to Service," *College and Research Libraries* 29:496-501 (November 1968).
Seventy-three smaller members of the Association of Research Libraries were surveyed to determine the extent of information desk services. Of those responding, 37 offered such services. Ten guidelines are given regarding information desks, based on the results of this study.

388. Lewis, Alfred J. "The Use of an Automatic Answering Service in Research Libraries," *College and Research Libraries* 31:107-108 (March 1970).
The author describes the advantage of an automatic answering service for use when the reference staff is not on duty. The patron can leave a record of his question and phone number and the question will then be taken care of the following morning. One advantage is that inexperienced non-professional personnel need not be used to deal with reference inquiries on off-hours and that all questions will be answered by experienced professional personnel. There is an advantage to the patron in that he is not likely to be inconvenienced by wrong or inadequate answers and does not need to call back at another time.

389. Maxton, L. P. "What Special Indexes Should be Maintained by the Reference Department of the Reading Public Library?" Unpublished Master's thesis, Drexel Institute of Technology, 1950. 41p.

390. Siebert, Grant W. "The Reference Catalog," *RQ* 8:262-263 (Summer 1969).
The author describes a "reference catalog," which would be based on frequently asked questions with the *best* source for particular subjects listed. It would refer users to encyclopedias, pamphlets, periodicals, almanacs, yearbooks, handbooks, and other types of reference sources. This reference catalog would make location of information quicker and easier and eliminate a great deal of guesswork and repetition of effort.

391. Swan, James. "Answer to the Term Paper Dilemma," *RQ* 11:50-51 (Fall 1971).

The Social Sciences Division of the Brigham Young University Library maintains a resource file to help students in preparing term papers. The subject-arranged file, maintained by the Reference Department, lists monographs, government documents, indexes and abstracts, and names and addresses of helpful organizations. The student is taught how to use the file and, in using it, learns a great deal about basic research procedures and library use in general. Staff are saved the necessity of repeatedly explaining search procedures in detail each time a popular subject re-occurs.

392. Wells, Dorothy. "How-To-Do-It Approach to Reference," *RQ* 10:331-335 (Summer 1971).

The Ball State University Reference Department reports on control of college catalogs, supply of pencils, use of labeling tape, housing of telephone directories, ready reference books, jiffy key-holders, expansion space, and a buzzer page code. A Roladex is utilized containing frequently requested titles, repeated reference questions under subject, names and addresses, phone directory holdings. One is also used for ready reference titles. Also described is a title index for *Masterplots* and *Masterpieces*.

ASSOCIATIONS

See also: Chapter 5, Reference Service (General Works)
Chapter 12, Cooperative Reference Service

This section includes materials about reference organizations on both national and state levels. The Reference and Adult Services Division of the American Library Association aims at identification of "the library interests and needs of present and potential users" (*ALA Handbook of Organization 1975-1976*, Chicago, 1975). Its official publication is *RQ* (quarterly), which contains information concerning RASD activities.

393. American Library Association. Standards Committee. "A Commitment to Information Services: Developmental Guidelines," *RQ* 14:24-26 (February 1974).

This draft report was prepared by the ALA Standards Committee to provide guidelines for reference service, including information services, developmental programs, and library instruction.

394. Barton, Mary N. "Progress Report on Reference Services Division," *ALA Bulletin* 52:347 (May 1958).

During its first year the Reference Services Division reached a membership of 3,307, including reference librarians from all types of libraries. During this year a statement of functions was prepared and local chapters were formed. An Isadore Mudge distinguished service award was established, conference plans were made, and committees were formed. Consideration was given to forming sections by subject and type of patrons.

395.   Cheney, Frances N. "The Reference Services Division: A Look Before and
        After," *RQ* 4:3-6 (November 1964).
Describes the background of reference organization. Discussed are the Reference
Librarians' Section of the Association of College and Reference Libraries and the
Reference Librarians' Section of the American Library Association's Public Libraries
Division. Describes the formation of the Reference Services Division of the Amer-
ican Library Association in 1957 and its subsequent activities.

396.   Geller, E. "Hypothetic Dialogues, the RSD Preconference," *Library Journal*
        96:2450-2451 (August 1971).
Described here is the RSD Preconference and the address by Robert Hayes. Hayes
speaks of the possibility of dissemination centers that provide SDI services on the
basis of the user's interest profiles. He stresses that these services would require the
utilization of reference librarians rather than by-passing them. The ERIC system is
described in an address by Josh Smith.

397.   "Reference Services Division," *ALA Bulletin* 63:1423-1427 (November
        1969).
Reference Services became a division in 1956. The Board of Directors, publications,
and committees, along with their purpose and membership, are listed here. The functions of this Division are improvement and extension of informational, bibliographical, and research activities in all types of libraries, at all levels, and in all subject
fields. Reference materials, inquiries and inquirers, indexes and indexing, bibliographies and bibliographic methods are considered. Issues of the *ALA Bulletin* often
contain reports of the Reference Service Division.

398.   Thackery, John T., Jr. "We Point with Pride: Reference Services Division
        Chapters," *RQ* 3:9-10 (January 1964).
Describes accomplishments of chapters in Maryland, New Jersey, Wisconsin, Ohio,
Tennessee, Florida, Michigan, the Potomac Valley, and also the chapter associated
with the Southeastern Library Association. Also notes special publications of some
of these groups.

399.   Waters, Richard L. "Reference Service Planned by Reference Librarians,"
        RQ 9:37-38 (Fall 1969).
Describes the Reference Round Table of the Texas Library Association, affiliated
with the Reference Services Division of the ALA. Growth and accomplishments are
described, including a survey of reference in Texas, two Preconference Institutes,
and a network survey.

CHAPTER 6

REFERENCE SERVICE IN TYPES OF LIBRARIES

ACADEMIC LIBRARIES

See also: Chapter 5, Reference Service (General Works; Subject Specialists and/or Generalists; Subject Departments and/or Centralized Service)
Chapter 7, Special Types of Reference Service
Chapter 9, The Reference Process (Users)
Chapter 11, Research in Reference (Measurement and Evaluation)
Chapter 13, Information Centers and Services (Academic and Special Libraries)
Chapter 14, Information Retrieval

Included in this section are works on reference service in academic or research libraries in general. Specific aspects of academic library reference service are included in appropriate sections, such as Administration of Reference Service and In-Service Training (both in Chapter 5). Surveys and other research pertaining to academic and research libraries are included in Chapter 11, Research in Reference (Measurement and Evaluation).

Bibliographical coverage of reference service in academic and research libraries can be found in Guy Lyle, *Administration of the College Library* (New York, H. W. Wilson, 1974); Everett Moore, "Reference Service in Academic and Research Libraries," *Library Trends* 12:363-372 (January 1964); Billy Wilkinson, *Reference Services for Undergraduate Students: Four Case Studies* (Metuchen, N.J., Scarecrow, 1972). Other bibliographies of interest on academic and research library service in general are: Friedrich Brose, *Junior College Libraries: A Checklist of About 750 Published and Unpublished Sources* (Washington, D.C., Educational Resources Information Center, 1971), 62p.; C. H. Millis, "Toward a Philosophy of Academic Librarianship: A Library-College Bibliography," *Library-College Journal* 3:49-56 (Summer 1970); also *Library-College Journal* 4:58-68 (Winter 1970) and 4:48-56 (Summer 1971); Irene Braden, *The Undergraduate Library* (Chicago, American Library Association, 1970), pp. 151-153 (ACRL Monograph, No. 31); Harrison Bryan, *Critical Survey of University Libraries and Librarianship in Great Britain* (South Australians' Librarian Board, 1966), pp. 210-245 (Occasional Papers in Librarianship, No. 4); Morell Boone, and others, ed., *Use, Misuse, and Nonuse of Academic Libraries* (New York Library Association, College and University Libraries Section, 1970), pp. 105-126; K. Allen, "Student and Faculty Attitudes," *Library-College Journal* 3:35-36 (Fall 1970); Elizabeth Mills, "The Separate Undergraduate Library," *College and Research Libraries* 29:144-156 (March 1968).

400. Bauer, Harry. "Information Wanted," *Library Journal* 78:1465-1469 (September 15, 1953).
Notes that reference work does not differ markedly by type of library. Typical reference questions and sources used are presented, along with general descriptions of reference service in a university library. Bibliographic centers are also discussed.

401. Boatman, Maurice W. "Reference '67: The Small College Library," *Illinois Libraries* 49:252-254 (April 1967).
The educational emphasis has changed from requiring students to collect facts to an emphasis on the process of critical thinking, and this requires a change in reference librarianship. Source materials must be expanded and a wide variety of points of view must be represented. The reference librarian must be informed on current trends and theories in education, as well as familiar with the literature of the various disciplines. He must also be able to communicate with faculty and students on the level of ideas.

402. Borden, Arnold K. "Reference Work in a College Library," *Libraries* 35:33-34 (January 1930).
Considers qualities needed by the college reference librarian, particularly a wide cultural background, well-developed cultural interests, and human interests. Discusses the reference interview and work with undergraduate students in general.

403. Cheney, Frances N. "The Reference Librarian Looks to the Faculty," *Peabody Journal of Education* 28:275-279 (March 1951).
The author discusses the relationship between the reference department and the faculty in terms of interaction. She suggests that reference departments should be informed of assignments requiring extensive library use. Faculty should assist in evaluating the collection in their subject areas. Graduate students should be guided away from research in areas where library resources are insufficient.

404. Dolby, James L. "University Libraries and the Information Needs of the Researcher," *Aslib Proceedings* 28:185-190 (July 1966).
Describes the nature of the demands on university libraries by researchers and discusses problems and solutions. Researchers usually refer to the library when other sources have failed and they need answers quickly. Solutions are provision of books for their office, telephone information service, and electronic devices. Electronic devices are promising, but much work remains to be done.

405. Fenton, Dorothy M. "Reference Librarian," *Journal of Higher Education* 9:153-156 (March 1938).
Services given by the reference librarian in a liberal arts college are considered. There is a discussion also of the way these services vary among colleges and universities.

406. Gore, Daniel. "Anachronistic Wizard: The College Reference Librarian," *Library Journal* 89:1688-1692 (April 15, 1964).
Points out that students who lean upon a reference librarian will be helpless in unlocking the resources of the library on their own in the future. Describes how reference librarianship developed to interpret the multiplicity of reference tools that became available in the twentieth century. The time is at hand, now, to begin

teaching students to master these tools as a regular part of their curriculum. Suggests and outlines such a formal couse and observes that it should be taught by professional librarians rather than by library school faculty.

407. Halvorson, Homer. "The Reference Function in the University and Research Library." In Butler, Pierce, ed., *The Reference Function of the Library*. Chicago, University of Chicago Press, 1943. pp. 103-124.
This classic essay discusses the nature and function of reference work in university and research libraries and shows how it differs from that in other types of libraries.

408. Harrer, Gustave A. "The University Library: Reference Librarians: Today and Tomorrow," *RQ* 5:29-31 (Winter 1965).
Reference, as the library's most essential service, has not received sufficient support in the past. There is an increasing need in reference work for subject specialists. The author discusses the effects on library services of the explosions in population, publication, and learning.

409. Haviland, Morrison C. "The Reference Function of the La Mont Library," *College and Research Libraries* 11:369-371 (October 1950).
The La Mont Undergraduate Library at Harvard emphasizes exposing students to books, and extensive aids to the collection are provided. Only basic works are available and students are helped to locate more specialized works in other libraries. The collection is constantly weeded and kept up to date to correspond to the changing curriculum.

410. Hernon, Peter, and Maureen Pastine. "Floating Reference Librarians," *RQ* 12:60-64 (Fall 1972).
The authors advocate that the "floating reference librarian" should work actively to communicate with faculty and students and to participate more fully in the educational process. They suggest more programs of specialized library instruction and special seminars in various subject fields.

411. Hoyle, N. "Academic Library Reference." In Katz, W., *Introduction to Reference Work*. New York, McGraw-Hill, 1969. Volume 2, pp. 145-163.
Considers reference service to undergraduates, graduates, and faculty. Discusses administration and organization of reference work. Describes ways in which outside resources such as library staff, faculty, and resources of other libraries can be utilized in reference service.

412. Jahoda, Gerald. "Planning Improved Library Service for Scientists in Universities," *College and Research Libraries* 28:343-346 (September 1967).
The point is made by the author that improvement in existing information services is not sufficient. He stresses that new information services must be developed and tested. He describes an experiment at Florida State University where new information services were offered to scientists as part of a study of personal indexes.

413. Jameson, R. D. "Consultant Service and the College Library," *College and Research Libraries* 3:230-234 (June 1942).

Comments that important problems faced by college libraries are the gulf between librarians and faculty and selection from among the vast number of new books. Describes the use of research faculty as consultants at the Library of Congress. Suggests that some faculty members have teaching loads reduced and be appointed library consultants. They could prepare and annotate checklists of needed materials, survey the collection in their area and recommend books for purchase, assist in reference work, and consult with students.

414. Laythe, Rosamund. "New Dimensions in Innovation: Who Are We?" *Learning Today* 6:16-17 (Winter 1973).

Describes the attempt to establish a general reference function in a library organized around six large subject areas. "Oases" of information are being set up, including vertical files, pamphlets, and paperbacks. Emphasis is on individual needs, inclusion of media, and more aggressive service in approaching the patron, going along with him and teaching use of resources.

415. Lyle, Guy, and others. **Administration of the College Library**. 4th ed. New York, H. W. Wilson, 1974. 320p.

The chapter on reference work, pages 90-100, covers objectives, organization, staff and qualifications, selection of reference materials, work with students, faculty, and outside users, and interlibrary loan. A bibliography is included.

416. Lyle, Guy. "The Reference Function in the College Library." In Butler, Pierce, ed., *The Reference Function of the Library*. Chicago, University of Chicago Press, 1943. pp. 81-103.

The author discusses the ways in which the reference function of the college library differs from that in the university or public library. Also considered are instruction in the use of libraries, direct reference service, faculty relations, research, and service to off-campus users.

417. Mills, Elizabeth. "The Separate Undergraduate Library," *College and Research Libraries* 29:144-156 (March 1968).

In 1949, the first separate library for undergraduates was established in a university. The author discusses the concept of the undergraduate library and analyzes those at Harvard, Michigan, and UCLA.

418. Moore, Everett T. "Reference Service in Academic and Research Libraries," *Library Trends* 12:362-372 (January 1964).

Reviews trends in reference service and cites relevant research. Considers the issues of subject specialists as opposed to generalists and departmentalization as opposed to centralization. Also discusses reference responsibility in regard to government publications, the pros and cons of separate undergraduate reference service, and the demand that reference librarians perform more specialized services, such as organizing special materials in subject fields. Discusses the need for interlibrary cooperation and suggests that the reference function should expand to direct provision of information rather than remain instructional in nature.

419.   Morrison, Perry D. "The Librarian—Warehouseman or Educator?"
       Improving College and University Teaching 3:7-10 (February 1955).
The author takes a moderate viewpoint between the extremes, believing that the
librarian has an important role as selector, arranger, and interpreter of information
sources and that in this he should work closely with the faculty. He should be
neither a warehouseman nor a psychologist.

420.   Palmer, Foster M. "Reference Section in the Harvard College Library,"
       Harvard Library Bulletin 7:55-72 (Winter 1953).
Reviews the development of reference service at the Harvard College Library to
1953. Describes each stage of development and includes discussion concerning
concepts of service, which led to physical changes in the building.

421.   Ranstead, Donald D. "Feed-Back to Faculty," *Library Journal*
       87:171-173 (January 15, 1962).
A particular problem in faculty feed-back is noted here by the author. The reference
librarian is often in a better position than the faculty member to observe and understand the problems and difficulties faced by undergraduates in completing their
assignments. Discussion between faculty and reference librarians might help prevent
"panic" questions and unproductive research efforts.

422.   Rogers, Rutherford, and David C. Weber. "Reference and Information
       Assistance." In *University Library Administration*. New York, H. W.
       Wilson, 1971. pp. 202-214.
Considers general policies of service and reviews the instructional versus informational functions. Also covers collaboration with faculty, elective courses in library
use, service to particular groups, reference desk and information desk service,
staffing, measurement and statistics, budgeting, and relations with other library
departments.

423.   Rogers, Rutherford D. "Undergraduate Reference Work," *College and
       Research Libraries* 3:248-251 (June 1942).
The author sees the role of the undergraduate reference librarian as helping to
locate subject information and bibliographical information, and instructing students in library use.

424.   Tanis, Norman. "Reference Service in Junior Colleges," *RQ* 9:105-106
       (Winter 1969).
This brief essay introduces a section of *RQ* devoted to junior college reference
service. The author suggests demonstration projects that would offer junior college
reference service of the very best quality. Since this is not possible, this series of
articles is intended to serve as a substitute for demonstration units.

425.   Tanis, Norman E. "Reference Service for Technology," *RQ* 9:121-123
       (Winter 1969).
Discusses the requirements of reference services for technical and vocational students at urban community colleges. The reference department should work closely
with industry libraries, special, university, and public technical libraries. All kinds

of sources should be utilized, particularly technical reports, periodicals, microfilm, and data banks.

426. Tannenbaum, Earl. "The College Library: An Experiment in Non-Mechanized, Human Reference Service," *Colorado Academic Library* 2:1-7 (Summer 1965).

While computer applications are useful, the most important aspect of reference service is the human interaction which it provides. The best reference service should be a person-to-person experience, and the best opportunity for this is in the small to medium-sized college library. Rather than receiving exhaustive computer-produced bibliographies, students should receive help in defining needs and analyzing and evaluating material. Personal reference service is cheaper and faster in this respect.

427. Tomlinson, K. R. "That Association of Teachers in Technical Institutions Document," *New Library World* 74:149-151 (July 1973).

This document, distributed by the ATTI, is significant in that it supports resource-based learning but sees the teacher, rather than the librarian, as the expert in resource management. Academic librarians are opposed to the appointment of non-librarians as "resource coordinators'. to oversee their functions.

428. Viet, Fritz. "Reference Service in the College Library," *Catholic Library World* 39:274-276 (December 1967).

The history and various philosophies of reference service are briefly reviewed. The author notes that today reference service is an indispensable function in the library. He discusses the need for college students to obtain reference service in libraries other than their own, and suggests supplementary area reference centers or agreements between libraries. He discusses computer-based reference service for larger areas as a solution.

429. Waldron, Rodney. "Reference Service—Pure, But Not Simple," *The Bookmark* 6:5-6 (September 1953).

This article describes reference service at the University of Idaho Library, including their philosophy of service and use of reference tools. Guidance is given to students on fundamentals to help them make more efficient use of time and to create good-will for the library.

430. Wallace, James O. "Reference Services in Junior Colleges," *RQ* 9:106-110 (Winter 1969).

The functions of reference service in the junior college are described as 1) use of all types of media, 2) individualized instruction, 3) participation by reference librarians in the academic program, 4) support of classroom instruction, 5) creativity, and 6) responding to area needs.

431. Wyer, James I. **Reference Work: A Textbook for Students of Library Work and Librarians**. Chicago, American Library Association, 1930. 315p.

The chapter entitled "Reference Work in University and College Libraries" covers the spectrum of reference work in academic libraries, including organization, administration, staffing, faculty relations, preparation of handbooks, and reference service in general.

PUBLIC LIBRARIES

See also: Chapter 5, Reference Service (General Works; Subject Departments and/or Centralized Service)
Chapter 7, Special Types of Reference Service
Chapter 8, Reference Service to Special Groups
Chapter 9, The Reference Process (Users)
Chapter 11, Research in Reference (Measurement and Evaluation)
Chapter 12, Cooperative Reference Service
Chapter 13, Information Centers and Services (Public Libraries)

Included in this section are only general works pertaining to reference service in public libraries. Specific aspects of public library reference service will be included in appropriate sections such as Administration of Reference Service and In-Service Training (both in Chapter 5). Surveys and other research pertaining to public library reference service are included in the section Measurement and Evaluation in Chapter 11.

Bibliographical coverage of reference service in public libraries is available in C. S. Toase, "Public Libraries' Reference Service," in *Five Years Work in Librarianship, 1961-1965* (London, Library Association, 1968); Katharine G. Harris, "Reference Service in Public Libraries," *Library Trends* 12:373-389 (January 1964); and Joseph Wheeler and Herbert Goldhor, *Practical Administration of Public Libraries* (New York, Harper, 1962). Other bibliographies relating to public library service in general are: Eleanor Brown, *Modern Branch Libraries in Systems* (Metuchen, N.J., Scarecrow, 1970), pp. 720-731; Mary Lee Bundy, *Metropolitan Public Library Users* (College Park, University of Maryland, School of Library and Information Service, 1967), pp. 124-130.

432.   "Brookyln Public Library Establishes 16 Reference Centers," *Library Journal* 88:982 (March 1, 1963).
A report from the Brooklyn Public Library that in 1961 sixteen agencies were designated as Reference Centers; they are attempting to build collections to take pressure off the main library.

433.   Bury, Peter. "Reference '67: The Suburban Library," *Illinois Libraries* 49:249-251 (April 1967).
The author describes the problems of the suburban library in giving reference service. He suggests that new reference library systems might provide the answer to some of these problems. He notes improvements that are needed in systems already existing.

434.   Chatwin, Dorothy B. "The Library and the Community: North York Public Library, Information Services," *International Library Review* 3:315-321 (June 1971).
Information service is discussed here in general and also in regard to Canadian libraries and the North York Public Library. A proposed reference center for this public library is described. Resources and metropolitan reference service are also discussed.

435.   Childers, Thomas. "Community and Library: Some Possible Futures,"
       Library Journal 96:2727-2730 (September 15, 1971).

Discusses some futures of the public library in view of population dispersing from
the center of cities and demand for duplication of services. Considers the possible
alternatives of 1) serving only as a cultural ornament, 2) denying service to the
richer elements of society who can afford to use commercial services, 3) providing
a very narrow range of special information/knowledge services for everyone.

436.   Christeson, Frances. "Twelve Lessons in Branch Reference Service,"
       Wilson Library Bulletin 30:380-382 (January 1956).

This article describes a course in reference service given by the Los Angeles County
Public Library by correspondence to staff at branch libraries. Improvements made
by staff after taking the course are described. The course outline, given here, includes
approach, objectives, content, materials, and evaluation.

437.   Collison, Robert L. W. "Information Services in Public Libraries," *Aslib
       Proceedings* 4:213-224 (November 1952).

Information services should be centered in the public library. In the United States
cooperation exists between public, university, and special libraries. In Great Britain
the more efficient public library can usually supply general periodicals, local history
and government, law, foreign language dictionaries, maps, and works on librarianship.
The Metropolitan Subject Specialization plan is described, and a plea is made for
improved service at the British Museum.

438.   Colombo, Elda. "Reference '67: The Large Public Library/Research Center,"
       Illinois Libraries 49:242-246 (April 1967).

The Chicago Public Library is one part of a library system that includes three other
reference and research centers in Illinois. The resources and responsibilities of each
of these four reference departments are described. Reference service with students
and other regular patrons of the Chicago Public Library is also discussed. The author
advocates the development of more library reference systems.

439.   Edwards, Elizabeth. "Reference '67: The Public Library System in a Rural
       Area," *Illinois Libraries* 49:247-248 (April 1967).

Problems of small rural area libraries are lack of communication, crowded shelves,
no book budgets, and limited ability to give reference service. The author describes
the types of reference requests made to the main library by members of the system.
She discusses improvements in the system and concludes that more and better
systems are needed.

440.   Gaines, Ervin J. "The Reference Librarian in an Urban Public Library,"
       Library Journal 91:2003-2007 (April 15, 1966).

Philosophy of librarianship and reference service as technology or intellectual voca-
tion are discussed. It is advanced that public libraries are much the same everywhere,
public library usage has not changed, aims and purposes are still not clearly defined,
and little progress has been made in researching users' needs and effectiveness of
service. The second part of the article concerns the Minneapolis Public Library and
reports on a survey that indicated that more than half of reference service was

concerned with the major activities in people's lives and, thus, of vital importance. The author comments that the reference librarian imposes order, shape, and form on the flow of knowledge. Emphasis is needed on human relations.

441.	Hargreaves, E. "The Public Reference Librarian," *Library Association Record* 60:215-219 (July 1958).
Public libraries in Great Britain tend to neglect reference librarianship. Qualifications of a reference librarian are discussed. The author describes problems in status and training and suggests solutions. Also considered are differences in American and British reference work.

442.	Harris, Katharine G. "Metropolitan Reference Service: Patterns, Problems, Solutions," *Library Journal* 88:1606-1611 (April 15, 1963).
The metropolitan areas of Detroit, Cleveland, Minneapolis, Boston, and Denver are discussed in regard to their provision of reference service. Among aspects covered are staffing and state support. Prominent trends noted are increasing departmentalization, telephone service, and service to business and industry.

443.	Harris, Katharine G. "Reference Service in Public Libraries," *Library Trends* 12:373-389 (January 1964).
Briefly reviews the historical development of reference service and cites relevant public library surveys and studies. Reference service in metropolitan and rural areas is compared. Other trends discussed are departmentalization, telephone reference service, change in types of questions, increased demands for service and development of reference systems, and interlibrary loan. The public library should serve as an information center rather than as a center for library instruction.

444.	Harrison, Kenneth C. **Public Libraries Today**. New York, Philosophical Library, 1963. 146p.
Chapter five gives an overview of reference work in the public library, covering collection, staffing, subject departments, bibliographic control, indexing, media, telephone questions, interlibrary loan, and library networks.

445.	Howard, Paul. "The Reference Function in the Small and Medium-Sized Public Library." In Butler, Pierce, ed., *The Reference Function of the Library*. Chicago, University of Chicago Press, 1943. pp. 35-61.
The function of reference is related to society, and the relationship of the library to other agencies is considered. Also discussed is the way in which the reference function is affected by the community served. Administration, the reference librarian, and the collection are covered.

446.	Jackaman, Peter. "Public Libraries, Information and the Community," *Assistant Librarian* 66:18-21 (February 1973).
The author describes the effect of the increasing number of information agencies on public library reference service. A brief review of the development of reference service is given.

447.   Labdon, P. R. "Rural Reference Library Services." In Mort, Geoffrey, ed. *Proceedings of the 17th Annual Conference and Study Group of the Library Association, Reference, Special and Information Section, Keele, March 28-31, 1969*. London, The Library Association, Reference, Special and Information Section, 1969. pp. 40-54.

Services to rural readers in Great Britain are inferior to those available to town dwellers. Mobile libraries and individual delivery services are not a complete solution. The following solutions are discussed: 1) central reference service available by phone, telex, or computer at all times; 2) central library unit with reference sources; 3) reference specialist for libraries serving 10,000 or more; 4) mobile reference librarians and collections traveling between branches; 5) subject enquiry forms to be answered by mail.

448.   McCombs, Charles F. "The Reference Function in the Large Public Library," In Butler, Pierce, ed. *The Reference Function of the Library*. Chicago, University of Chicago Press, 1943. pp. 16-35.

The reference function in a large public library is defined, and five elements are discussed, including physical facilities, sources of information, users, reference librarians, and methods.

449.   Meyer, Edith P. **Meet the Future: People and Ideas in the Libraries of Today and Tomorrow.** Boston, Little, Brown and Co., 1964. 278p.

Includes a discussion of public library reference service and describes how reference questions are handled in a large departmentalized public library. A list of sample questions is given.

450.   Severns, Hannah. **Reference Services in a Small Public Library**. Chicago, American Library Association, Small Libraries Project, Library Administration Division, 1962. 12p.

Coverage of broad aspects of reference service, including principles of service, reference books and selection, types of material and arrangement. Suggestions are given regarding the importance of local history, knowing the collection, meeting readers, and using publicity.

451.   Toase, C. A. "Public Libraries' Reference Service." In Sewell, P. H., ed., *Five Years Work in Librarianship 1961-1965*. London, The Library Association, 1968. pp. 334-346.

Surveys and reviews the literature and research in regard to British and American public libraries from 1956 through 1965. Discusses staff in regard to number required, characteristics, education and in-service training, the reference collection, subject departmentalization, users, and cooperative arrangements. Also covers hours of service, user knowledge of availability of reference service, student users, and facilities. Discusses increase in inquiries, philosophies of service, mail and phone inquiries, search strategy, and measurement and evaluation. Reviews organizations and publications.

452.   Tucker, Harold W. "Greater Role in Education Seen for Public Libraries: New York Librarian Outlines Aid Needed to Maintain Staff, Develop New Services," *Library Journal* 92:2322-2324 (June 15, 1967).
Described here is a statement by Tucker to the National Advisory Commission on Libraries. He foresees increasing demands for reference service and discusses the problems faced by public libraries in regard to maintaining sufficient well trained reference staff.

453.   Walker, Estellene P. "Improving Reference Service," *Wilson Library Bulletin* 33:669-670, 677 (May 1959).
Describes the problems facing reference service in South Carolina's public libraries. Improvements in service were made with funds from the Library Services Act. Some improvements made were the hiring of a consultant, establishment of interlibrary loan, purchase of new reference sources, and a conference on reference. There are plans for a statewide central reference and interlibrary loan service.

454.   Wand, M. W. "Reference and Information Services in County Libraries," *Librarian and Book World* 45:94-97 (May-June 1956).
Described here are county reference services in the English counties of Lancashire, Derbyshire, Herfordshire, and Middlesex. The basic aim of these services is to encourage users to come to local service points for information and books; if necessary, requests will then be referred to larger libraries.

455.   Wyer, James I. **Reference Work: A Textbook for Students of Library Work and Librarians**. Chicago, American Library Association, 1930. 315p.
Discussed in the chapter entitled "Reference Work in Public Libraries" are the public library constituency and the distinctive aspects of public library reference work. Also considered are public libraries of different sizes, branches, group work, telephone service, and translation of classics.

SCHOOL LIBRARIES

See also: Chapter 7, Special Types of Reference Service (Readers Advisory Service)
Chapter 9, The Reference Process (Users)
Chapter 10, Sources of Information (Reference Materials—Selection and Evaluation)
Chapter 11, Research in Reference (Measurement and Evaluation)

Included here are works pertaining to reference work in school libraries and reference work with children. Studies of school library reference work are included in the section Measurement and Evaluation, in Chapter 11. Neither reading guidance in the schools nor instruction in library use will be covered, since bibliographies already exist in these areas. Some materials on reading guidance will be included in the section Readers Advisory Service, in Chapter 7. Bibliographies of reading guidance appear in: Florence Cleary, *Blueprints for Better Reading: School Programs for Promoting Skill and Interest in Reading.*

2nd ed. (New York, H. W. Wilson, 1972); H. M. Robinson and S. Weintraub, "Research Related to Children's Interests and to Developmental Values of Reading," *Library Trends* 22:81-108 (October 1973).

Bibliographical coverage of school library service in general can be found in: Ruth Ann Davies, *School Library: A Force for Educational Effectiveness* (New York, Bowker, 1969), pp. 372-378; Jean E. Lowrie, *Elementary School Libraries*, 2nd ed. (Metuchen, N.J., Scarecrow, 1970), pp. 223-230; J. Lowrie, "Review of Research in School Librarianship." In Herbert Goldhor, *Research Methods in Librarianship: Measurement and Evaluation* (Urbana, Illinois University, Graduate School of Library Science, 1968), pp. 65-69; Ernest Roe, *Teachers, Librarians and Children: A Study of Libraries in Education* (Hamden, Conn., Shoestring, 1965), pp. 175-182.

456.　Aceto, Vincent. "The Children's Librarian—Passive Provider or Active Agent for Change?" *RQ* 7:74-78 (Winter 1967).

Reference service is defined as assistance to individuals in resolving uncertainty. Reference service to children involves instruction in use of books and libraries, guidance in choice of books, and information services. Children should be taught to discover and use the entire resources of the library, including media. Respect for the child's intellect should be the cornerstone of service.

457.　Berry, June. "The IMC in the Continuous Progress School," *School Library Journal* 11:25-28 (November 1964).

The Brigham Young University Laboratory School, high school section, maintains an instructional materials center which is described here. Reference service to teachers includes preparation of bibliographies and collection and preparation of materials. The librarian also visits classes and departmental meeting to discuss needed materials and aids in previewing films.

458.　Browning, Elizabeth. "Solving the Mystery of Reference: Use Calendar Clue," *School Library Journal* 22:71-74 (October 1975).

Describes a game called "Calendar Clue," which teaches the use of reference materials for elementary school students. The game is played on a weekly basis. The author reports that teachers became interested and played also.

459.　Cleary, Florence. **Blueprints for Better Reading: School Programs for Promoting Skill and Interest in Reading**. 2nd ed. New York, H. W. Wilson, 1972. 312p.

Sections cover "Reading Guidance: Foundations and Perspectives," "Approaches to Reading Guidance Programs," and "Programs in Reading Guidance." Notes and references at the end of each chapter.

460.　Davies, Ruth Ann. **The School Library Media Center: A Force for Educational Excellence**. 2nd ed. New York, Bowker, 1974. 484p.

Discusses the role of the school librarian as a curriculum consultant and materials specialist. Also considers the relationship of the school library to programs in English, social studies, science and mathematics, guidance, and study skills. Bibliography.

461.   Delaney, Jack J. **The New School Librarian**. Hamden, Conn., Shoe String
       Press, 1968. 201p.
In the chapter titled "Waiting on Pupils and Teachers," the author discusses reference
services and includes part of a questionnaire to be used in evaluating the school
library program.

462.   Delaney, Jack. **The School Librarian: Human Relations Problems**. Hamden,
       Conn., Shoe String Press, 1961. 183p.
The chapter titled "School Library Service" covers types of service, limits to service,
and evaluation. Included is an evaluation form.

463.   Dobson, Marjorie. "Stimulating the Use of Reference Materials," *Education*
       84:198-201 (December 1963).
Suggests ways to stimulate use of reference materials by elementary school students.
Describes use of reference tools to facilitate development of basic skills. Discusses
encyclopedias, dictionaries, atlases, indexes, and special subject area books in terms
of children's needs for information. Concludes by advocating that children learn
to consult as many sources as possible in order to learn how to evaluate information.

464.   Donehue, B. K. "Use of Reference Materials in the High School," *Education*
       84:217-220 (December 1963).
The future success in life of high school students often depends on their ability to
find, interpret, and synthesize information. The high school library must provide
students with a wide variety of information sources and guidance in locating and
interpreting information. The Knapp School Libraries Project demonstrated that
when standards are met, excellent service can be provided.

465.   Florence, A. L. "Library Service Centre," *Manitoba Library Association
       Bulletin* 14:2-3 (Winter 1966).
Library service to 85 schools in Winnepeg, Canada, is coordinated by a Library
Service Centre. Three professional librarians provide reference service and offer
reading guidance.

466.   Freiser, Leonard, H. "Information Retrieval for Students," *Library Journal*
       88:1121-1123 (March 15, 1963).
The Toronto, Canada, Board of Education established an Education Centre
Library in 1960 for the Toronto school system of 95,000 students and
4,000 professionals in 115 schools. It is unusual in that it is based on the
concept that the difficulties of library use often prevent students from
obtaining the information and, consequently, the knowledge they are seeking. Students are supplied with photo-reproductions of needed materials and
bibliographies, which include descriptions of search procedures. Advantages
are student time saved and protection of costly reference tools.

467.   Freiser, Leonard. "Reconstruction of Library Services." In Linderman, W.,
       ed. *The Present Status and Future Prospects of Reference/Information
       Service.* Chicago, American Library Association, 1967. pp. 48-56.
Proposes replacing the public school and the public library with a resource center.
This would be a campus-type complex with total information services in print, radio,
telephone, film, video, computer, studios, shops, laboratories, conference rooms,
playrooms, stadium, and theatre. The staff would be professionally heterogeneous,
permanent, and drawn from the community. The center could be extended through
mobile units, mail, film discs, telephone computer circuits, video, and printout.
Goes on to consider theoretical and practical aspects of this proposal.

468.   Freiser, Leonard H. "Students and Librarians," *Phi Delta Kappan* 44:444
       (June 1963).
The new Education Centre Library of the Toronto, Canada, Board of Education is
described. Information is supplied directly to students in the form of photocopied
material. Publisher's approval is secured when a number of copies are made.

469.   Freiser, Leonard H. "Students and Spoonfeeding," *Library Journal*
       88:3251-3253 (September 15, 1963).
In this article Freiser answers those who disagree with the philosophy of information
retrieval for students as carried out at the Education Centre Library in Toronto. He
argues that locating and obtaining information is often so time-consuming that
students no longer take time or have time to interpret and evaluate what they have
found. Thus, direct provision of information to students is justified.

470.   Freiser, Leonard H. "Toronto's Education Centre Library," *Saturday
       Review* 48:76, 79 (April 17, 1965).
Describes the unique program of information service for high school students in
the Education Centre Library. Students may approach ECL with questions and
ECL, in turn, informs them of things they may need. This type of service is based
on having the student expend his energy on working with information rather than
finding it. Teaching basic library skills is not enough. It may only give a sense of
false adequacy. Describes the library and the way students interact with it. Considers in more depth the philosophy behind this kind of service.

471.   Henne, Frances. "Learning to Learn in School Libraries," *School Libraries*
       15:15-23 (May 1966).
Discusses objectives, content, and methods of library instruction. Considers the relative importance in learning of having the answers on one hand, or of knowing the
sources and how to find answers on the other. Comments, "Deploring the spoonfeeding of students, as librarians so frequently do, may actually mean deploring a
more intelligent use of a student's time and efforts; and self-directed study or learning is not necessarily synonymous with self-directed finding of materials."

472. Henne, Frances. "The Reference Function in the School Library." In Butler, Pierce, ed. *The Reference Function of the Library*. Chicago, University of Chicago Press, 1943. pp. 61-81.

The reference function in the school library is considered in regard to five areas, including the educational function, reference work with students and with teachers, reference materials, and problems needing further investigation.

473. Kline, Donald. "Developing Resource Units," *Education* 84:221-225 (December 1963).

Discusses unit teaching and the preparation of resource units. Describes how reference books can be used in this process by teachers and students. Also considers use of overhead projectors and community resources.

474. Leopold, Carolyn. "School Librarians: Are We For Real?" *Library Journal* 96:1424-1428 (April 15, 1971).

The author takes a middle ground in the controversy over the philosophy of reference service in school libraries. She argues that the Toronto Information Centre retrieval plan actually restricts free access to information and concludes that the school library is "the best medium to teach basic cognitive capabilities."

475. Lowrie, Jean E. **Elementary School Libraries**. 2nd ed. Metuchen, N.J., Scarecrow, 1970. 238p.

Discusses philosophy and scope of the elementary school library and considers curriculum and reading guidance as well as other aspects of school library service. The chapter "How Do I Find . . . ?" discusses library instruction and reference work with children. Bibliography.

476. Michael, Mary Ellen. "Reference Materials Found in a Sample of Illinois School Library Media Centers," *RQ* 13:313-319 (Summer 1974).

The study was done to determine which reference books are most widely held, the age breakdown of reference titles held, and the relationship between size of school and size of reference holdings.

477. Orsini, Lillian. "Observations on Reference Service to Children," *RQ* 7:60-62 (Winter 1967).

Problems in children's reference service are noted here as follows: 1) children's reference collections are inadequate, 2) review media are not sufficiently helpful, 3) too much time is spent in teaching library skills, 4) teachers do not play a sufficient role in teaching use of reference tools, 5) cooperation among teachers is not sufficient, 6) not enough research has been done on reference service to children.

478. Pacific Northwest Library Association. **Library Development Projects Reports**. Seattle, Wash., University of Washington Press, 1960. 4v. *Elementary and Secondary School Libraries of the Pacific Northwest*. Edited by Morton Kroll. Volume 2. 330p.

Included here are data from elementary, junior high, and high school libraries in Idaho, Montana, Oregon, Washington, and the Province of British Columbia. In the first chapter, "Role of the School Library in the Schools of the Pacific Northwest," by Richard Darling, reference collections and teacher usage of these collections are analyzed.

479.   Reynolds, Judith A. "Redefinition of Reference Materials," *RQ* 9:149 (Winter 1969).

Centralized elementary school libraries face a problem in regard to circulation of reference materials. When activities are in progress in the library, use of reference materials at the same time creates difficulties. The author suggests that some circulation of reference materials is necessary to meet classroom needs.

480.   Roe, Ernest. **Teachers, Librarians and Children: A Study of Libraries in Education**. Hamden, Conn., Archon, 1965. 189p.

Written as the result of five years spent by the author in investigative studies on the role of libraries in education. Deals with theoretical, educational, philosophical, and sociological issues and makes constructive proposals concerning libraries and education. Bibliography.

481.   Rossoff, Martin. "The Forgotten Key," *Library Journal* 91:5126-5128, 5141 (October 15, 1966).

The author uses examples of Library of Congress subject headings to show difficulties encountered by students in both card catalog and index use. Two possible ways to overcome this barrier between students and information needs are to teach students to master the intricacies of subject headings or to establish resource centers that will furnish the information directly to students, as is done in the Education Centre Library in Toronto.

482.   Rothstein, Samuel. "For the Sake of Argument: The School Library as an Information Center," *BCL Quarterly* 21:35-38 (January 1958).

483.   Shores, Louis. "The Other Half—Where to Find It," *Education* 84:202-206 (December 1963).

Discusses the lack of knowledge of reference materials on the part of students of all ages. Considers the proper utilization of dictionaries, describing and comparing features of major dictionaries. Discusses encyclopedias as an educational medium and analyzes and compares major English and foreign language encyclopedias. Concludes with a brief discussion of sources of current information.

484.   Shores, Louis. "Reference Becomes Learning: The Fourth 'R'." In Rowland, Arthur, ed., *Reference Services*. Hamden, Conn., Shoe String Press, 1964. pp. 228-237. (Contributions to Library Literature, No. 5).

Discusses the importance of libraries in the educational process. Considers the slogan "half of knowledge is knowing where to find it." Reference is defined as the process of locating information and as such constitutes at least half of learning. Skills of reference must be extended to more students and teachers who must learn to use reference tools more effectively. Gives examples of the kinds of information to be found in encyclopedias. Comments on the importance of reference in helping children to become sufficiently informed to make good choices of future directions.

485.   Spain, Charles. "Reference Materials in the Modern School," *Education*
        84:195-197 (December 1963).
Discusses the purpose of reference tools in education and presents four criteria for
evaluation. Suggests three policies that should be implemented in order to provide
a suitable reference collection.

486.   Spain, Charles, ed. "The Use of Reference Materials," *Education*
        84:195-225 (December 1963).
This feature section includes eight articles as follows: 1) "Reference Materials in
the Modern School," by Charles Spain; 2) "Stimulating the Use of Reference Materials," by Marjorie Dobson; 3) "The Other Half—Where to Find It," by Louis Shores;
4) "Using the Dictionary," by Helen Barron; 5) "Using the Encyclopedia, by
Frances N. Cheney; 6) "Using the Elementary School Library," by George Butler;
7) "Use of Reference Materials in the High School," by Bernice Donehue; and 8)
"Developing Resource Units," by Donald Kline.

487.   Stookey, M. M. "Study of High School Reference Work." Unpublished
        Master's thesis, Drexel Institute of Technology, 1950. 39p.

488.   Williams, Dorothy. "Adventures in Finding Out," *Wilson Library Bulletin*
        43:456-457 (January 1969).
Considers how a child can be guided in using reference sources. Describes feelings of
a child in his first contact with a reference librarian in a public library.

489.   Wirth, Suzanne. "Reference Service to Adults Interested in Children's
        Books and Reading," *RQ* 7:63-67 (Winter 1967).
This article describes the Cooperative Children's Book Center of Madison, Wisconsin,
opened in 1963. Its function is to serve as a depository for an historical collection
of children's books. Its services include training sessions and a reference center for
adults, which gives assistance in research in children's literature and publishes
bibliographies.

490.   Wofford, Azile. **The School Library at Work**. New York, H. W. Wilson,
        1959. 256p.
Chapter 4, on use of materials in the school library, covers reading guidance and
reference work. Aspects of reference work discussed are types of reference materials, selection, reference questions, practical helps in reference, and the importance
of reference work. On pages 169-170 are sample questions received from senior and
junior high schools and elementary schools.

491.   Wright, John G. W. "The Politics of the School Library," *APLA Bulletin*
        30:75-79 (September 1966).
The author considers the concept of the school library as it operates in Saskatchewan,
Canada. He describes six services—media, reference, reading, technical, instructional,
and administrative. These services need to be implemented at the district or provin-
cial level.

492. Wyer, James I. **Reference Work: A Textbook for Students of Library Work and Librarians**. Chicago, American Library Association, 1930. 315p.

In the chapter titled "Reference Work in School Libraries" the role of the school library is discussed and the distinctive aspects of reference work in school libraries are considered. Also covered are the school library as a centralizing agency, group instruction, and library use.

SPECIAL LIBRARIES

See also: Chapter 7, Special Types of Reference Service
Chapter 9, The Reference Process (Users)
Chapter 11, Research in Reference (Measurement and Evaluation)
Chapter 13, Information Centers and Services
Chapter 14, Information Retrieval

Included in this section are general works pertaining to reference service in special libraries. Specific aspects of reference service are included in appropriate sections, such as Administration of Reference Service and In-Service Training, both in Chapter 5. Surveys and other research pertaining to special library reference service are included in the Measurement and Evaluation section in Chapter 11.

Bibliographical coverage of special library reference service is provided in Mary E. Anders, "Reference Service in Special Libraries," *Library Trends* 12:390-404 (January 1964) and Wilfred Ashworth, *Handbook of Special Librarianship and Information Work* (London, Aslib, 1967). Other sources of bibliographical coverage are also provided in Gertrude Schutze, *Information and Library Science Source Book* (Metuchen, N.J., Scarecrow, 1972). See also *Bibliography of Research Relating to Communication of Scientific and Technical Information* (New Brunswick, N.J., Rutgers State University, 1967), and Ronald Havelock, *Bibliography on Knowledge Utilization and Dissemination* (Ann Arbor, University of Michigan, Institute for Social Research, 1972).

493. Amiel, Esther. "The One Man Show Reference Business: The Satirical Approach." In *Reference Work—Background and Implications*. Tel Aviv, Israel Society of Special Libraries and Information Centres, 1971. pp. 23-29. ERIC Document ED056714.

The author describes reference work in science and technology as an information officer working alone in an organization. She discusses personal qualities needed and problems encountered. She describes six lessons to be learned in the preliminary stage after first taking a job. The second stage, of beginning to work in a scientific manner, is then described. She concludes with a number of suggestions on how to reach the clients and what will be expected in special library work.

494.   Anders, Mary Edna. "Reference Service in Special Libraries," *Library Trends* 12:390-404 (January 1964).

The author summarizes the background and development of special libraries from approximately 1900 to early in 1960 and describes the types of organizations that have special libraries. The primary aspects of special library reference service are 1) direct provision of information, 2) literature searches, 3) preparation of bibliographies, 4) current awareness service. Auxiliary services include interlibrary loan, indexing and abstracting, publishing services, translation, and photo-duplication. The relative roles of technical information specialists and reference librarians are discussed and further implications considered. The use of automation and the influence of special library reference service on other types of libraries are also covered.

495.   Ashworth, Wilfred, ed. **Handbook of Special Librarianship and Information Work**. 3rd ed. London, Aslib, 1967. 624p.

The fifth chapter, "Information Retrieval" (pp. 141-232), by J. R. Sharp, covers a wide variety of aspects of information retrieval. Chapter 10, "Subject Inquiries and Literature Searching," by C. W. Hanson (pp. 415-452), covers reference staff, types of inquiries, the reference interview, search strategy, and sources of information. Appendices include an annotated list of guides to subject literature and directions for preparation of guides to sources of information.

496.   Beyerly, E. "International Reference Service: Requiem or Revival?" *International Library Review* 7:427-443 (October 1975).

Reviews philosophy and development of reference service. Describes a special international reference service which is part of the Unesco Library. Discusses location of the service, reference collection, and catalog. Describes the provision of reference service to patrons on a variety of subjects in a variety of languages. Also discusses other activities of reference librarians, including selection, weeding, and in-service training. Objectives include bringing people and information together and keeping the collection current and viable.

497.   Bird, Jack. "Organization of Reference Work in a Special Library," *UNESCO Bulletin for Libraries* 14:6-9 (January 1960).

Covered here are selection and acquisition of materials, organization, staff, and provision of direct reference service.

498.   Burton, Elizabeth. "New Trends in Special Library Reference Service," *Indiana Slant* 24:7+ (February 1962).

Comments on the trend toward increasing specificity of questions and attributes this to the "exacting requirements of the space age."

499.   Carlson, Walter M. "The Research Librarian in a Challenging Age," *Special Libraries* 55:11-19 (January 1964).

Activities sponsored by the scientific and technical information program of the Department of Defense are explained. The system of Defense Research Libraries is described.

500. Cohan, Leonard, and K. Craven. **Science Information Personnel**. New York, Modern Language Association of America, 1960. 107pp. ERIC Document ED 013365.

The importance of foreign languages in science information work is stressed. Main areas of discussion in this report are the creation and organization of information, the occupation of science information specialists, recruiting and using science information personnel, recommended undergraduate and graduate programs in science and language, and predictions for the future of science information work.

501. Goodwin, Harry B. "Some Thoughts on Improved Technical Information Service," *Special Libraries* 50:443-446 (November 1959).

Discusses the five types of information required by scientists. Four of the five items relate to the "keeping up" process.

502. Gray, Dwight. "General Problems of Information Services," *Special Libraries* 48:313-320 (September 1957).

Describes ways of exchanging information and focuses on a few of the principal problems that confront organized information services. Should there be automatic or selective dissemination and how should it be carried out? Should technical reports be organized by subject, corporate author, or number? Discusses problems in handling requests and using machines. Other problems include finding materials in other collections, security classification of materials, and need for improvements in technical writing.

503. deWit, Pauline. "The Rivalry: Routines and Reference." In Rowland, Arthur, ed., *Reference Services*. Hamden, Conn., Shoe String Press, 1964. pp. 101-103. (Contributions to Library Literature, No. 5).

Discusses the problem of the librarian in the small library who must take care of both record-keeping and reference service. Gives suggestions on how record-keeping can be streamlined.

504. Forman, Dorothy J. "How to Approach the Reference Question," *Special Libraries* 46:354-357 (October 1955).

Suggests an approach to reference problems as applied to metallurgy but applicable to other areas. Techniques described are 1) fitting the inquiry into a broad subject area, 2) determining whether new or older information would contain the answer, 3) using good judgment in questioning, 4) treating all inquiries as equally important. Also described are evaluating reference tools, use of outside information sources, and translating.

505. Goodrum, Charles A. "The Reference Factory," *Library Journal* 82:122 (January 15, 1957).

The author discusses the use of subject analysts in the Legislative Reference Division of the Library of Congress: " . . . as long as the service was asked to provide factual answers to specific questions, the librarian was most efficient. But when the inquiries began demanding either broad analysis of past situations or anticipated results of some theoretical future move, we had to have more specialized personnel."

506. Gwinn, Nancy. "How Automation and the New Congressional Reference Center Have Helped LC Provide Instant Answers for Congress on Capitol Hill's Hot Line," *Library Journal* 100:640-643 (April 1, 1975).

Describes the services of the CRS, or Congressional Research Service. Gives brief history and present status and describes the installation of small branches in House and Senate Office Buildings to make material available in closer locations.

507. Klempner, I. M. "Special Library Reference Service." In Katz, W. *Introduction to Reference Work*. New York, McGraw-Hill, 1969. Volume 2. pp. 167-172.

Considers ways in which the special librarian gives personalized reference service to researchers, administrators, technologists, and other types of specialized personnel. Such reference service must provide access to information from a variety of specialized viewpoints.

508. Lewton, Lucy. "The Roving Librarian," *Special Libraries* 36:75-79 (March 1945).

Describes a change from broader questions asking for general information on a subject to more specific questions exemplified by "What's in it?", "Who makes it?", and "Where does he work?"

509. Mann, Margaret. "Research and Reference in the Special Library," *ALA Bulletin* 18:185-190 (August 1924).

Discusses the influence of business on our national life and the importance of reading to our democracy. Describes the development of special libraries of two types, those limited to special subject fields and those serving special organizations and businesses. The function of each type is discussed. Also discussed is the handling of quick reference questions and longer research questions. Research services and compilations of bibliographies for a fee are discussed.

510. Saffady, William. "Reference Service to Researchers in Archives," *RQ* 14:139-144 (Winter 1974).

Reviews the literature on reference service to researchers in archives and notes that little attention has been given to this subject. Archival reference service is important because of differing classification systems and because researchers lack education in archival research methods. Describes five types of archival reference questions and concludes that most archival reference service is instructional in nature rather than informational because 1) the researchers need orientation, 2) historians often do not have precisely formulated needs. Most important for archival reference service is depth in subject specialization and familiarity with the collection. Technology offers promise of improving subject access to archival materials, but there is danger that it also may increase the tempo of work so as to crowd out time for reference service.

511.   Whitford, Robert H. "To Show or to Know," *Special Libraries* 29:253-256
       (October 1938).
Considers whether the librarian or subject specialist should predominate in the special library. Points out the need for the special librarian to be able to understand
the technical field in order to answer questions effectively. Concludes that the most
important function is to be a librarian, but the possession of subject knowledge is
an important advantage.

CHAPTER 7

SPECIAL TYPES OF REFERENCE SERVICE

TELEPHONE AND MAIL SERVICE

See also: Chapter 5, Reference Service (Administration of Reference Service)
Chapter 8, Reference Service to Special Groups
Chapter 9, The Reference Process (Users)
Chapter 11, Research in Reference (Measurement and Evaluation)
Chapter 12, Cooperative Reference Service
Chapter 13, Information Centers and Services

Included in this section are works on telephone and/or mail reference service in all types of libraries. Some bibliographical coverage is provided by Terence Crowley and Thomas Childers, *Information Services in Public Libraries* (Metuchen, N.J., Scarecrow, 1971).

512.   Auster, Ethel. "A Field Service Reference Program for Educational
        Administrators," *Special Libraries* 66:111-115 (March 1975).
Describes a special field reference service of the Reference and Information Service of the Library of the Ontario Institute for Studies in Education for educational administrators at remote locations in the Province. Questions arrive at the Library by mail or phone and reference librarians compile bibliographies and other materials, including photocopied articles, descriptions of the search plan, names of persons and schools to contact, and other useful information. This is then packaged and mailed. Describes users of the service, types of requests, and subjects of bibliographies compiled.

513.   Baky, J. "Library Line 1974," *Connecticut Libraries* 16:5-9 (June 1974).
Believes the Library Line program has significant potential despite the criticism in *Library Journal* (99:1105, April 15, 1974). Gives a short history of the project and insight into its present workings. Library Line is a statewide program centered in the Connecticut State Library, which answers or refers questions telephoned in from all over the state. Library Line staff handle some 250 calls per day. The author concludes that this high usage by the public is because of the convenience of having one number and one place to call and because it is a consumer-oriented service not related to governmental boundary lines.

514. "Code for the Handling of Reference Inquiries Received by Mail," *College and Research Libraries* 13:364-365 (October 1952).
This code was taken from the Report of the Committee on the Referral of Reference Inquiries, Reference Librarian's Section, ACRL. The purpose of the code is described and the text of the code is given.

515. Crowley, Terence, and Thomas Childers. *Information Services in Public Libraries: Two Studies.* Metuchen, N.J., Scarecrow, 1971. 210p.
The authors attempted to determine whether the statistics on reference service as reported by the New Jersey State Library and the claims of success made by reference librarians were consistent with the quality of reference service as actually experienced by patrons using the service. Two case studies are reported here where questions of fact were asked of reference librarians who were unaware that a test was being carried out. Results indicate that the quality of service "does not support the claims made for it."

516. Gifford, Florence. "Telephone Reference Service," *Wilson Library Bulletin* 17:630-632 (April 1943).
Policies and procedures in regard to telephone reference service at the Cleveland Public Library are outlined. Important guidelines for telephone reference are 1) it should be fast and accurate, 2) some kind of time limit should be observed, 3) judgment should be made as to which questions can be answered easily and which will require that the librarian return the patron's call.

517. Heneghan, Mary A. "The Telephone and Mag Selection," *RQ* 11:253-255 (Spring 1972).
Describes training reference assistants in answering telephone reference queries. The assistant first listens to senior staff members answering telephone questions and then the assistant answers while the staff member listens. Selection of new magazines is also discussed.

518. Kinney, Mary R. "Reference Inquiries Received by Mail," *College and Research Libraries* 24:309-313 (July 1963).
Discusses the handling of reference inquiries by mail in medium-sized public libraries. The reasons why this service is needed are considered and a code concerning this type of inquiry is discussed.

519. Petrella, J. A. "Survey of Telephone Reference Questions at the Business Information Bureau, Cleveland Public Library." Unpublished Master's thesis, Western Reserve University, 1951 . 51p.

520. Rohlf, Robert. "Let's Consider a Telephone Department," *Library Journal* 83:50-53 (January 1, 1958).
Some reasons for the increasing need for telephone reference service are described, such as decentralization of population, transportation problems, and lack of parking. Telephone contact is a trend particularly followed by business and industry and is bound to increase.

521. Shields, G. R. "Sorry, the Library Line Is Busy," *Library Journal* 99:1105
    (April 15, 1974).
This editorial comments adversely on an East Coast State Library that has inaugurated a new program called "Library Line," which averages 200 to 300 calls per day.
Criticized are lack of helpfulness and refusal to answer any but "serious" questions.
Quotes such as "we get calls for homework questions they could answer themselves"
illustrate this attitude. Also criticized is the manning of the service by volunteers
without special library training.

522. Souder, L. E. "Telephone Reference Service of the Missouri State Library."
    Unpublished research paper, University of Missouri, 1973. 14p.

CURRENT AWARENESS SERVICES

See also: Chapter 13, Information Centers and Services
          Chapter 14, Information Retrieval

Included in this section are works concerned with both manual and computerized current awareness services in all types of libraries. Listed here are
articles concerning SDI (Selective Dissemination of Information) and other
current awareness services.
    Bibliographical coverage is provided by T. R. Savage, *SDI Bibliography—1*
(Santa Barbara, Calif., Share Research Corp., 1968), 26p.; J. H. Schneider,
"Selective Dissemination and Indexing of Scientific Information," *Science*
173:300-308 (July 23, 1971); E. M. Housman, "Selective Dissemination of Information," in *Annual Review of Information Science and Technology, Volume 8*
(Washington, D.C., American Society for Information Science, 1973); Gertrude
Schultze, *Information and Library Science Source Book* (Metuchen, N.J., Scarecrow,
1972); *Bibliography of Research Relating to Communication of Scientific and Technical Information* (New Brunswick, N.J., Rutgers State University, Graduate School
of Library Service, 1967); Ronald Havelock, *Bibliography on Knowledge Utilization
and Dissemination* (Ann Arbor, University of Michigan, Institute for Social
Research, 1972).

523. Burton, H. D. "User Dependent SDI System: They Said It Could Not Be
    Done," *Special Libraries* 64:541-544 (December 1973).
Describes an SDI system in operation in the U.S. Department of Agriculture. Users
develop and modify their own profiles rather than relying on an intermediary. This
requires minimal staffing and makes it possible for a wide number of users in various
disciplines to have access to a variety of commercial tape services. Describes other
benefits of this sytem.

524. Carmon, James L. "SDI—Where Are We? The Challenge of the Future: The Information Dissemination Center View." *Paper Presented at the 37th Annual Meeting of the American Society for Information Science, October, 1974, Atlanta, Georgia* 19p. ERIC Document ED096997.

The historical background and current status of information dissemination centers is reviewed, with emphasis on the user interface. Technical problems have been solved and there are now many well-established information dissemination centers. Competitive data bases are often available in the same subject area. User interface, now generally requiring an intermediary, presents the greatest problem. An intermediary will probably be necessary for some time in the future but a breakthrough is needed in the understanding, modelling and simulation of the man-machine interfaces which the intermediary now handles.

525. Davis, Charles H., and Peter Hiatt. "An Automated Current-Awareness Service for Public Libraries," *Journal of the American Society for Information Science* 21:29-33 (January-February 1970).

Describes a computerized current-awareness demonstration project in a public library situation. The Dewey Decimal Classification is used as a basis for reading interest check sheets. Resulting reader interest profiles are then matched against new acquisitions. Printouts include patron's name and address and basic bibliographic information on recently acquired books in his subject area. Cost and other data indicate that this system is feasible.

526. Davis, Charles H., and Peter Hiatt. "SDI: A Program for Public Libraries," *American Documentation* 8:139-145 (July 1967).

Discusses the use of the computerized COMIT program for retrieving non-fiction and fiction in the public library situation. Describes the retrieval on non-fiction by Dewey numbers. Fiction is retrieved by author names or categories such as westerns, mysteries, science fiction, etc. Describes how this program was carried out for the public library system in Lake County, Indiana.

527. Davis, Charles H. "SDI Is for People," *Library Journal* 96: 3573-3575 (November 1, 1971).

This article gives brief background on reading interests and describes how this study on the use of SDI was conducted in small public libraries in Indiana, using a checklist of the Dewey Decimal categories. This personalized service was well received. The most important change suggested was that fiction should be included by subject. Included is the reading interest check sheet and a sample printout.

528. Downie, Currie, and others. **Selective Dissemination of Information in Practice: Survey of Operational and Experimental SDI Programs.** Springfield, Va., Federal Clearinghouse for Scientific and Technical Information, 1967. 19p. ERIC Document ED019103.

An overview of the operational and experimental systems for selective dissemination of scientific and technical information. Based on results of two recent surveys, it reveals the existence of some 45 SDI services in operation. Trends are toward capitalizing on products from large systems, toward increased use of group profiles, and toward commercial subscription services.

529.   East, H. "Development of SDI Services," *Aslib Proceedings* 20:482-491
        (November 1968).
Described here are seven SDI systems in Great Britain. These systems are discussed
and compared in categories of data input, strategies of profile matching, output,
and cost analysis. Evaluation of the systems is considered in regard to relevance,
ratio of documents selected to documents scanned, and measure of the number
of descriptors that actually participate in selection of documents (termed selection-
participation ratio).

530.   Fidoten, Robert F. "Current Awareness Service." In *Encyclopedia of
        Library and Information Science*. Allen Kent and Harold Lancour, eds.
        Vol. 6. New York, Dekker, 1971. pp. 332-336.
Discusses various definitions of current awareness service and its impact on information retrieval.

531.   Holt, J. A. "Selective Dissemination of Information: A Review of the
        Literature and the Issues." Unpublished Master's thesis, University of
        California, 1967. 38p.

532.   Housman, E. M. "Selective Dissemination of Information." In *Annual
        Review of Information Science and Technology, Volume 8*. Washington,
        D.C., American Society for Information Science, 1973. pp. 221-224.
Introduces SDI and presents highlights in this area in 1971. Covers the following
key aspects of SDI: data bases, interest profiling, search problems, announcement
media, costs, SDI service centers, and systems evaluation. Extensive bibliography.

533.   Kolder, Hansjoerg, and Irwin Simpkins. "Selective Dissemination of
        Information and the Academic Science Library," *College and Research
        Libraries* 28:53-57 (January 1967).
Discusses the role of current awareness services in the academic science library. The
author stresses the inadequacies of biomedical bibliographic services and the cost
of personal information storage and retrieval systems.

534.   Macgrill, Rosemary, and Charles H. Davis. "Public Library SDI: A Pilot
        Study," *RQ* 14:131-137 (Winter 1974).
Report of a study done in the Flint, Michigan area and sponsored by the Midwestern
Michigan Library Cooperative and the University of Michigan School of Library
Science.

535.   Mauerhoff, G. R. "Selective Dissemination of Information." In *Advances
        in Librarianship*, Volume 4. New York, Academic Press, 1974. pp. 25-62.

536.   Parker, Steve, and Kathy Essary. "A Manual SDI System for Academic
        Libraries," *RQ* 15:47-53 (Fall 1975).
Describes a manual SDI system pilot project, RECAST, carried out at the University
of Arkansas. Seven faculty members with research projects participated. The purpose
of the project was to identify relevant current material in all formats and in six
languages. Describes how profiles were produced. Staff then determined which

abstracts and indexes should be examined and these were searched regularly. New books were also examined. Citations were then combined and sent to the researchers weekly. A comparison of the effectiveness of the RECAST program with that of MEDLINE showed that RECAST identified all of the same relevant citations found by MEDLINE, plus seven more relevant citations not found by MEDLINE.

537. Savage, T. R. *SDI Bibliography—1*. Santa Barbara, Calif., Share Research Corp., 1968. 26p.
Lists some 200 papers on all aspects of SDI published through 1967.

538. Schneider, J. H. "Selective Dissemination and Indexing of Scientific Information," *Science* 173:300-308 (July 23, 1971).
Notes that formal classification schemes have received little attention in this country in regard to computer-based systems. This appears to be due to emphasis on thesauri and post-coordinate indexing. Bibliography.

READERS ADVISORY SERVICE

See also: Chapter 8, Reference Service to Special Groups
Chapter 11, Research in Reference (Measurement and Evaluation)

This section contains works pertaining to readers' advisory service and selected works on aspects of reading guidance.
Bibliographical coverage is provided by Lee Regan, "Status of Readers' Advisory Service," *RQ* 12:227-233 (Spring 1973).

539. "Across the Desk of the Readers' Adviser," *Adult Education and the Library* 3:19-22 (February 1928).
Stresses the availability of free unstructured education as one of the main assets of the public library. For those dropping out of school, the public library, "unhampered by creeds, doctrines, or scholastic requirements," should provide an educational alternative.

540. Ahern, M. E., ed. "Individualizing Library Service," *Libraries* 33:279-300 (June 1928).
Methods of individualizing readers' advisory service are discussed, including acquisition of bibliographies, compiling lists, contacting subject authorities and organizations, acquiring catalogs and references of all local educational opportunities, tutors, and lecturers.

541. Bacon, Virginia Cleaver. "Possibilities of Informal Education Under Library Guidance," *ALA Bulletin* 21:317-319 (October 1927).
Stresses the opportunities of libraries for continuous informal adult education and the friendly relationships with patrons that develop out of readers' advisory service and thus make "permanent library students."

542.   Bryan, Alice. "The Psychology of the Reader," *Library Journal* 64:7-12 (January 1, 1939).

The author suggests that, contrary to prevailing educational philosophy, the reading of books can create emotional reactions as intense as those created by "real life" experience. Discusses reading guidance from a psychological point of view. It is important to know what motivates the reader and how different books will affect him. Reading planned with an understanding of the reader in terms of his personal needs, goals, frustrations, and conflicts, can help him work out constructive solutions to his problems. Considers studies of reading interests and attitude changes and the need for expanded services and bibliotherapy. Suggests that psychologists be available to consult with readers' advisors in diagnosing needs of readers who are really seeking advice on deeper problems.

543.   Bryan, Alice. "The Reader as a Person," *Library Journal* 65:137-141 (February 15, 1940).

Discusses the importance of understanding the human personality and social behavior.. Communications, interpersonal relations, psychology, and sociology should be studied in regard to reading habits. It is necessary to know why the patron reads. Motivations discussed are 1) economic or emotional security, 2) new experience (adventure, escape), 3) response and recognition (shared experience, communion).

544.   Chancellor, John. "Helping Readers with a Purpose," *ALA Bulletin* 25:136-139 (April 1931).

Describes goals of readers' advisory service to be 1) thoughtful personal time and attention given to readers, 2) emphasis on consecutive reading and depth of knowledge—really to know the subject approached, 3) teaching people to "read with a purpose," rather than haphazardly.

545.   Cohan, Leonard, ed. *Reader's Advisory Service: Selected Topical Booklist.* New York, Science Associates, 1974— . Annual.

This new serial reprints topical subject bibliographies, booklists, annotated reading lists, and guides to the literature prepared by leading libraries and information centers.

546.   Dunlap, Florence, and Jeanne Rose. "The Reader's Advisor: Is This Reference Work?" *RQ* 7:25-26 (Fall 1967).

The reference librarian who also acts as a readers' advisor is discussed. For readers' advisory work it is important to be familiar with a wide variety of novels and books on all levels of knowledge. This can also aid in locating useful bits of factual information.

547.   Dunn, A. M. "Nature and Functions of a Reader's Advisory Service as Revealed by a Survey of the Literature of the Field, 1935-1950." Unpublished Master's thesis, Western Reserve University, 1950. 32p.

548. Ennis, Phillip. **Adult Book Reading in the U.S.** Chicago, National Opinion
Research Center, 1965. 113p. ERIC Document ED010754.
Findings of a pilot study of personal use of books. Includes a personal view of reading from interviews with businessmen, housewives, and students, and sections on
patterns of reading and availability of books. Graphs and tables included.

549. Farquhar, Alice. "Tools for the Readers' Advisor," *Library Journal*
55:1008-1010 (December 15, 1930).
The increased number of library patrons and the increase in publishing have made it
difficult for readers' advisors to keep up. There is a definite need for more "brains
and bibliographies." Tools and special aids are described.

550. Feinstein, Leonore. "A Philosophy of Readers' Advisorship," *Wilson
Library Bulletin* 26:386 (January 1951).
A philosophy of readers' advisorship is related to the basic purpose of the library.
"Practically any public library where a censor has not been at work contains more
ideas than any school curriculum." A creative education is possible through the
library.

551. Flexner, Jennie, and Byron Hopkins. **Readers' Advisors at Work: A Survey
of Development in the New York Public Library**. New York, American
Association for Adult Education, 1941. 77p.
This survey, among other findings, indicated that those branches of the New York
Public Library maintaining readers' advisors improved circulation 9.7 percent while
those without advisors showed a decline of 1.4 percent.

552. Flexner, Jennie, and Sigrid Edge. **A Reader's Advisory Service**. New York,
American Association for Adult Education, c1934. 59p.
Covers history, publicity, interviewing, list making, books wanted, supplying the
reader with books, tools for building lists, other sources of information, the reader
and his reading, and responsibilities of a reader's advisor.

553. Hart, Richard. "Reader Guidance," *Minnesota Libraries* 19:73-77
(September 1958).
Discusses the findings of the Public Library Inquiry of 1949 that readers' advisory
service is going out of fashion. "The tendency is to provide such service through the
staff generally rather than through a particular sub-division of the staff. . . . The
present practice is to consider every librarian who comes in contact with the public
as a readers' advisor."

554. Heath, Eleanor. "Some Aspects of Reading Guidance," *Minnesota Library*
22:33-34 (Summer 1967).
A report on the Reading Guidance Institute planned by the University of Wisconsin
Library School in cooperation with the American Library Association's Adult
Services Division in June 1965. The keynote speech emphasized that "constant,
thoughtful, adventurous reading is essential to a full life." Methods of guidance
include personal consultation, lists, displays, collection arrangement, radio and TV
presentation. Abilities and qualities required include empathy, tact, assessing

reading level, and interests, adaptability to people of different backgrounds, education, and familiarity with books. Responsibilities include guidance toward the best available and away from "quack" books, explanations of content of books and of the way in which one differs from another.

555.   Jackson, Evalene P. "The Essential Task of the Librarian," *Tennessee Librarian* 11:48-50 (April 1959).
Discusses the public image of readers' advisors as attempting to elevate readers' tastes. Feels the older readers' advisors erred in planning lists of "informational" or "cultural" reading, rather than encouraging simple reading for simple enjoyment.

556.   Jordan, Eloise. "Adult Reference Service and Reading Guidance," *Illinois Libraries* 48:523-526 (September 1966).
Reference service in general for adults is discussed, including the roles of the reference librarian, personal contact with the patron, catalog use, and sources of information. Readers' advisory service is described and suggestions are made for displays, exhibits, book lists, and collection arrangement.

557.   Kelley, Grace. "Reader's Adviser Still Keeps Faith," *Library Journal* 74:695-697 (May 1, 1949).
The author feels that more should be done "in building programs that . . . strengthen the human side of our profession."

558.   Money, Darlene. "What Ever Happened to Reader's Advisory Service?" *Ontario Library Review* 55:14-16 (March 1971).
Reader's advisory service has declined in importance due to the emphasis on aid to patrons who are seeking information. Library schools also emphasize information work and reference sources, neglecting reader's advisory service. More emphasis is given to groups rather than individuals. Reading for pleasure and general purposes is still paramount in public libraries.

559.   Norvell, George. **The Reading Interests of Young People**. East Lansing, Michigan State University Press, 1973. 516p.
An investigation of reading interests covering studies of all types of reading materials. Includes tabulations of data.

560.   Polette, Nancy, and Marjorie Hamlin. **Reading Guidance in a Media Age**. Metuchen, N.J., Scarecrow, 1975. 267p.

561.   Rast, P. C. "Reader's Advisory Service: A Survey of its Development in Relation to Other Adult Education Services." Unpublished Master's thesis, University of Chicago, 1958. 83p.

562.   Regan, Lee. "Status of Reader's Advisory Service," *RQ* 12:227-233 (Spring 1973).
Reviewed here is the history and present status of reader's advisory service in public libraries. Examples of the way various U.S. public libraries handle this type of service are discussed and the effectiveness of various techniques is considered. References.

563. Shortt, May. "Advisers Anonymous, Arise!" *Ontario Library Review* 59 [i.e., 49] : 81-83 (May 1965).

Describes the problem of librarians faced with a difficult reader's advisory interview. Notes that library schools stress reference tools and do not prepare students to work with fiction. Fiction readers have been reduced to second-class status. Discusses reader's advisory service and the types of patrons who use it.

564. Smith, Eleanor T. "Reader Guidance: Are We Sitting Down on the Job?" *Illinois Libraries* 48:527-532 (September 1966).

Discusses the decline in adult reader guidance, which should be a vital area of service. Describes the training given in reader's advisory service at the Brooklyn Public Library. Librarians should circulate to see if people are finding what they want. Opportunities to provide reading guidance along with reference work should be stressed. Describes effective techniques such as regular reading improvement conferences with patrons, special hours for reader's advisory services at branch libraries, and outreach services where book talks are given and manned exhibits of books are taken to community meetings to reach non-library users.

565. Smith, Eleanor. "Return of the Reader's Advisor," *Library Journal* 90:3215-3216 (August 1965).

Describes the well-attended Institute sponsored by the University of Wisconsin's Library School and University Extension Division's Department of Library Science in cooperation with ALA's Adult Services Division. Its purpose was to reinstate reader guidance as a fundamental library service. Describes and discusses content of papers presented and panel sessions.

INNOVATIONS

See also: Chapter 6, Reference Service in Types of Libraries
Chapter 8, Reference Service to Special Groups
Chapter 12, Cooperative Reference Service
Chapter 13, Information Centers and Services

Included in this section are innovative and unusual reference services in academic, public, special libraries, as well as independent reference services.

Bibliographical coverage of innovative and unusual services may be found in Carolyn Forsman, "Resource Guide," *RQ* 12:350-354 (Summer 1973) and Eleanor Brown, *Library Services to the Disadvantaged* (Metuchen, N.J., Scarecrow, 1971). Another bibliography of interest is J. Lebovitch, *College Libraries and Tutor Librarianship: An Annotated Selected Bibliography* (Hertis, 1971), 28p.

566. Aspnes, Grieg. "INFORM: An Evaluation Study," *Minnesota Libraries* 24:171-185 (Autumn 1974).

Included here is the author's report to the Board of Directors of INFORM, an experimental consortium of libraries in the Minneapolis-St. Paul metropolitan area designed to provide "in-depth" reference service to clients for a fee. The author shows a rise of use up 115 percent in the second year and 53 percent in the third year, and concludes that this shows need for the service. In regard to the success of INFORM, pro and con comments from users and non-users are studied. Also considered is whether the service is justifiable or not; a number of criticisms are raised and answered. The advantages and disadvantages of fees are listed and discussed. The future of INFORM is discussed.

567.　Auld, Larry, and Irene Voit. "Library Group Practice," *College and Research Libraries* 34:54-58 (January 1973).

"No longer can the highly qualified and thoroughly experienced specialist devote a substantial share of his time to sitting at the reference desk." The authors expand on these views and describe the group practice library as one where upon entering, the patron is met by an information clerk who determines the level of service required and directs the patron to a person who can be of assistance and sets up an appointment. Reference and other librarians should do no clerical work but function only at the level for which they are trained.

568.　"Baltimore Shopping Center Gets Reference Service," *Library Journal* 97:3270 (October 15, 1972).

A brief note of a new ready-reference service through the Enoch Pratt Free Library. An information booth has been set up in a shopping center area and the hours and types of service are discussed.

569.　Berry, J. N. "Building an Information Constituency," *Library Journal* 100:705 (April 15, 1975).

This editorial comments on Galvin's conclusion that the quality of reference and information service has not improved as much as should have been expected over the years. (Galvin, "The Education of the New Reference Librarian," *Library Journal*, 100:727-730, April 15, 1975). The author is hopeful that improvement in service is coming about and describes a number of specific instances of publications and projects where reference librarians are working hard to provide, collect, and compile the information that people want and need.

570.　Borden, Arnold. "The Research Librarian Idea," *Library Journal* 58:104 (Feburary 1, 1933).

Describes the subsidization by the Carnegie Corporation of special bibliographic assistants to be at the disposal of professors doing research in social sciences and humanities. It was hoped that this would lead to the establishment of a service to those subject departments whose work centered in the library which would be as effective as the aid available for those doing laboratory research.

571.　"California State College 24-Hour Reference Service," *Library Journal* 98:3336 (November 15, 1973).

This brief announcement describes the inauguration of a 24-hour reference service at the California State College Library. During times when there is no reference service in the library, patrons can call a reference librarian at home for service. Reference librarians work from duplicate ready reference collections in their homes.

572. Cheren, Mark. "Franklin County Learning Exchange," *Bay State Librarian* 63:12-13 (April 1974).
Describes a learning exchange program of the Greenfield Public Library where people who wish to share hobbies and interests or particular knowledge and learning are matched with each other. About 400 matches have been made, about half of which were successful. The author describes how the exchange functions and concludes that participation was good and that it provided person-to-person learning experiences through the public library.

573. Doebler, Paul. "Seek and Ye Shall Find," *Publisher's Weekly* 302:39-42 (October 16, 1972).
Discusses the FIND information service operated by ICH (Information Clearing House) and sold by subscription to business and other organizations. It is associated with SVP, a similar service in Paris, begun 25 years ago. Questions are dealt with by telephone. Advantages of the service are an in-house index to 5,000 information sources, a collection of often-used reference materials, and reciprocal agreements with the worldwide SVP network and with other information centers. FIND has been in operation for a year and is expected to become self-supporting after 18 months.

574. Dowlin, Kenneth E. "CATV + NCPL = VRS," *Library Journal* 95:2768-2770 (September 1, 1970).
Referred to in the title of this article is "Community Antenna Television plus the Natrona County Public Library equals Video Reference Service." A test was made of the use of this service, which resulted in 78 questions over a 22-hour period. It is felt the service could be developed over a period of years since the test indicates its feasibility. Cost figures are needed to determine economic feasibility.

575. Evans, Susan, and Maurice Line. "Personalized Service to Academic Researchers: The Experimental Information Service in the Social Sciences at the University of Bath," *Journal of Librarianship* 5:214-232 (July 1973).
An experimental program was offered at the University of Bath in which the following services were provided: manual current awareness, bulletins, retrospective searches, press cutting, and MARC tapes current awareness for monographs. Users evaluated each current awareness citation that they received. Relevance was considered good and most references were new to the users. The service was rated highly by users and considered to have a high priority in regard to university funding.

576. "FIND: Information on Demand," *BCLA Reporter* 17:19 (January 1974).
FIND is a commercial information service with headquarters in New York, which currently answers some 1,000 questions per month for some 2,000 executive users. Staff includes skilled researchers and subject specialists who use a proprietary index of over 3,000 information sources. Services include simple and complex questions, bibliographies, literature searches, definitions, market data, names, locations, dates, and provision of copies of specific materials.

577.   Fusaro, Janiece B. "Media Counseling: A New Dimension for Reference
       Service," *RQ* 9:114-116 (Winter 1969).
Under ideal circumstances in a junior college library there would be extensive media
use, due to emphasis on self-study. In addition to traditional duties, reference librarians should be able to provide "media counseling," guiding individuals toward
appropriate media, both hardware and software, to meet their needs.

578.   Gopinath, M. A. "Personalized Reference Service," *Library Herald* 12:1-10
       (April 1970).
Described here is personalized documentation service which consists of five stages:
1) reader presents his question, 2) question is analyzed using a freely-faceted classification scheme, 3) question is matched with entries of documents, 4) the class
number is located, 5) documents are located and supplied, and their relevance is
evaluated on the basis of the reader's reactions.

579.   Hahn, Robert. "Hospital Reference Service," *RQ* 12:283-284 (Spring 1973).
The author suggests a program where student reference aids would act as "supervised
intermediaries between hospital librarians and the reference materials and collections
of a resource library." After a training period, students and librarians would communicate by mail and phone and students would conduct literature searches, fill bibliographic requests, and perform other services.

580.   Jones, R. J. "Pay as You Learn," *Assistant Librarian* 66:166-171 (October
       1973).
Suggests providing readers in the public library with new in-depth information service in order to encourage library use. Discusses such a service in terms of that personalized information service provided by Collier-Macmillan to those who purchase
a set of its encyclopedias.

581.   Kepple, Robert R. "Serving Readers in a Special International Library,"
       College and Research Libraries 28:203-207, 216 (May 1967).
This article is concerned with the International Atomic Energy Library. User
characteristics are discussed. Methods of introducing users to the library are
described, including an initial interview, a "field-of-interest register," and a personalized UDC schedule.

582.   Kochen, Manfred. "Referential Consulting Networks." In Rawski, Conrad,
       ed. *Toward a Theory of Librarianship*. Metuchen, N.J., Scarecrow, 1973.
       pp. 187-220.
Referential consulting is suggested by the author as a new type of expanded reference
service. The reference consultant provides aid on any question of importance to people in their daily lives. The question is dealt with by an expert within the referntial
consulting network or is referred to outside agencies or organizations.

583.   "Librarians on Call 24 Hours a Day," *American Libraries* 4:598 (November
       1973).
California State College has extended reference assistance to a 24-hour service. There
are 84 weekly hours when no reference librarian is on duty and service is provided
from the librarian's home. The request may be handled by giving directions to a

student assistant at the library, by using a duplicate ready reference collection in the librarian's home, or by the librarian returning to the library, if necessary.

584.   Martin, Gordon. "What They Are Asking: A Very Public Reference Desk," *RQ* 4:5 (July 1965).
Discusses the Library/USA information center operated by ALA at the U.S. Pavillion at the New York World's Fair. In addition to the UNIVAC Real Time Computer, staff provided a reference service which answered some 100,000 reference questions during the 1964 season. In addition, annotated reading lists on 75 subjects were supplied to 200,000 people by the computer.

585.   Maxfield, David K. "Counselor Librarians Stimulate Reading and Learning," *Improving College and University Teaching* 3:34-35 (February 1955).
The author describes a program of the Chicago Undergraduate Division of the University of Illinois. A Department of Library Instruction and Advisement was set up and specially trained librarians provided reference help, general counseling, information, and advice. Possibly as a result of the program, circulation of books increased, more reading was done, and elementary reference questions decreased.

586.   Maxfield, David K. "Counselor Librarianship at U.I.C.," *College and Research Libraries* 15:161-166 (April 1954).
The author describes the Department of Library Instruction and Advisement at the Chicago Undergraduate Division of the University of Illinois. Librarians with special training counsel students, giving reference help, general information, and advice. They guide students toward educational, vocational, and personal counseling and also undertake liaison activities. The program centers its concern on the student and his problems, even to the point of psychological help.

587.   Michelman, C. A. "Counselor and Librarian," *Library Journal* 78:291-294 (February 15, 1953).
Describes similarities in functions of librarians and counselors. The librarian's role should include the following: 1) providing the best information about vocations, educational opportunities, social relationships and personal development; 2) assisting in locating and interpreting pertinent information for problem solving; 3) aiding in orientation to educational opportunities; 4) obtaining information and utilizing available information about the individual to aid in working more effectively with him; 5) providing opportunities for development; 6) providing such counseling services as are appropriate. The author explains these points in detail and describes how counselors and librarians can work together.

588.   "Missouri's Legislative Hot Line," *American Libraries* 4:466-467 (September 1973).
Local public libraries are linked with the Missouri State Library on a toll-free line in order to deal with questions concerning the status of bills in the state legislature. The rationale for this hot line is described, and its operation and services are discussed.

589. *"The NCPL Scene 1980: Script for Videotape."* Casper, Wyoming, Natrona County Public Library, 1974. 4p.

In 1971, the Natrona County Public Library in Wyoming established full-time use of a cable TV channel for reference service. High-speed microfilm equipment was also acquired. It is planned to develop a computerized index to all traditional reference tools and a microfilm retrieval system. A videotape library, a computerized data base, and cable TV communications with library patrons would be added.

590. "Natrona County Library Opens Cable TV Outlet," *Library Journal* 97:960-961 (March 15, 1972).

Describes the cable TV reference service of the Natrona County Public Library in Wyoming. Reference service is given daily from 2:00 P.M. to closing. As an example, a patron who has requested a map can be shown the map on TV. Descriptions and photographs of equipment are given, and costs and type of use are discussed.

591. "New Advisory Services Tried by College Libraries," *Library Journal* 100:912 (May 15, 1975).

This brief note reports on an advisory program at the University of California at Berkeley where graduates and some undergraduates in humanities and social sciences receive assistance in their bibliographic work, including interviews, consultations, introduction to the literature, and advice in locating and acquiring relevant materials. A similar program may be set up at the University of Arizona in Tucson.

592. Orne, Jerrold. "An Experiment in Integrated Library Service," *College and Research Libraries* 16:353-359 (October 1955).

A special program was developed at the Air University Library, Maxwell Air Force Base, to encourage use of the library by those who had been away from the academic world for some years. Subject specialist librarians went directly to students, faculty, and staff, attending classes, lectures and activities in their subject area. Details of this program are given and its success is evaluated.

593. Pritchard, Hugh. "Reference Work at Amherst College Library," *College and Research Libraries* 14:172-173 (April 1953).

An unusual program is described in which a student doing research registers with a reference librarian and a conference is held to discuss scope and sources of information. When further information or help is available, a note is left for the student on a "call board." A card is kept with each student's name and topic and notes are clipped to it containing helpful information and suggestions. The student then copies these and the original notes are saved for further use. Much heavier use of reference sources and government documents has been reported as a result of this program.

594. *Project Aurora: An Experiment in Expanding Library Awareness, July 1970 to June 1972. Final Report.* Columbus, Ohio, Ohio Library Foundation, 1973. 104p. ERIC Document ED088456.

Reported here is Project Aurora, a new form of library extension in which four non-professionals, after a six-week training course, made monthly vists to homes. Their purpose was to provide books, to stimulate interest in the library, and to discover local needs. Families participating came from all socioeconomic groups and included both library users and non-users. Results of a questionnaire filled out by families in the Project indicated that the program stimulated an interest in reading but not necessarily library use. A need for library service to those unable to get to the library was shown.

595.   "Teamwork Pays Off: Librarians Have Accompanied Staff Physicians on Their Morning Rounds," *American Libraries* 5:353-354 (July 1974).
Describes a new program where medical librarians accompany physicians, interns, and other medical personnel on their morning rounds. When a question is encountered which needs to be researched, the librarian, on returning to the library, performs a Medline search and receives a printout which is then made available that afternoon to physicians.

596.   "Video Reference Service Set Up at Alabama Library," *Library Journal* 97:2031 (June 1, 1972).
The Mobile Public Library in Mobile, Alabama, has set up a video reference center. Information is given on types of materials used, costs, and equipment. Similar operations by the Natrona County Public Library (Wyoming) are mentioned.

597.   Wagner, Walter. "On Integrating Libraries and Classrooms: An Experiment Worth Continuing," *Learning Today* 6:48-62 (Winter 1973).
Described here is an experimental program at Upsala College in 1972, where librarians attempted to integrate the library and the classroom. Two courses were selected, and faculty and librarians revised the course syllabi to include library research projects.

598.   Warner, A. S. "An Independent Librarian Looks at: Information Services: New Use for an Old Product," *Wilson Library Bulletin* 49:440-444 (February 1975).
Discusses Warner-Eddison Associates, an independent information service business founded by the author and an associate, both librarians, which provides information to customers on a fee basis. The business aspects of the service are described and typical inquiries are given. Methods and resources include a small reference collection, other libraries, telephone calls, computer data bases, and travel.

599.   Yanchisin, D. A. "Portable Librarian," *RQ* 11:340-341 (Summer 1972).
Suggests that large libraries use a free-wheeling reference librarian who would circulate through the building assisting patrons who are timid about asking for help. This method might assist in making library personnel more approachable. Points out the disadvantages but feels that the benefits would be worth the effort.

CHAPTER 8

REFERENCE SERVICE TO SPECIAL GROUPS

Included here are *highly selective* works on information needs of special
groups of library users and reference or information service to these groups, as
well as selected works on library service in general to special groups. See the
closely related Chapter 13, Information Centers and Services, particularly the
section, Public Libraries.

Special groups will be defined here as those groups of the general population which share certain characteristics and needs and for whom special services
might be developed to meet these needs. Such groups included the disadvantaged,
the handicapped, the institutionalized, ethnic minorities, and any other groups
with special needs.

Bibliographical coverage is provided by T. A. Childers and J. A. Post,
Information Poor in America (Metuchen, N.J., Scarecrow, 1975). See also
Joanne Boelke, *Library Service to the Visually and Physically Handicapped:
A Bibliography* (ERIC Clearinghouse for Library and Information Sciences,
1969), 20p.); C. J. Stoffle, "Public Library Service to the Disadvantaged: A
Comprehensive Annotated Bibliography, 1964-1968," *Library Journal*
94:141-152, 505-515 (January 15, 1969); and *Institutional Library Services:
A Plan for the State of Illinois* (Chicago, American Librarian Association,
1970), pp. 107-110. Bibliographies are also provided in E. F. Brown, *Library
Services to the Disadvantaged* (Metuchen, N.J., Scarecrow, 1971); Charles
Booth and others, *Culturally Disadvantaged: A Bibliography and Keyword-
Out-of-Context (KWOCK) Index* (Detroit, Wayne State University Press, 1967).

600.   Bendix, Dorothy, ed. *Library Service for the Undereducated*. Philadelphia,
       Drexel Institute of Technology, 1966. 54p. (Drexel Library School Series,
       Vol. 15).
Consists of papers from a conference on the role of librarians in the fight against
poverty. Discusses programs in the New Haven Library Center, Enoch Pratt Free
Library, the Free Library of Philadelphia, the Kalamazoo Public Library, and the
Brooklyn Public Library.

601. Brown, Eleanor Frances. **Library Services to the Disadvantaged**. Metuchen, N.J., Scarecrow, 1971. 560p.

The first section of this book covers staffing, cooperation with other agencies, general problems, and programs. Other sections cover individual groups, including economically disadvantaged, physically handicapped, mentally retarded, mentally ill, institutionalized, Black Americans, older citizens, those with a language barrier, illiterates, and migrants. Also considered are the place of the neighborhood library center, out-reach programs, and research and experiments. Appendices include conferences, workshops, and institutes, booklists, and bibliographies.

602. Bundy, Mary L. "Urban Information and Public Libraries," *Library Journal* 97:161-169 (January 15, 1972).

The greatest barrier to fulfilling urban information needs is the lack of minority group members in librarianship. More minority personnel should be recruited and white participation accordingly limited. Urban information needs and failure to meet these needs are discussed. The public library's information functions are reducing access barriers, collecting needed information, and widespread dissemination of that information. Eight information services, such as an advisory service, are suggested and described. A new philosophy of service is needed for urban information work.

603. Childers, T. A., and J. A. Post. **The Information Poor in America**. Metuchen, N.J., Scarecrow, 1975. 182p.

A literature search was conducted to learn what is known about the information universe of disadvantaged adults. More than 700 documents were discovered bearing on information needs, use, and information-seeking behavior of the aged, blacks, native Americans, Chicanos, migrants, and the poor and other disadvantaged. An overview of the documents and a profile of the information-poor is provided. The bibliography section lists more than 700 relevant documents.

604. Forsman, Carolyn. "Crisis Information Services to Youth: A Lesson for Libraries?" *Library Journal* 97:1127-1134 (March 15, 1972).

Crisis services to youth are described, such as switchboards, free clinics, and hotlines. They are easily utilized, located in store-fronts or available by telephone, and give advice on food, housing, birth control, and the draft. Study of these services and their hours, personnel, training, and public relations might be of value to librarians concerned with reaching non-users.

605. **Frontiers in Librarianship. Proceedings of the Change Institute of 1969**. Westport, Conn., Greenwood, 1972. 440p.

This Institute attempted to bring together librarians of all ages from all areas and types of libraries to examine social issues in relation to library service. Some subjects covered are "Dissident Elements in the Culture," "The Disadvantaged: Reorienting the Urban Setting to New Goals and New Commitments," and "The City as Change Milieu."

606.   Josephine, Helen. "Serving the Unserved Majority: The Women's Resource Librarian," *Library Journal* 99:88-89 (January 15, 1974).
The Women's History Library is described and its materials are discussed. Many requests for information cannot be answered due to lack of both staff and local information. It is desirable that libraries and women's centers should set up special areas for women's resources and supply trained reference service in this area.

607.   Lipsman, Claire. **The Disadvantaged and Library Effectiveness**. Chicago, American Library Association, 1972. 204p.
Programming for the economically disadvantaged in 15 target cities is studied. Covered are 1) goals and objectives as related to community and user needs, 2) planning and implementation, 3) carrying out objectives, 4) program results, 5) objectives met, 6) satisfaction of patron needs, 7) program costs in relation to results.

608.   Lyman, Helen. **Library Materials in Service to the Adult New Reader**. Chicago, American Library Association, 1973. 614p.
The purposes of this book are to review the literature on the reading of the adult new literate, to consider the sociological context of this reading, to provide new data from a national survey of new adult readers, to present criteria for selection of materials, and to relate the above factors to national programs of adult reading instruction. This book is organized in four general sections—background, population study, materials evaluation, and comments on indigenous literature.

609.   Lyman, Helen H., ed. "Library Programs and Services to the Disadvantaged," *Library Trends* (October 1971). (Whole Issue).
This issue of *Library Trends* contains 20 articles related to programs and services for the disadvantaged. Sections relate to 1) minorities and the library, 2) multi-media approaches, 3) research in reading, 4) changing environments and agencies, 5) library's responsibility to youth and students, 6) education and training for service.

610.   McCrossan, John. **The Reading of the Culturally Disadvantaged**. Urbana, Illinois University, Graduate School of Library Science, 1966. 42p.
Surveys aspects of reading of culturally disadvantaged adults and children based on research and literature in this area. Considers reading ability, causes of reading problems, reading interests, and library use. Recommendations for libraries are made. Bibliography and tables included.

611.   Miles, Bill. "From Prostitutes to Meter Maids—Unholy Sources of Urban Information," *RQ* 15:13-18 (Fall 1975).
Questions whether library schools are adequately preparing reference personnel for urban information work. Library schools should become involved in contemporary action, in trying to use contemporary resources and persons who can give insights into the social problems of today. Describes and lists a large number of sources of information used by professional information seekers (FBI, credit bureaus, etc.). Notes 15 information needs of the urban poor and discusses a wide variety of community residents who can provide and analyze key urban information.

612. Moses, Richard. "Hindsight on High John," *Library Journal* 97:1672-1674 (May 1, 1972).

The author describes the formation and development of the High John program, designed to reach ghetto residents. He sums up what was learned as a result of this experience: 1) the program should begin with getting to know residents by knocking on doors, etc.; 2) learning for a service profession must involve honest on-the-job responsibility; 3) library service must become less class-oriented; 4) community support is vital. He notes that, due to backlash, such projects will probably not succeed in the future.

613. Oko, Dorothy, and Bernard Downey. **Library Service to Labor**. New York, Scarecrow, 1963. 313p.

Discusses labor groups, need of library services in terms of reference services to labor unions, building collections, and other projects.

614. Owens, Major R. "Information Power for Inner-City Communities," *Southeastern Librarian* 25:9-16 (Fall 1975).

Describes the need for information as the fourth necessity after food, shelter, and clothing, and shows how lack of adequate information can alter people's lives. Describes and discusses the 10 most important areas of information needs for inner-city residents. Gives examples of how information for decision-making at crucial times can influence the future of a community. Six reasons are given why the public library is best suited for a community information center. Describes ways the public library can develop an effective urban information center.

615. Plotnik, Art. "Library Life on the West Coast. Part II: The Why-Nots and the Have-Nots," *Wilson Library Bulletin* 48:812-820 (June 1974).

Describes unique and unusual library and other related services on the West Coast, both public and private. Covers public and school libraries, information services, outreach programs, and volunteers.

616. Sherrill, Laurence, ed. **Library Service to the Unserved**. New York, Bowker, 1971. 116p. (Library and Information Science Studies, No. 2).

A collection of papers presented at a conference held at the University of Wisconsin–Milwaukee School of Library and Information Science, November 16-18, 1967. Objectives of the conference were to explore relationships between the library and the community, to focus on problems of the unserved, and to aid participants in becoming more effective in serving this group.

617. Smith, Joshua, ed. **Library and Information Services for Special Groups**. New York, Science Associates/International, 1974. 337p.

Reviews and discusses what has been done to meet the needs of special groups in regard to library and information services. Also evaluates these programs in terms of needs as perceived by the groups themselves. Chapters cover American Indians, Appalachia, black academia and black studies, correctional institutions, and Mexican Americans.

618.   White, Carl M. "Services to Scholars," *Library Trends* 3:148-163
        (October 1954).
The differences between serving scholars and serving other types of users are considered. Collection building is also discussed in regard to meeting the needs of
scholars.

CHAPTER 9

THE REFERENCE PROCESS

Since works on the reference process are basically theoretical in nature, the reader is advised to refer to Chapter 2, Theory and Philosophy (Communication and Reference Process Theory). Works on separate aspects of the reference process are covered below in the sections on Communication and the Reference Interface, Reference Questions, Search Strategy and Reference Techniques, and Users.

COMMUNICATION AND THE REFERENCE INTERFACE

See also: Chapter 2, Theory and Philosophy
Chapter 3, Teaching of Reference
Chapter 5, Reference Service (General Works)
Chapter 7, Special Types of Reference Service
Chapter 9, The Reference Process (Reference Questions; Users)
Chapter 11, Research in Reference (Measurement and Evaluation)
Chapter 13, Information Centers and Services

Included in this section are works concerning the reference interface and selected works on communication in general. Works on the reference interface cover such areas as the reference interview, relationship with the patron, and other interpersonal relationships in reference work. Those works which are primarily theoretical in nature are included in the section on Theory and Philosophy. Studies and research on communication and the reference interface are included in the Measurement and Evaluation section in Chapter 11.

Bibliographical overviews of this area are outlined in Chapter 2, Theory and Philosophy. Other bibliographies are Patrick Penland, *Communication for Librarians* (University of Pittsburgh, 1971); Patrick Penland, *Communication Science and Technology* (New York, Dekker, 1974); Patrick Penland, *Interviewing for Counselors and Reference Librarians* (University of Pittsburgh, 1970); Patrick Penland, *Advisory Counseling for Librarians* (University of Pittsburgh, 1970); and Franklin Fearing, "Toward a Psychological Theory of Human Communication," *Journal of Personality* 22:71-88 (September 1953).

619.   Anderson, L. W. "Reference Librarians and Psychology," *Library Journal* 81:1058-1060 (May 1, 1956).
Comments on the human qualities needed by reference librarians as described in an article by Sarah Reed. Understanding the patron is as important as helping to answer questions. More preparation should be given in library school in psychology and

human relations. "The slow process of learning on the job can be appreciably shortened by formal education."

620. Benjamin, Alfred. **The Helping Interview**. New York, Houghton Mifflin, 1969. 171p.
Covered in this book are physical arrangements, general interview orientation, notetaking, problems in understanding, and appropriate verbal responses. Examples of verbatim responses illustrate the above aspects of the interview and also serve to show what may be expected in typical interviews.

621. Bunge, Charles. "Seekers vs. Barriers: Getting Information to People: Your Role," *Wisconsin Library Bulletin* 70:76-78 (March 1974).
Notes on a speech by the author at a reference workshop of the Wisconsin Valley Library Service. Describes such barriers as 1) the complexity of the library, 2) lack of knowledge on the patron's part of what librarians can and will do to help them, 3) lack of ability to express information needs clearly. The goal of the reference interview is to help the patron clarify his information need and to help the librarian determine the patron's need clearly enough to help him.

622. Burr, Robert L. "Librarians, Libraries, and Librarianship: A Model," *Libri* 23:181-209 (No. 3, 1973).
Contacts between librarians and patrons are related to the Johari Window Model for interpersonal relations. This model indicates that some relationships are improved by more openness and some by more secrecy. It is hypothesized here that interaction between librarians and patrons should be characterized by more openness.

623. Crum, Norman J. "Customer Relationship: Dynamics of Filling Requests for Information," *Special Libraries* 60:269-277 (May-June 1969).
Describes and discusses the interpersonal relationship between librarian and patron from the time the inquiry is presented until the entire reference transaction is completed. Particular emphasis is given to problems in communication created by physical, psychological, linguistic, and personality factors. Solutions to these problems are suggested. Sensitivity to the patron's needs is recommended as the most effective way to improve interpersonal relations in the reference interview. A flow chart is included.

624. Dexter, Lewis. **Elite and Specialized Interviewing**. Evanston, Ill., Northwestern University Press, 1970. 205p.
Major attention is given to in-depth interviewing. Some topics covered are oral history interviewing, how to determine if the informant is telling the truth, conducting and recording the interview, notetaking, and tape recording. Specialized interviewing, in which the interviewee structures his own information, is discussed.

625. Donovan, W. A. "Seemingly Unjustified Complaints Repay a Second Look," *RQ* 8:265-267 (Summer 1969).
The dominance/submission roles in interpersonal exchange are considered in relation to the reference interview and in regard to whether patron or librarian should "manage" the interview. Reference librarians must be flexible enough to understand

and adjust to the various attitudes of those they deal with. As professionals they should not let ego-involvement interfere in interpersonal contacts and should not let the patron down by failure to communicate with him.

626.   Fearing, Franklin. "Toward a Psychological Theory of Human Communication," *Journal of Personality* 22:71-88 (September 1953).
The author considers communication within the framework of personality-perceptual theory. The relationship between communicator and interpreter is discussed in terms of perceived instabilities, and restructuring the situation toward greater understanding.

627.   Flood, Barbara. "Referencemanship," *RQ* 7:3-4 (Fall 1967).
Humorous article written as an example of what not to do. Shows how the patron is often put on the defensive in the reference interview. Demonstrates how to put the patron in his place by playing the game of "one-upmanship," which keeps him at a constant disadvantage. The author notes that when the librarian and patron become opponents, the real value and purpose of reference service are lost.

628.   Hall, Edward T. **The Silent Language**. New York, Doubleday, 1959. 240p.
Considers the importance of cross-cultural communication. Relates communication and culture in terms of primary message systems (PMS). These primary message systems include: 1) interaction with the environment, of which speech is a form; 2) associational patterns; 3) subsistence; 4) basic sexual culture; 5) territoriality; 6) temporality—cycles, tempo of life; 7) learning—adaptive mechanisms; 8) play; 9) defensive techniques; 10) exploitation of environment—adjustment of organisms to meet specialized environmental conditions.

629.   Hickey, Doralyn. "Advanced Referencemanship," *RQ* 7:93-94 (Winter 1967).
Based on the article by Barbara Flood, which gave a humorous description of the game of "referencemanship" designed to assert the librarian's superiority and put the patron in his place. The author here describes a more intricate and advanced version of this game.

630.   Hoggart, Richard. **On Culture and Communication**. New York, Oxford University Press, 1972. 111p.
This book consists of six essays from the author's 1971 BBC Reith lectures. He defines communication as the sharing of representative experiences and believes it is both vital and possible to achieve. The social communication within individual cultures and that between cultures is discussed. The mass media must become an instrument of honest communication as well as serving an entertainment function.

631.   Horn, Roger. "Why Don't They Ask Questions?" *RQ* 3:225-233 (Spring 1974).
Discusses problems in reference service that can be created by the physical setting and arrangement of the library, by lack of communication between librarian and patron, and by the administrative structure of the library. Describes how administrative practices can interfere with good reference work.

632.   Hurst, D. S. "Reducing Communicative Interference in Reference Situations," *Oklahoma Librarian* 23:15-17 (October 1973).

633.   King, Geraldine. "Open and Closed Questions: The Reference Interview," *RQ* 12:157-160 (Winter 1972).
Many reference librarians do not perform skillfully in the reference interview, often because they have not received training in this area in their professional education. "Open" and "closed" questions are discussed, "closed" questions being those which can be answered by "yes" or "no." Open questions, on the other hand, cannot be answered by "yes" or "no," and encourage the patron to talk, thus bringing forth additional helpful information. The question "why" is often productive in determining the patron's needs and what type of material would best meet them. The need for reference librarians to learn and practice interview skills is emphasized.

634.   Library Association. Reference and Special Libraries Section. **Proceedings of the 3rd Annual Conference, Stockport, 1955**. London, The Section, 1955. pp. 7-13.
Discusses problems in inquiry techniques, including use of forms to pinpoint the initial inquiry.

635.   Mosher, Frederic. "Sermon for Beginning Reference Librarians," *Rub-Off* 12:1-4 (January 1961).
Discussed here is the problem of the reference librarian in dealing with questions which, on the surface, appear to be direct and accurate but which actually contain misinformation and inaccuracies. The librarian must consider information skeptically, must see the possibility of error everywhere, and must be prepared to solve such problems effectively.

636.   Mount, Ellis. "Communication Barriers and the Reference Question," *Special Libraries* 57:575-578 (October 1966).
Psychological, intellectual, and physical factors often cause poor communication in the reference interaction. The author is particularly concerned with the problem of determining what the patron actually wants and needs. Users often ask questions that are incomplete or not relevant to their real needs. Nine of the reasons for communication difficulties are examined, with suggestions on how to overcome these barriers, which stand in the way of good service.

637.   Peck, Theodore. "Counseling Skills Applied to Reference Services," *RQ* 14:233-235 (Spring 1975).
Discusses the similarities between reference service and counseling and explores the common ground shared by reference and the helping professions. Discusses the ways in which reference librarians can improve the reference interview in sections on empathy, attentive behavior, and content listening.

638. Penland, Patrick. **Advisory Counseling for Librarians**, Pittsburg, University of Pittsburgh, Graduate School of Library and Information Sciences, 1970. 181p.

The first section discusses the background, purpose, and functions of advisory counseling. The second considers the interrelationships of information transfer and flexibility in moving from one frame of reference to another. The third section discusses the principles and functions of counseling and guiding. The fourth section considers techniques for interview and question analysis, and the fifth section presents methods of evaluation and research. The appendix contains items developed for teaching of interpersonal communications.

639. Penland, Patrick. **Communication for Librarians**. Pittsburgh, University of Pittsburgh, Graduate School of Library and Information Sciences, 1971. 189p.

Designed to help the library profession address significant communication problems. Three major areas are covered: 1) history and theory of communication, communication institutions, communication structures in biological and social organization; 2) transfer of meaning, processing of messages in different media, analysis of message content and systems; 3) individual behavior, social interaction, attitude formation and change, public opinion, and consequences of exposure to different methods. Extensive bibliography.

640. Penland, Patrick, ed. **Communication Science and Technology: An Introduction**. New York, Dekker, 1974. 205p.

An introduction discusses media, library, and information science, generalized patroncy, and professional systems. Chapters cover "Adaptive Control Organisms," "Community of Genkind," "Genkind's Helping Profession," "Coordinating Genkind's Behavior," "Behavior Design," "Persuasion," and "Infrastructure." Includes bibliography.

641. Penland, Patrick. "Interview as Communication," *Library Occurent* 24:422-444 (May 1974).

Describes steps in helping the patron solve his problem. Patrons achieve self-actualization by tactics of self-observation, identification of their own likes and dislikes, and identification of possible opportunities. Suggests interview techniques: 1) encourage the patron to talk, and don't rush; 2) be alert to hidden problems; 3) ask clear and relevant questions; 4) use open-ended questions and a wide variety of leads; and 5) summarize and restate.

642. Penland, Patrick R. **Interviewing for Counselors and Reference Librarians**. Pittsburgh, University of Pittsburgh, Graduate School of Library and Information Sciences, 1970. 140p. ERIC Document ED049802.

Chapters discuss the following aspects of interviewing in librarianship: orientation, interface, counseling in librarianship, interpersonal aspects and psychological aspects of librarian counseling, and interview question analysis. References are included with each chapter. Appendices include sample interviews of the non-directive, directive, and functional types.

643.   Pierson, Robert M. "Is Moby Dick the Whale or the Captain?" *RQ* 7:21-24 (Fall 1967).
This article is concerned with the problem of analyzing the patron's need by means of the reference interview. Questions in literary criticism are used as examples. The problem of student plagiarization of sources is also considered.

644.   Powell, Janice. "Effective Communication: The Key to Reference Service," *Hawaii Library Association Journal* 27:3-5 (June 1970).
A broad program to develop reference technique was carried out by the Humanities Reference Department of the Hamilton Library at the University of Hawaii. Two communication seminars were held in which librarians observed and discussed their own communication and that of others, noting strong and weak areas.

645.   Pritchard, Hugh. "Sensitivity at the Reference Desk," *RQ* 11:49-50 (Fall 1971).
Eighteen problems encountered in reference service are described here, and suggestions are made for handling these problems with concern for the feelings of both patron and librarian. These suggestions and guidelines, if followed, should serve as an aid to improved communication and interpersonal relations in reference service.

646.   Sexton, Kathryn. "The Reference Interview and the Young Adult," *Top of the News* 30:415-419 (June 1974).
One of the most important aspects of the reference interview is clarification of the questions, particularly with young adults who may not be accustomed to using the library. After their needs have been determined, they should join in the search and learn use of library resources. It is often desirable to approach young adults who are reluctant to ask for help rather than have them leave the library with their needs unsatisfied. A well-conducted interview will help them to find the library materials they need, and successful library experiences at this stage will encourage future use.

647.   Smith, Nathan M., and Stephen Fitt. "Vertical-Horizontal Relationships," *Special Libraries* 66:528-531 (November 1975).
Discusses the need for sensitivity in the progress of question-negotiation. The librarian with vertical tendencies, or "movement against one's fellows," is insensitive and fails in communication. Such individuals may either feel deficient or worthless or, on the other hand, feel superior to others and act dictatorially. Horizontal relationships are positive and non-threatening and the status of these individuals is not dependent on making others feel they do not belong.

648.   Swope, Mary Jane, and Jeffrey Katzer. "Why Don't They Ask Questions?" *RQ* 12:161-166 (Winter 1972).
Reviews the literature and research in regard to communication between reference librarians and patrons. Describes results of a study done at Syracuse University's Carnegie Library. Library users were selected randomly from different areas of the library and asked whether they had questions and, if so, whether they would ask a reference librarian. Forty-one percent of the sample did have questions. Sixty-five percent of those having questions would not ask a reference librarian for help. The major reasons were, in order of frequency 1) dissatisfaction with the past service

of the librarian, 2) their question was too simple for the reference librarian, 3) they did not want to bother the reference librarian. Other findings were that users prefer to ask directional rather than reference questions. This is borne out by the fact that 87 percent of the respondents' reference questions were never asked.

649.   Taylor, Robert S. "Question Negotiation and Information Seeking in Libraries," *College and Research Libraries* 29:178-194 (May 1968).
Presented here is the author's theory that the patron develops his question on four levels: 1) the actual need to know, felt on the visceral level; 2) the conscious unspoken description of the need; 3) the need formalized into a statement; 4) the compromised need as actually presented. The librarian and patron then attempt to arrive at a mutual understanding of the last need. To achieve this, the librarian must determine the subject and the patron's motivation and personal characteristics, and must relate his question to library resources and to possible answers.

650.   Tibbets, Pamela. "Sensitivity Training—A Possible Application for Librarians," *Special Libraries* 65:493-498 (December 1974).
T-group sensitivity training has been shown by numerous studies to be effective in producing short- and long-term attitude and behavior changes. It provides opportunities for 1) increasing self-assurance, 2) receiving feedback, 3) achieving more effective interpersonal relations, 4) exploring of values, 5) lowering need for defense mechanisms, 6) gaining insight, 7) becoming more sensitive, 8) becoming aware of non-verbal communication. Librarians should utilize this method in order to improve communication.

651.   Wallace, Sarah L. **Patrons are People: How to be a Model Librarian**. Rev. ed. Chicago, American Library Association, 1956.
Discusses techniques for dealing with problem situations that may arise between patron and librarian. Gives suggestions for improved interpersonal relations in the library setting.

REFERENCE QUESTIONS

See also: Chapter 2, Theory and Philosophy
Chapter 7, Special Types of Reference Service
Chapter 9, The Reference Process (Communication and the Reference Interface)
Chapter 11, Research in Reference (Measurement and Evaluation)
Chapter 14, Information Retrieval (Search Strategy and the Subject Approach to Information)

Included in this section are records and discussion of questions and requests in all types of libraries, analysis and classification of questions, and works concerning the nature of the question/answer process. Also included here are all surveys and research concerned primarily with the collection and analysis of reference questions.

Bibliographical coverage is provided in R. S. Taylor, "The Process of Asking Questions," *American Documentation* 13:391-396 (October 1962); N. D. Blemap, *An Analysis of Questions: Preliminary Report* (Santa Monica, Calif., System Development Corp., 1963); and J. G. Fetros, "The Value of the Reference Question in Training Programs," *Californian Librarian* 33:164-168 (July 1972). Other bibliographies are available in Caroline Hieber, *An Analysis of Questions and Answers in Libraries* (Bethlehem, Pa., Lehigh University, 1966); George Gardiner, "The Empirical Study of Reference," *College and Research Libraries* 30:130-155 (March 1969); Samuel Rothstein, "Measurement and Evaluation of Reference Service," *Library Trends* 12:456-472 (January 1964); and Terry Weech, "Evaluation of Adult Reference Service," *Library Trends* 22:315-335 (January 1974).

652.   Beatty, Patricia, and John Beatty. "Stalking the Wayward Query," *American Libraries* 4:141-144 (March 1973).
The authors, writers of historical fiction, express their gratitude to reference librarians who have helped them in the past. Examples of the type of questions they have asked are given.

653.   Blemap, N. D., Jr. **An Analysis of Questions, Preliminary Report**. Santa Monica, Calif., System Development Corp., 1963. 160p.
The logical syntax of questions and answers is discussed. A question is determined by the alternatives it presents and the request it makes. This analysis is demonstrated by cross-clarification of questions into different types. Three kinds of questions are considered.

654.   Charters, W. W. "College Preparation for Reference Work," *School and Society* 27:150-152 (February 4, 1928).
The author describes his work in preparing a "curriculum study" textbook on reference work for the ALA. Most helpful was the study by Martha Connor (*Library Journal*, 52:415-418, April 15, 1927) who collected classified samples of questions at the Carnegie in Pittsburgh. The author extended that study by obtaining parallel figures from 18 libraries—large and small public libraries, library commissions, and special and university libraries. A table is given showing the percent of questions in each Dewey classification. Results and trends are discussed in detail.

655.   Chase, J. W. "Analysis of the Reference Questions Received at the Bremerton, Washington, Public Library." Unpublished Master's thesis, University of Washington, 1954. 54p.

656.   Christ, Robert W. "Recording Reference Service," *College and Research Libraries* 8:23-27 (January 1947).
Considered here are methods of classifying and recording questions and discussion of the value of attempting to record reference service. Questions are categorized in five divisions: telephone, individual requests, building questions, use of catalog questions, and unanswered questions.

657. Cole, Dorothy E. "Some Characteristics of Reference Work," *College and Research Libraries* 7:45-51 (January 1946).

Questions can be classified by time required to answer, by user's occupational background, by skill required to answer, by sources of information used, by unanswered questions, and by subject. The author discusses results of a questionnaire survey done in 1941 and suggests a new classification scheme for questions. Classification is useful to show changes in subject emphasis, to aid in selection, and to determine qualifications of personnel.

658. Cole, P. F. "Analysis of Reference Question Records as a Guide to the Information Requirements of Scientists," *Journal of Documentation* 14:197-207 (December 1958).

Examined here are the ways in which analysis of reference questions can aid in organizing and making available the large body of technical literature appearing each year.

659. Conner, Martha. "What a Reference Librarian Should Know," *Library Journal* 52:415-418 (April 15, 1927).

The author studied 24,727 reference questions at the Pittsburgh Public Library from September to December in each of the years 1905, 1910, 1915, 1920, and 1925. Findings indicated that questions heavily emphasized the social sciences and science and technology. Various types of these questions which are likely to be asked of reference librarians are presented and discussed. These are related to the type of training and preparation needed by reference librarians.

660. Erlandson, Ruth. "An Analysis of the Work of the Information Desk at the University of Illinois," *College and Research Libraries* 5:36-43 (December 1943).

Describes the work done at the information desk stationed near the catalog in the University of Illinois Library. The history of this service is reviewed. All questions recorded during the first three years of information service are analyzed. Questions are divided into the following types: general information, card catalog and classification questions, and subject questions. There are sub-groups under these categories. Describes character and subject matter of information requested. Also discusses qualifications needed by information desk personnel and library handbooks.

661. Fetros, John G. "The Value of the Reference Question in Training Programs," *Californian Librarian* 33:164-168 (July 1972).

The author emphasizes the importance of practical work in education for reference work and believes that the "question" approach should be utilized rather than a materials approach. Cross sections of patrons in certain types of libraries are essentially interested in the same types of information. The author gives 14 questions from the Liverpool Public Library in England and 50 questions from the San Francisco Public Library. He also lists and describes a number of specific articles and books that contain collections of reference questions for various types of libraries.

662.   Flood, Barbara. "Analysis of Questions Addressed to a Medical Reference
        Retrieval System: Comparison of Question and System Terminologies,"
        American Documentation 18:216-227 (October 1967).
Four hundred and eighty-three subject reference questions asked at the Library of
the College of Physicians of Philadelphia were analyzed for the number of question
terms matching system subject headings, number of question terms translatable to
system subject headings, number of stop-list words, number of untranslatable
words, using the judgment of the author. There were no significant differences
between doctors' and lawyers' questions or between questions received orally or
in written form in regard to the above factors. Requestors rarely stipulated type
of material to be covered, language, time period, cost, or time for completion.

663.   Hieber, Caroline. **An Analysis of Questions and Answers in Libraries**.
        Bethlehem, Pa., Lehigh University Center for Information Sciences, 1966.
        56p. (Studies in the Man-System Interface in Libraries. Report No. 1).
        ERIC Document ED014995.
This report is based on the author's analysis of a number of reference questions.
Traditional methods of classification of questions are discussed. The author suggests
a classification scheme by format of answer desired, and gives the following categories; exact reproduction, fill-in-the-blank, short descriptive, information about,
and list of references. Further research needed on this scheme is described, and its
value in terms of the library is discussed.

664.   Horn, Roger. "The Adequate Answer," *RQ* 9:150-153 (Winter 1969).
The author describes three types of reference questions—the scavenger hunt, the
puzzle, and the genuine question. The first two are thought by the questioner to
have an answer. There may not be an answer to the genuine question. Types of
answers are correct, right, adequate, and good. The correct answer is the fullest
possible, the right answer is less exhaustive, the adequate answer satisfies the
patron. The good answer is the sum of all and is, in a sense, the perfect answer.

665.   Jacobs, F. G. "Analysis of Reference Enquiries in a Technical Library."
        Unpublished Master's thesis, University of Chicago, 1959. 54p.
A study done in the John Crerar Library which indicates that "even in a highly
specialized technical library more use could be made than is now being made of
non-professional personnel in handling of reference questions."

666.   Jahoda, Gerald, and Mary Culnan. "Unanswered Science and Technology
        Reference Questions," *American Documentation* 19:95-100 (January
        1968).
Records of unanswered science and technology reference questions were kept by
26 science, technology, and chemistry libraries for one month. The authors, as a
result of analyzing these questions, make suggestions for needed improvements.

667.   Joseph, E. C. "What the Patrons Ask," *Louisiana Library Association
        Bulletin* 27:85-86 (Summer 1964).
Examples of types of questions are given here, ranging from directional to those
requiring considerable research. Telephone requests are also described.

668. Kronick, D. A. "Varieties of Information Requests in a Medical Library," *Medical Library Association Bulletin* 52:652-669 (October 1964).

One thousand three hundred and fifty requests for information presented at the Cleveland Medical Library over a two-year period were analyzed. Fifty percent of the requests were for reference on a specific subject, 25 percent for verification of citations, 12 percent for factual information, and 9 percent for biographical and directory information. Requests in each of the above categories were also studied in regard to volume and characteristics.

669. Ludewig, Christel W. "Information Needs of Scientists in Missile and Rocket Research as Reflected by an Analysis of Reference Questions." Unpublished Master's thesis, University of North Carolina, 1965. 67p.

670. Mackay, D. M. "Informational Analysis of Questions and Commands." In Cherry, C., ed. *Information Theory*. London, Butterworths, 1961. pp. 469-476.

Discusses the difference between questions and commands in relation to development of effective interactive systems.

671. Mackay, D. M. "What Makes A Question?" *The Listener* 63:789-790 (May 5, 1960).

The inquirer who formulates a question is characterized in this article as having a "certain incompleteness in his picture of the world—an inadequacy in what we might call his 'state of readiness' to interact purposefully with the world around him."

672. Miller, Mary M. "Two Days at the Reference Desk," *RQ* 8:107-111 (Winter 1969).

All reference questions at the Warder Public Library, Springfield, Ohio, were recorded for a two-day period by the staff in order to provide a picture of reference work in a medium-sized public library. Actual questions are presented here, grouped in categories of "easy," "harder" (required more than one reference tool or more time than a quick search), and "research." Also given is a list of off-desk activities engaged in by reference staff.

673. Nelson Associates. **Public Library Systems in the U.S.** Chicago, American Library Association, 1969. pp. 362-365.

Test reference questions used by the survey team to evaluate public library service are given here. Intended to be typical of those asked at most reference desks.

674. Potts, Rinehart S. "This Is the Way the Questions Go: Have Book, Will Answer," *RQ* 5:35-37 (Winter 1965).

The author presents a picture of the types of questions that come across a public service desk, drawn from his own experience as a reference librarian at the New Jersey State Library. Techniques and sources used to answer questions are described.

675.   Rees, Allan, and Tefko Saracevic. "Conceptual Analysis of Questions in Information Retrieval Systems." In Lynn, H. P., ed. *Automation and Scientific Communication. Annual Meeting of the American Documentation Institute, October 6-11, 1963.* New York, Kraus Reprint, 1963. pp. 175-178.

The various stages and aspects of the question-asking process are described and analyzed. Presents a flow chart of this process.

676.   Rowland, Mrs. C. W. "Dusty Answers," *Virginia Librarian* 19:7 (Winter 1972/1973).

A partly unanswerable question is one of the most challenging aspects of reference service because it forces the reference librarian into action. A complete and satisfactory answer is a dead answer.

677.   Shores, Louis. "What Americans Wanted to Know in 1951," *Saturday Review* 35:36-39 (February 9, 1952).

The author appraises reference questions asked during one year in eight public libraries. He concludes that five categories predominated—current events, questions relating to contests and quiz shows, household problems, people and places, and curiosities. Most frequently consulted sources included dictionaries, encyclopedias, almanacs, atlases, indexes, and biographical sources.

678.   Smith, Ann Lewis. "Relationship of the Type of Reference Question to the Occupation and Education of the Patron." Unpublished Master's thesis, University of North Carolina, 1967. 47p.

679.   Smith, R. T. "Analysis of Inquiries Made at the Reference Desk in the Trevor Arnett Library." Atlanta University, 1963. 23p.

680.   Stewart, S. A. "Survey of Reference Questions at Locke Branch Library, Toledo, Ohio." Unpublished Master's thesis, Western Reserve University, 1950. 66p.

681.   Swift, Iva I. "Classifying Readers' Questions," *Wilson Bulletin for Libraries* 8:274-275 (January 1934).

A tentative chart for classification of types of questions is given. This chart should be adapted to the reference work of each individual library, and it is hoped that it will serve as an aid in evaluation.

682.   Taylor, R. S. "The Process of Asking Questions," *American Documentation* 13:391-396 (October 1962).

Analyzes questions and answers in regard to question formation, level of question, question asking, state of readiness, and available answers. Problems are considered in regard to question type.

683.   Wofford, Azile. **The School Library at Work**. New York, H. W. Wilson, 1959. 256p.

Pages 169-170 contain sample questions received from senior and junior high schools. Includes 37 questions.

SEARCH STRATEGY AND REFERENCE TECHNIQUE

See also: Chapter 2, Theory and Philosophy
Chapter 9, The Reference Process (Reference Questions; Users)
Chapter 11, Research in Reference (Measurement and Evaluation)
Chapter 14, Information Retrieval (Search Strategy and the Subject
Approach to Information)

Included here are all works concerned with the process of search strategy
or problem-solving behavior directed toward finding solutions to reference
problems presented by patrons. Both known-item searching and subject searching are covered. This section includes works discussing, analyzing, or presenting
flow-charts concerning the intellectual process of planning, decision-making, and
source selection in seeking answers to reference requests. The process of carrying
out a literature search and any techniques that contribute to more effective
resolution of reference problems are covered.

Bibliographical coverage is provided by H. R. Astall, "The Techniques of
Reference," *Library Association Record* 70:42-43 (February 1968); Alfred
Beltran, "The Craft of Literature Searching," *Sci-Tech News* 25:113-116 (Winter
1971); F. S. Stych, "Decision Factors in Search Strategy," *RQ* 12:143-147
(Winter 1972); Charles Bunge, *Professional Education and Reference Efficiency*
(Springfield, Illinois State Library, 1967); George Gardiner, "The Empirical
Study of Reference," *College and Research Libraries* 30:130-155 (March 1969);
S. D. Neill, "Problem Solving and the Reference Process," *RQ* 14:310-315
(Summer 1975). Both subject and known-item searching are covered in Gertrude
Schutze, *Information and Library Science Source Book* (Metuchen, N.J.,
Scarecrow, 1972), and known-item searching in Bohdan Wynar, *Library Acqui-
sitions: A Classified Bibliographic Guide to the Literature and Reference Tools*,
2nd ed. (Littleton, Colo., Libraries Unlimited, 1971). Bibliographical coverage
of the search process is also available in William Katz, *Introduction to Reference
Work*, Vol. II (New York, McGraw-Hill, 1974).

684.   Alexander, Carter. "Technique of Library Searching," *Special Libraries*
27:230-238 (September 1936).
The search process is described step by step. Techniques and procedures are described
for each step to aid in more effective searching.

685.   Astall, H. R. "The Techniques of Reference," *Library Association Record*
70:42-43 (February 1968).
Reviews the literature on reference techniques and the reader-librarian-enquiry
approach. Examples of this literature can be found in the Reference Libraries
column, 1936-1964, in the *Library Association Record*, in Margaret Hutchin's
Introduction to Reference Work, and through use of the *Bibliography of Library
Economy, 1876-1909*. The author continues to review literature sources up to the
date of the article. British sources are emphasized, but American sources are considered also. A bibliography is given, including a number of articles in *Library
Association Record*, relating to aspects of the reference process.

686.   Beltran, Alfred. "The Craft of Literature Searching," *Sci-Tech News* 25:113-116 (Winter 1971).
Describes steps involved in in-depth literature searching as 1) defining the background and scope of the search with requestor, 2) subject familiarization through texts and encyclopedias, 3) search strategy—sources of headings, 4) preliminary search of one year in each source and re-evaluation, 5) time and cost estimate, 6) discussion and clarification with requestor, 7) search, 8) final preparation of results, 9) evaluation.

687.   Benson, James, and Ruth Maloney. "Principles of Searching," *RQ* 14:316-320 (Summer 1975).
Describes a generalized model of the search process. Points to be considered are the query, purpose, scope, subject interrelationship, time frame, place, level of language comprehension, form desired, and time needed. Other steps discussed include identifying the system, translating into language, conducting the search, and delivery of the information. Failure to locate information may be due to system failure or searcher failure. Reasons for searcher failure are 1) failure to recognize answer when found, 2) modifying the query in terms of preconceived knowledge, 3) misunderstanding the query, 4) relying upon the accuracy of the query, 5) relying upon the accuracy of the information within the system. Failures should be systematically analyzed to develop future searching capabilities.

688.   Bunge, Charles. "Charting the Reference Query," *RQ* 8:245-250 (Summer 1969).
Presented here is a flow chart describing the reference process from the initial question to the final resolution. The chart is based on the author's study of seven Midwest libraries where matched pairs of professional and non-professional reference librarians were given the same set of reference questions to answer.

689.   Carlson, G. **Search Strategy by Reference Librarians: Part 3 of the Final Report on the Organization of Large Files**. Sherman Oaks, Calif., Hughes Dynamics, Inc., Advanced Information Systems Division, 1964. 41p.
Search procedures of reference librarians in a university medical library are analyzed. Conclusions are 1) human search behavior has elements of regularity which can be codified, 2) procedures and techniques used by reference librarians are not consistent and could be improved, 3) certain search routines can lend themselves to computerization.

690.   Coates, E. J. "Classification in Reference Service," *Annals of Library Science* 1:152-161 (September 1954).
Suggests that reference service and classification be taught together. The limitations of relying on memory and subject specialization alone are demonstrated by use of examples. The usefulness in reference service of an effective classification system, such as the "patterned" colon type classification used by the British National Bibliography, is discussed. Search procedures, helped by this type of classification, are described and the implications of this type of classification for the dictionary catalog are explained.

691.   Doyle, James M. "Searching Education Literature," *RQ* 11:227-230
       (Spring 1972).

The search strategy outlined here is designed basically for doctoral research. Steps
in the search process are given and basic sources are suggested.

692.   Fetros, John. "Literature Search Observations," *RQ* 10:201-204 (Spring
       1971).

When doing a literature search, significant information may be overlooked if all
relevant subject headings are not used. Examples are given that demonstrate the
problems encountered in working with the wide variety of subject headings in
various indexes. The Universal Reference System is helpful in locating related
subject headings, which can then be searched in other indexes.

693.   Fizette, Marjorie, Bruce Jones, and Robert Gibson, Jr. "Bibliographic
       Research Team," *Special Libraries* 49:253-255 (July-August 1958).

Describes the method of literature search used at Battelle Memorial Institute. The
bibliographic research team consists of a literature specialist and an information
specialist. The information specialist consults the subject specialist for boundaries,
dates of coverage, relevant sources, and the significance of the subject areas. As the
search proceeds, the literature specialist also checks the references for quality and
relevance.

694.   Fristoe, Ashby. "The Bitter End," *Library Resources and Technical
       Services* 10:91-95 (Winter 1966).

Discusses the most efficient methods of bibliographical searching. The author
hypothesizes that the results of a search for bibliographical information on a number of specific titles will be affected by the number of available tools, and by the
sequence and depth of the search. A sample experiment was done using 100 order
cards picked at random from 1965 American imprints which were searched in
1) *Cumulative Book Index*, 2) LC proof slip file, 3) *National Union Catalog*,
4) *American Book Publishing Record*, 5) *Publishers Weekly*, 6) *Publishers Weekly
Announcements*. A "bitter end" search in all six tools found 71 titles after 940
searches. But if the LC proof slip file, *Publishers Weekly Announcements*, and
Cumulative Book Index were searched in that order, 71 titles were located after
228 searches.

695.   Hanson, C. W. "Subject Inquiries and Literature Searching." In Ashworth,
       W., ed. *Handbook of Special Librarianship and Information Work*. 3rd ed.
       London, Aslib, 1967. pp. 415-444.

Searching techniques and approaches are described for requests for simple information, representative information, "all the information," and detailed and specific
information. Also considered are very recent information and foreign language
literature.

696.   Howison, Beulah. "Simulated Literature Searches," *Drexel Library
       Quarterly* 7:309-320 (July-October 1971).

Described here is a simulated literature search planned for the purpose of instructing
students. The search was planned by a professor and a librarian.

697.   Jahoda, Gerald, and Paul E. Olson. "Analyzing the Reference Process,"
       RQ 12:148-156 (Winter 1972).

The author defines the reference process as the sum total of steps taken to answer the question. Several models of the reference process are shown in diagrams.

698.   Jahoda, Gerald. "Reference Question Analysis and Search Strategy
       Development by Man and Machine," *Journal of the American Society
       for Information Science* 25:139-144 (May-June 1974).

Nine steps are outlined in the reference process and then considered in relation to the possibility of automation. It was concluded that such automation was not feasible.

699.   Josel, Nathan. A. "Ten Reference Commandments," *RQ* 11:146-147
       (Winter 1971).

The author provides ten practical recommendations for effective reference service. Included are: 1) assume patron's information may be incorrect, 2) doublecheck the most likely source if the answer is not found, 3) do not rely on the accuracy or completeness of another person's search, 4) check coincidences, 5) utilize a "query" file for difficult questions, 6) utilize special indexes, 7) utilize tracings, 8) think in synonyms, 9) list sources consulted as you go along, 10) "no" is never an answer. Referral to other substitute sources is better than nothing.

700.   Lowy, George. **A Searcher's Manual**. Hamden, Conn., Shoe String, 1965.
       104p.

Describes bibliographic searching procedures used by acquisitions department workers who need to determine for a book 1) exact author and title, 2) its relationship to other editions, 3) bibliographic history, 4) whether it is held by the library, 5) the correct entry, 6) cost and source. Instructions are given on searching procedure for the card catalog and major bibliographic tools.

701.   Rice, Barbara. "Teaching Bibliographical Reference in a Reports Collec-
       tion," *Special Libraries* 64:203-206 (April 1973).

Describes a method of teaching non-professional assistants how to identify government reports and documents. Assistants are trained to use a request form in order to gather as much information as possible. Presents a table of bibliographic tools relating to technical reports and their contents to be used in training. Gives a number of hints on search strategy.

702.   Stevens, Charles H., Marie Canfield, and Jeffrey Gardner. "Library
       Pathfinders: A New Possibility for Cooperative Reference Service,"
       College and Research Libraries 34:40-46 (January 1973).

Library "pathfinders" are brief guides to the literature of specific subject areas and include all types of sources. A systematic exchange of pathfinders on a national level would provide an opportunity to share reference methodology. Pathfinders, which are available for a wide range of subjects, save the time of library users. A detailed description of the use of pathfinders in reference service is given, along with a description of their success at the MIT Engineering Library.

703. Stych, F. S. "Decision Factors in Search Strategy," *RQ* 12:143-147
(Winter 1972).   *LIBS*

Suggestions are made to those teaching reference work in regard to students with no reference experience. Factors involved in reference decisions are discussed. The logical basis on which reference librarians' choices and decisions are made is examined. Bibliography.

704. Stych, F. S. "The Flow Chart Method and Heraldic Enquiries," *RQ*
6:169-174 (Summer 1967).

Describes types of heraldic enquiries and lists basic works. Presents a flow chart showing search strategy based on consultation of these same works. Indicates what information must be obtained first and the order and way in which the sources should be consulted.

705. Swenson, Sally. "Flow Chart on Library Searching Techniques," *Special
Libraries* 56:239-242 (April 1965).

This two-page flow chart was prepared for the users of Northern Electric's Research and Development Laboratories Library. The search process is described in six steps and related to basic library resources, including indexes and other research aids. It is hoped that the chart will help the user in conducting his own effective search.

706. Voress, H. E. "Searching Techniques in the Literature of the Sciences,"
College and Research Libraries 24:209-212 (May 1963).

Attempts to reduce searching procedures to a numbered sequence. Outlines 15 steps to be followed, including 1) determining subject scope, 2) time period, 3) depth, 4) literature and reference tools to be used, 5) familiarize self with indexes to be used, 6) determine subject headings, 7) scan indexes, 8) check abstracts for relevance, 9) prepare author list of selected references, 10) scan author indexes for additional references, 11) prepare list of corporate authors, 12) scan corporate author indexes for additional references, 13) arrange in order, 14) edit, 15) compose copy. Each step is discussed in detail.

USERS

See also: Chapter 2, Theory and Philosophy
Chapter 6, Reference Service in Types of Libraries
Chapter 7, Special Types of Reference Service
Chapter 9, The Reference Process (Communication and the
Reference Interface)
Chapter 11, Research in Reference (Measurement and Evaluation)
Chapter 13, Information Centers and Services
Chapter 14, Information Retrieval (User Interaction)

The purpose of this section is to provide background on library use. Covered on a selective basis are works related to both users of information and users of libraries. Some areas included are attitudes toward information, information needs, uses of information, information gathering habits, and information transfer patterns. Also included are general use studies in all types of libraries and works about user research. Those works on information transfer that are primarily theoretical in nature can be found in Chapter 2, Theory and Philosophy. Studies on users of reference service in particular will be found in the section Measurement and Evaluation, in Chapter 11.

Bibliographies and reviews of user studies are given below at the beginning of the section. Other bibliographies and reviews can be found in Robert Coover, "User Needs and Their Effects on Information Center Administration: A Review, 1953/66," *Special Libraries* 60:446-456 (September 1969); and yearly in *Annual Review of Information Science and Technology*, 1966– . A bibliography of public library use studies is contained in Mary Bundy, "Metropolitan Public Library Use," *Wilson Library Bulletin* 41:896-961 (May 1967). Another useful bibliography is that of R. A. Davis, and C. A. Bailey, *Bibliography of Use Studies* (Philadelphia, Drexel Institute of Technology, School of Library Science, 1964).

Other bibliographical coverage is provided in Gertrude Schutze, *Information and Library Science Source Book* (Metuchen, N.J., Scarecrow, 1972); *Bibliography of Research Relating to Communication of Scientific and Technical Information* (New Brunswick, N.J., Rutgers University, 1967); Ronald Havelock, *Bibliography on Knowledge Utilization and Dissemination* (Ann Arbor, University of Michigan, 1972); Thomas J. Waldhart and Enid Waldhart, *Communication Research in Library and Information Science* (Littleton, Colo., Libraries Unlimited, 1975).

Bibliographies and Reviews

707. Atkin, Pauline, comp. **Bibliography of Use Surveys of Public and Academic Libraries, 1950-1970**. London, The Library Association, 1971. 84p.
An annotated bibliography of 700 library use studies arranged in classified order with a subject index. International coverage.

708. Brittain, J. M. **Information and Its Users: A Review with Special Reference to the Social Sciences**. New York, Wiley, 1971. 208p.
Surveys some 500 user studies. Arranged in five sections: 1) terminology and relationships between information science and user studies, 2) methodology, 3) studies in the social sciences, 4) studies of communication artifacts, 5) neglected aspects of users and their information requirements.

709. FID/II Information for Industry, comp. **Index to User Studies**. The Hague, International Federation for Documentation, 1974. 103p.
References with abstracts to more than 200 studies in the past 10 years over 20 countries.

710. Havelock, Ronald. **Bibliography on Knowledge Utilization and Dissemination**. Ann Arbor, University of Michigan, Institute for Social Research, 1972. 250p. ERIC Document ED061466.
Includes periodical articles, dissertations, books. Unannotated. Covers such areas as adoption, application, and assimilation of new knowledge. Also covered are information flow and transmission.

711. Jain, Aridaman, and Carroll De Weese. **Report on a Statistical Study of Book Use, Supplemented With a Bibliography of Library Use Studies.** Springfield, Va., Clearinghouse for Federal Scientific and Technical Information, 1967. 337p. ERIC Document ED018244.

Appendixes to this study include: 1) a state of the art examination of use studies, 2) a bibliography of 547 use studies prepared by De Weese, which supplements and updates the 1964 bibliography of Richard A. Davis and C. A. Bailey, and 3) bibliography of 84 items by the author of this study.

712. **Library Surveys and Development Plans.** Bibliography Series Number 3. Minneapolis, Minn., University of Minnesota, ERIC Clearinghouse for Library and Information Science, 1969. 43p. ERIC Document ED 031609.

An annotated bibliography of 104 library surveys and development plans at the state or national level published since 1965. Includes most of the post-1965 titles listed in Galen Rike's *Statewide Library Surveys and Development Plans: An Annotated Bibliography, 1956-67.*

713. Waldhart, Thomas, and Enid S. Waldhart. **Communication Research in Library and Information Science: Bibliography on Communication in the Sciences, Social Sciences, and Technology.** Littleton, Colo., Libraries Unlimited, 1975. 168p.

Covers communication patterns and behavior of research workers. Arranged in sections of "General," "Structures of Communication," "Discipline-Oriented Studies," "Communication Barriers," and "Communication Innovations." Citations are to journal articles published between 1964 and 1973.

714. Wood, D. N. "User Studies: A Review of the Literature from 1966 to 1970," *Aslib Proceedings* 23:11-23 (January 1971).

Updates the paper by Fishenden (*Journal of Documentation,* September 1965), which covered a limited number of British use studies up to 1965. This paper covers the literature of use studies from 1966 to 1970 in more detail. A wide variety of use studies, mainly British and American, are considered. Bibliography included.

General Works

715. Adams, Golden V., Jr. "A Study: Library Attitudes, Usage, Skill and Knowledge of Junior High School Age Students Enrolled at Lincoln Junior High School and Burns Union High School, Burns, Harney County, Oregon, 1971-72." Research Paper, Brigham Young University, 1972. 114p. ERIC Document ED077538.

Grade level, sex, GPA, formal library science classes and reading achievement level were studied in relation to library attitudes, usage, skill, and knowledge. The card catalog, vertical file, periodicals, and reference books were evaluated. Conclusions are presented in regard to use of reference books, with the *Reader's Guide* being the least used reference tool. The two main finding skills were browsing and asking the librarian. Skill in using reference books was definitely increased by taking a reference class. Other results are presented regarding usage.

716. American Library Association. **Student Use of Libraries: An Inquiry into the Needs of Students, Libraries, and the Educational Process, Papers of the Conference within a Conference, July 16-18, 1963, Chicago, Illinois.** Chicago, American Library Association, 1964. 212p.

The purpose of this conference was to study the library needs of students and to establish concerns that would result in improvements. Six background working papers are presented along with comments and recommendations.

717. Benford, John Q. "The Philadelphia Project," *Library Journal* 96:2041-2047 (June 15, 1971).

Describes results of a survey undertaken by the Philadelphia Free Library, the Philadelphia School District, and the Roman Catholic Archdiocese School System and aided by an Office of Education grant. Ten thousand students, 184 teachers and staff in 51 school and nine public branch libraries were surveyed to 1) determine library requirements and evaluate existing resources and 2) develop joint planning between public and school libraries. Results indicated that resources are not sufficient for the urban poor. Community library and student centers were recommended to close the separation between the community and the public and school libraries.

718. Budington, William S. "Access to Information." In *Advances in Librarianship*, Vol. 2. Edited by Melvin Voight. New York, Seminar Press, 1971. pp. 1-43.

The significance of access to information and problems that arise in regard to this are discussed. Also covered are financing, management, and improvement of information provision. The philosophy of access to information should be based on a commitment to intellectual freedom and on the right of each individual to self-fulfillment.

719. Bundy, Mary. "Metropolitan Public Library Use," *Wilson Library Bulletin* 41:896-961 (May 1967).

Discusses ways in which current trends will affect public library use. Reports on a survey of library users in metropolitan Maryland which surveyed some 21,385 library users in 1966. Every fifth adult patron entering one of the libraries was asked to fill out a questionnaire. Survey questions covered the user's age, education, occupation, subject interests, getting to the library, why they came, and what they did while there. Findings are reported in detail and analyzed. Comments on reference service and other subjects are included. Unanswered questions raised by the survey and implications for the future are discussed.

720. Burton, Hilary D. "Personal Information Systems," *Special Libraries* 64:7-11 (January 1973).

Personal information systems are described in terms of their effect on use of formal and secondary information services. The author concludes that personal information systems are not "personalized libraries." Formal library services should try to develop complementary programs. References.

721.   Chapin, Richard. "Limits of Local Self-Sufficiency." In *Proceedings of the Conference on Interlibrary Communication and Information Networks*. Edited by Joseph Becker. Chicago, American Library Association, 1971. pp. 54-58.

The author considers self-sufficiency by type of library. Information needs and patterns of library use are also considered for science and technology, social sciences, and humanities.

722.   Clapp, Verner W. "The Problem of Specialized Communication in Modern Society." In Egan, Margaret, ed. *Communication of Specialized Information. Papers Presented Before the 17th Annual Conference of the Graduate Library School of the University of Chicago, August, 1952.* Ann Arbor, Mich., Cushing-Malloy, Inc., 1954. pp. 1-13.

Library work is only a part of the total informational process. The communication of specialized information is complex and costly and requires interrelationships with other agencies. Control of specialized information is also a problem. There must be new directions in professional training. Some basic concerns in communication of specialized information are registration of publications, secondary publications, and information retrieval.

723.   Coover, Robert. "User Needs and Their Effects on Information Center Administration: A Review, 1953-1966," *Special Libraries* 60:446-456 (September 1969).

The administrative role in planning for and meeting user needs in an information center is discussed. Methods of investigation of user needs, such as diaries, interviews, and questionnaires, are considered and major studies of user needs are reviewed.

724.   Crane, Diana. **Invisible Colleges: Diffusion of Knowledge in Scientific Communities.** Chicago, University of Chicago Press, 1972. 213p.

The author studies sociometric networks in science in relation to information-seeking behavior of scientists. Particular attention is given to working groups of scientists, referred to as "invisible colleges." Two research areas, rural sociology and mathematics of finite groups, are used as examples to illustrate the diffusion of knowledge.

725.   **DOD User Needs Study.** L. H. Berul, and others. Philadelphia, Auerbach Corp., 1965. 2v. (Report No. 1151-TR-3; AD-615 501, AD 615 502).

Reports on a survey of information needs of research personnel. One thousand two hundred seventy-five researchers were interviewed in depth. Findings were 1) engineering data is vitally important, 2) users tend to rely heavily on local environment, 3) formal information systems were not widely used, 4) formal and informal systems should be integrated.

726.   Davis, Diana L. "New Approaches to Studying Library Use," *Drexel Library Quarterly* 7:4-12 (January 1971).

Considers measurement of library use by both non-specialist and specialist patrons. Describes and discusses methods and techniques such as questionnaires, interviews, observation, diaries, and critical incident study.

727.   Doyle, L. B. **Information Retrieval and Processing.** Los Angeles, Melville, 1975. 410p.

The chapter on users of information covers scientific and technical information use, methods of conducting user studies, relating typical users to "ideal" information systems, and the scientific-user as an information processor. Concludes with an overview of the user.

728.   Dunlap, Leslie W. "Services to Readers," *Library Trends* 1:49-57 (July 1952).

The author concludes that little is known about the actual needs and capabilities of library users. Many assumptions have been made and widely accepted but have never been substantiated. As an example, the assumption is given that if users have direct access to books they will find one to meet their needs. Academic library studies of users' needs are discussed, and further directions for research are suggested.

729.   Ebert, Mary Hilda. "Contrasting Patterns of Specialized Library Use," *Drexel Library Quarterly* 7:13-27 (January 1971).

The author discusses patterns of library use characteristic of certain professions and types of students. Considered are psychiatrists, anthropologists, engineers, historians, and graduate students.

730.   Egan, Margaret, ed. **The Communication of Specialized Information.** Chicago, University of Chicago Press, 1952. 128p. (The University of Chicago Studies in Library Science).

Covers the problems of specialized communication, new patterns in research and publication, technical reports, unpublished reports, restricted dissemination, professional organization and training, trends in production and use of social data, industrial relations and communication, and emergence of a new structure for dissemination of specialized information.

731.   Egan, Margaret, and H. H. Henkle. "Ways and Means in Which Research Workers, Executives, and Others Use Information." In *Conference on the Practical Utilization of Recorded Knowledge—Present and Future, Documentation in Action.* Edited by Jesse Shera. New York, Reinhold, 1956. pp. 137-159.

Covers use of recorded knowledge in the research situation and use of recorded knowledge in the decision-making process. Concludes with a summary. Bibliography covers guides to the literature, systematic investigation, questionnaires and interviews, analysis of current use, selective judgment of specialists, tabulations of references, and reviews of studies.

732.   Ennis, Phillip. "The Study of the Use and Users of Recorded Knowledge," *Library Quarterly* 34:305-314 (October 1964).

Contends that "empirical studies of reference service are among the weakest in all library research."

733.   Felten, Suzanne Y. "Attitudes and Values Associated with Information,"
        Drexel Library Quarterly 7:42-47 (January 1971).
Examined here are the types of attitudes that occur in response to certain types of
communication in the areas of science and behavioral science.

734.   Fishenden, R. M. "Information Use Studies: Past Results and Future Needs,"
        Journal of Documentation 21:163-168 (September 1965).
In the first part of this paper information use studies are reviewed and needs for
further research are noted. The second part of the paper considers the future of
information services.

735.   Focke, Helen. "Library Users of Information and Their Needs." In Linderman,
        W., ed. *The Present Status and Future Prospects of Reference/Information
        Service*. Chicago, American Library Association, 1967. pp. 21-33.
Concentrates on the "bread and butter" patron and touches only briefly on the
more sophisticated user. Poses many questions that need to be answered in regard
to users themselves, the type and subjects of their questions, the reference interview,
and the reference process. Discusses ways in which reference librarians can participate in this kind of research. Suggests establishment of a "data bank" of information about patrons and the questions they ask, maintained on a continuing basis
for use in research.

736.   Ford, G. "Research in User Behavior in University Libraries," *Journal of
        Documentation* 29:85-106 (March 1973).
Reviews the state of the art and cites relevant literature in user behavior in university
libraries. Considers factors affecting the demand for library services, including available information sources, end uses of information, individual users, systems of which
the user is a part, and consequences of use. Also considers interaction between the
libraries and users, including catalog use and instruction in library use. Utilization
of library materials covers studies on book usage, quality of use, and reading habits.
Concludes that the area of most needed research is in utilization of library resources.
More longitudinal studies should be done. Extensive bibliography.

737.   Goodwin, Harry B. "Some Thoughts on Improved Technical Information
        Service," *Special Libraries* 50:444 (November 1959).
Discusses the five information needs of scientists and notes that four of the five
items relate to the "keeping-up" process. Knowledge of new and stimulating
developments in related fields is important to scientists.

738.   Grose, Daphne. "Some Deprived Information Users," *Aslib Proceedings*
        26:9-23 (January 1974).
The author discusses results of a survey which indicated that certain categories of
the British population were deprived for one reason or another of information to
satisfy their needs. Groups discussed are teachers, lawyers, local government offi-
cials, and Trading Standards Officers. The author concludes that the best solution
is a single number to call where all types of questions can be handled.

739.   Hall, J. "Analysis of Factors Related to Channels of Patron Input and Feed-
        back for Policy Making Used by Academic Library Directors." Unpublished
        Ph.D. dissertation, Florida State University, 1972. 220p.

740.   Harmon, Glynn. **Human Memory and Knowledge: A Systems Approach.**
        Westport, Conn., Greenwood Press, 1973. 159p.
Attempts to "explore the relationships between human memory limitations and the
formation of various fields of systematic knowledge." This inquiry compares the
formation of a limited number of sub-disciplines, disciplines, and interdisciplinary
fields. Special emphasis is given to the rise and development of information science,
"the focal discipline of the study."

741.   Hazzard, R. M. "User Consistency in Repeated Relatedness and Usefulness
        Evaluations Made on Bibliographic References to Journal Articles." Unpub-
        lished Master's thesis, University of Chicago, 1970. 57p.

742.   Herner, Saul, and Mary Herner. "Information Needs and Users in Science
        and Technology." In *Annual Review of Information Science and Tech-
        nology, Volume 2*. New York, Interscience, 1967. pp. 1-34.
Reviews and analyzes studies that consist of direct analysis of information gathering.
Also covers some indirect studies of user activities.

743.   Ladendorf, Janice. "Breaking the User Barrier," *RQ* 11:337-339
        (Summer 1972).
The author discusses reasons people don't use the library. A library must sell its
service, and the first step is a market analysis to determine the type of patrons
served and their needs. Then the library must be redesigned to fit the clientele.
Examples are given of ways this might be done.

744.   Landau, Herbert B. "Methodology of a Technical Information Use Study,"
        Special Libraries 60:340-346 (July-August 1969).
Describes a user needs survey of internal technical information needs and the existing corporate technical information network. Describes techniques of user needs
surveys, including data gathering techniques, selection of sample populations, conducting interviews, responses from interviews and analysis of data gathered.

745.   Lane, Gorham. "Assessing the Undergraduates' Use of the University
        Library," *College and Research Libraries* 27:277-282 (July 1966).
The results of four studies on undergraduates' use of the library are reported here.
Covered are students' use of the library, the purpose behind their visits, and statistics
on withdrawals of books by class and sex. A questionnaire was used to find out what
materials they were using and had used in the previous week and the nature of the
work they were doing. It was concluded that the educational potential of the
library is greater than is now being realized.

746.   Lehigh University. Center for Information Science. **Studies in the Man-System Interface in Libraries.** Bethlehem, Pa., The Center, 1966-1967. 4 reports.

A series of reports: 1) "An Analysis of Questions and Answers in Libraries," by Caroline Hieber; 2) "Application of Psychometric Techniques to Determine the Attitudes of Individuals toward Information Seeking," by V. Rosenberg; 3) "Question Negotiation and Information Seeking in Libraries," by R. S. Taylor; 4) "GRINS, an On Line Structure for Negotiation of Inquiries," by J. S. Green.

747.   Line, M. B. "On the Design of Information Systems for Human Beings," *Aslib Proceedings* 22:320-335 (July 1970).

Suggests that research is needed on user performance for 1) centralized or decentralized libraries, 2) book or conventional catalogs, 3) classified or alphabetical catalogs, 4) arrangement of abstracting journals. Notes that increased use of computers and microfilms could lead to a narrowing of readers' interest since browsing would no longer be possible.

748.   Line, Maurice B. "University Libraries and the Information Needs of the Researcher: A Provider's View," *Aslib Proceedings* 18:178-184 (July 1966).

Discusses the responsibility of the university to provide access, not only to its own materials, but to all materials as well. When subject boundaries are not clearly defined, grouping could be done by subject taught or by use made of materials. Efforts should be made to bring unusual sources to researchers' attention, and emphasis should be on the library as a provider of both simple and complex bibliographical services. Information transfer can be facilitated by providing an information officer for each research team or by introduction of national or international indexing services similar to *MEDLARS.* More translations should also be provided.

749.   Little, Thompson M. **Use and Users of Library Literature.** Albany, State University of New York, 1968. 35p. ERIC Document ED050745.

Paper prepared for the Conference on the Control of Library Science Literature, State University of New York, Albany, April 19-20, 1968. Reviews the growth and general characteristics of library literature. Describes main criticisms of those who have done studies of library literature as 1) poor literary style and execution, 2) superfluity, repetition, 3) belaboring the obvious, 4) no new ideas, 5) no scholarly approach, 6) lack of evidence of research. Citation analysis of library literature is discussed. The information needs of users and channels of use of library literature must be examined.

750.   Lubans, John. "Nonuse of an Academic Library," *College and Research Libraries* 32:362-367 (September 1971).

Describes results of a survey at Rensselaer which shows that successful graduation was possible for non-library users but that non-use can be detrimental to one starting on a professional job. Increased library use is shown as students advance in academic status. A table is included showing major reasons for non-use.

751. Marquardt, J. F. "Reading Habits of 290 Faculty Members in Ohio State Universities." Unpublished Master's thesis, Kent State University, 1955. 127p.

752. Menzel, Herbert. "The Information Needs of Current Scientific Research," *Library Quarterly* 34:4-19 (January 1964).
Focuses on the needs of research scientists. Covers concerns and directions, the multiplicity of functions of science-information systems, importance of informal and personal communication, and research on the information needs of scientists. Distinct needs of scientists which must be satisfied are 1) current awareness, 2) up-to-date answers to specific questions (reference function), 3) exhaustive searches, 4) brush up on a new field. These needs can be further divided by data, procedures, concepts, and by the researcher's own field versus other fields.

753. Nelson, C. E., and Donald Pollock. **Communications among Scientists and Engineers.** Lexington, Mass., D. C. Heath, 1970. 346p.
Based on a conference, "Communication among Scientists and Technologists," sponsored by Johns Hopkins University and supported by the National Science Foundation. Its purpose was to bring together researchers and systems developers to discuss the communication process, to review and synthesize research, and to relate it to development of future systems. The three major sections of this volume deal with 1) the structure of science and the production of scientific information, 2) utilization of scientific information, and 3) the development of scientific information systems.

754. Parker, Edwin, and others. **Patterns of Adult Information Seeking.** Stanford, Calif., Stanford University, Institute of Communication Research, 1966. 275p. ERIC Document ED010294.
Reports on a study done with U.S. Office of Education funds, where 1,869 adult residents of two California cities were interviewed on their information seeking habits, including library use. Results reveal the wide diversity of sources used by those interviewed.

755. Redmond, Donald, Michael Sinclair, and Elinore Brown. "University Libraries and University Research," *College and Research Libraries* 33:447-453 (November 1972).
Analyzes the research information cycle in terms of three stages—origin of the message, informal communication, and formal communication. A circular representation is given, beginning with personal communication to a colleague, oral group communication (lectures, etc.) producing primary literature. This is extracted and compiled, becomes standard fact and is, in turn, superseded by new research.

756. Robertson, Andrew. "Behavior Patterns of Scientists and Engineers in Information Seeking for Problem Solving," *Aslib Proceedings* 26:384-390 (October 1974).
Five subjects from universities, industry, and government research kept tape-recorded diaries. Results are arranged in tabular form in 10 broad categories of information seeking events, four internal-personal informal and formal, and six external-personal

informal. The different patterns of information seeking are shown, with three out of five working close to their information services or libraries.

757.   Rosenberg, Victor. **The Application of Psychometric Techniques to Determine the Attitudes of Individuals toward Information Seeking.** Bethlehem, Pa., Lehigh University, Center for the Information Sciences, 1966. 53p. (Studies in the Man-System Interface in Libraries, No. 2).

Concerned with preferences of professional personnel toward eight different information gathering techniques, including use of a library and consulting a reference librarian. It was found that people preferred methods that were easy to use even if other methods promised more information.

758.   Rothwell, Roy. "Patterns of Information Flow during the Innovation Process," *Aslib Proceedings* 27:217-226 (May 1975).

Traces the patterns of search through the various phases of the innovation process, discusses the different information seeking habits of scientists and technologists, describes the effect of firm size on the pattern of information search, and highlights the necessity of matching the degree of complexity of a message to the level of sophistication of its recipient. Concludes 1) information seeking behavior depends on the phase (with outward-looking attitude during "idea generation" to introspection during "problem solving"), 2) scientists primarily use extra-organizational sources and rely on primary sources, while technologists use primarily in-house sources and secondary literature, 3) larger organizations react more with external agencies than smaller ones, 4) information must be made more accessible and must be presented in a form understandable to the user.

759.   Rzasa, Philip V., and John Moriarty. "The Types and Needs of Academic Library Users: A Case Study of 6,568 Responses," *College and Research Libraries* 31:403-409 (November 1970).

Academic library users were surveyed to determine their primary and secondary reasons for visiting the library and type of materials used while there. The responses of faculty, graduate, and undergraduate students were compared in regard to the above factors.

760.   Shaw, Ralph R. **Use of Scientific Literature by Scientists.**Metuchen, N.J., Scarecrow, 1971 (c1956). 139p.

A study made under a National Science Foundation Grant which consists of 1) a review of previous studies of use of scientific literature by scientists with a critique of methods, 2) two pilot studies of the diary method at the Forest Products Laboratory of the Forest Service, U.S. Department of Agriculture, at Madison, Wisconsin. The two pilot studies are compared and the conclusion is reached that the diary method, even with better than average cooperation or supervision, is not reliable enough to justify further studies over extended periods of time.

761.   **A Survey of the Attitudes, Opinions, and Behavior of Citizens of Colorado with Regard to Library Services, Volume 2: Secondary School and College Student Summary**. Denver, Colo., State Library, 1974. 55p.

One hundred student responses are examined in sections: 1) library usage by Colorado students, 2) secondary students' evaluation of their school libraries,

3) college students' evaluation of their school libraries, 4) evaluations of local public libraries, usage and potential usage of selected library services, 5) student attitudes toward libraries and their purpose, 6) an assessment of the information needs of college students.

762. Wellisch, Hans. "Information Education at the Grass Roots," In *Reference Work: Background and Implications*. Tel Aviv, Israel Society of Special Libraries and Information Centers, 1971. pp. 1-10. (Contributions to Information Science 5; Clarissa Gadiel Memorial Issues). ERIC Document ED056714.

Discusses the failure of libraries to provide usable information. We must educate the reader about existing information services and how to make best use of them. Notes that little research has been done on needs of non-scientific and non-professional users. Discusses how to overcome obstacles to provide a meaningful exchange between the person in need of information and the information center.

763. Wolek, Francis W. "Preparation for Interpersonal Communication," *Journal of the American Society for Information Science* 23:3-10 (January-February 1972).

It is important to understand the rationale behind the interpersonal flow of information. Illustrated here are three methods used by scientists and engineers in doing research: 1) keeping the information need in mind in hopes of eventual discovery of the desired information, 2) consulting an associate, 3) reviewing the literature. Included is a flow chart and bibliography.

764. Woods, W. E. "Factors Influencing Student Library Use: An Analysis of Studies." Unpublished Master's thesis, University of Chicago, 1965. 52p.

765. Ziman, J. M. "Information, Communication, Knowledge." In Saracevic, Tefko, ed. *Introduction to Information Science*. New York, Bowkers, 1970. pp. 76-84.

Considers the current system of scientific communication. Discusses quality and authority of information, speed of communication, informal exchange, information in print, mechanized indexing, inefficient computers, specialized journals, and published proceedings. Stresses the importance of knowledge rather than just information. Emphasizes that traditional sources such as abstract journals in bound form and treatises are often more effective and efficient in gaining information than mechanized information retrieval and explains why this is so.

CHAPTER 10

SOURCES OF INFORMATION

See also: Chapter 2, Theory and Philosophy
                Chapter 6, Reference Service in Types of Libraries
                Chapter 7, Special Types of Reference Service
                Chapter 8, Reference Service to Special Groups
                Chapter 11, Research in Reference (Measurement and Evaluation)
                Chapter 13, Information Centers and Services

This chapter includes sections on human resources in reference service, the card catalog, and reference materials.

HUMAN RESOURCES IN REFERENCE SERVICE

766.   Baron, Michael. "The Answer Is in the Media," *RQ* 9:30-31 (Fall 1969).
A reference librarian should be flexible in considering all types of sources of information, rather than relying solely on conventional printed sources. Telephone calls to government, private agencies, and industry are often the most effective way to locate certain kinds of information.

767.   Dame, Katherine. "What Is Reference Work?" *Wilson Library Bulletin* 5:450-452 (February 1931).
Advocates use of resources other than printed materials in giving reference services. Suggested are use of special resource persons, and doing translating for fees.

768.   Hoey, P. O'N. "Systematic Utilization of Human Resources as an Integral Part of Information Science Work," *Journal of the American Society for Information Science* 23:384-391 (November-December 1972).
Considered here are "indexes to people," which are discussed in regard to informal communication networks and traditional sources of information. Examples are given of existing or planned files of this type. Bibliography.

THE CARD CATALOG

See also: Chapter 5, Reference Service (Special Aids and Devices and Information Desks)
                Chapter 7, Special Types of Reference Service
                Chapter 11, Research in Reference (Measurement and Evaluation)

This section includes selected works on the use of the card catalog in reference service, some catalog use studies, relationships between cataloging and reference staff, and selected works on the approach to information through subject headings. It also includes selected works on the computerized catalog. A solid review of catalog use studies is presented by Richard P. Palmer, *Computerizing the Card Catalog in the University Library* (Littleton, Colo., Libraries Unlimited, 1972), pp. 19-45.

Additional bibliographical coverage is provided by the following: Carlyle Frarey, "Studies of Use of the Subject Catalog," In Maurice Tauber, ed., *Subject Analysis of Library Materials* (New York, Columbia University, 1953), pp. 147-163; Concetta Sacco, "Book Catalog Use Study," *RQ* 259-266 (Spring 1973); James Krikelas, *The Effect of Arrangement on the Use of Library Catalogs—An Experimental Study of a Divided and a Dictionary Catalog* (Urbana, Illinois University, Library Research Center, 1967; ERIC Document ED020767); Eleanor Montague, "Card Catalog Use Studies, 1949-1965" (Unpublished Master's thesis, University of Chicago, 1967); Renata Tagliacozzo and Manfred Kochen, *Information-Seeking Behavior of Catalog Users* (Ann Arbor, University of Michigan, Mental Health Research Institute, 1970).

769.   Astbury, Effie C. "Catalog Code Revision: Implications for the Reference Librarian," *Wilson Library Bulletin* 36:450-455 (February 1962).
Considers possible effects of changes in the ALA Catalog Code on reference service. Changes discussed are in regard to personal authors, corporate entries, governmental materials, and unknown authors. The author concludes that the result of these changes will be to make the catalog less useful as a reference tool but provide increased worldwide standardization in cataloging.

770.   Ayres, F. H., and others. "Author Versus Title: A Comparative Survey of the Accuracy of the Information Which the User Brings to the Card Catalog," *Journal of Documentation* 24:266-272 (December 1968).
Users of the catalog at the British Atomic Weapons Research Establishment were surveyed in regard to the accuracy of their citations. Less than 75 percent of author information was correct while 90 percent of title information was correct.

771.   Brett, William H. "Use of the Subject Catalog by the General Reference Service of a University Library," *Journal of Cataloging and Classification* 7:16-19 (Winter 1951).
A study was done to determine how important the subject catalog is to reference service at the University of California Library. The investigator recorded 135 reference questions during selected hours, of which 70 required the use of the subject catalog. Thirty reference tools were used as alternatives to the subject catalog. The final conclusion of the author was that "although the subject catalog was the most valuable single tool at the disposal of the reference librarian, its use could not be considered indispensable."

772. Brett, W. H. "Use of the Subject Catalog by the General Reference Service of the University of California Library." Master's thesis, University of California, 1949. 64p.

773. Brown, Emily. "The Use of the Catalog in a University Library." Unpublished Master's thesis, University of Chicago, 1950. 60p.
This study was designed to identify the users of the catalog in a university library in terms of their purposes and types of materials desired.

774. Brown, Margaret. "The Graduate Student's Use of the Subject Catalog," *College and Research Libraries* 8:203-208, 217 (1947).
Thirty-three graduate students in sociology agreed to take part in an investigation of the use of the subject catalog in a large university library. The author interviewed and observed each student as he or she worked with the subject catalog. Studied were the student's selection of subject terms, the order in which the terms were searched, the specificity of terms used, the source of terms, use of subdivisions, understanding of subject as opposed to title entries, and selection of titles under a given subject. Problems in use of the subject catalog were 1) some current and very specific subjects were best suited to periodical indexes, 2) students did not know what the catalog could do and what they might expect to find listed there, 3) they often failed to find information that was readily available due to lack of experience and skill.

775. "Catalog Reference Service," In Swihart, S. J., and B. F. Hefley. *Computer Systems in the Library*. Los Angeles, Melville, 1973. pp. 163-184.
Covered in this chapter are author/title searches, retrospective subject searches, and current awareness service, all utilizing automated catalog records. Batch and on-line searches are described. Current awareness services are considered in regard to public announcement, individual notification, establishing and maintaining profiles. Compares the general purpose public announcement bulletin, individual current awareness, and retrospective searches. Concludes with a comparison of mechanized and manual retrieval methods by discussing advantages and disadvantages. Computerized searches are desirable when 1) there are too many inquiries for staff to handle, 2) extensive printed output is desired, 3) searches have many descriptors with complex interrelationships.

776. Christ, John M. **Concepts and Subject Headings: Their Use in Information Retrieval and Library Science**. Metuchen, N.J., Scarecrow, 1972. 174p.
This study examines the structure, meaning, and function of subject headings in the area of the social sciences in academic library catalogs to see how closely they match the terminology actually used by social scientists. The first chapter compares 665 general social science terms with those found in the Library of Congress subject heading list. Chapter 2 relates subject headings and interdisciplinary social science terms. Chapter 3 compares subject headings and sociological terms. Chapter 4 compares subject headings and social science subdivisions. Chapter 5 compares the term "value," and Chapters 6 and 7 consider how well subject headings refer to important basic books in the field. The author concludes that there is a need for a more contemporary approach to social science subject headings.

777. Dunkin, Paul S. "Cataloging and Reference: The Eternal Triangle," *RQ* 3:3-6 (March 1964).

The author considers whether the card catalog should be a finding tool or an encyclopedia. The historical development of the catalog is reviewed from its conception by Dewey as a finding tool, through its development into an encyclopedic reference tool. The present-day trend is toward a return to the catalog as a finding tool. The author concludes that the catalog should be a finding tool and gives reasons why an encyclopedic catalog is unnecessary.

778. Fern, L. "Library Catalogs as Reference Sources." Unpublished Master's thesis, University of Chicago, 1962. 48p.

779. Foskett, D. J. "Catalog and Reference Service," *Librarian and Book World* 41:213-218 (November 1952).

The complexities and difficulties of subject heading work in the catalog are examined. The catalog is considered in regard to helpfulness as a guide to a subject when there is nothing at the classification number for that subject in the collection. The classified and dictionary catalogs are compared in regard to advantages and disadvantages. The closely classified catalog is considered by the author to be better, though this judgment depends on the classification system used.

780. Frary, Carlyle J. "Studies of Use of the Subject Catalog: Summary and Evaluation." In Tauber, Maurice, ed. *The Subject Analysis of Library Materials*. New York, Columbia University, School of Library Science, 1953. pp. 147-166.

Reviews the studies of card catalog use. Concludes that subject use of the catalog has been found to be about equal to author use.

781. Harris, Ira. "Reader Services Aspects of Book Catalogs," *Library Resources and Technical Services* 8:391-398 (Fall 1964).

Reviews the literature regarding use of book catalogs and presents both pro and con opinions. Works are cited and major conclusions are quoted for each work. Concludes that neither pro or con opinion is solidly based on research.

782. Irwin, R. R. "Use of the Card Catalog in the Public Library." Unpublished Master's thesis, University of Chicago, 1949. 87p.

783. Jackson, Sidney. **Catalog Use Study**. Edited Vaclav Mostecky. Chicago, American Library Association, Resources and Technical Services Division, Cataloging and Classification Section, Policy and Research Committee, 1958. 86p.

A study for the purpose of identifying user demands and adequacy of the catalog in meeting these demands, isolating areas for further investigation, and producing reliable interview forms and related tools. Five thousand four hundred ninety-four interviews were conducted in 39 libraries of different types.

784.   Krikelas, James. **The Effect of Arrangement on the Use of Library Catalogs—An Experimental Study of a Divided and a Dictionary Catalog.** Urbana, Illinois University, Library Research Center, 1967.

A study was done in two university libraries using randomly selected undergraduates. Subjects were to select appropriate subject references in response to a set of search questions. Results indicated that there was no evidence that one type of catalog is superior to the other.

785.   Kuhlman, Clara A. "How Catalogers Can Help the Reference Librarian," *Wilson Library Bulletin* 26:267-269 (November 1951).

There must be cooperation between the reference and cataloging departments to assure that the catalog is of maximum helpfulness to users. Complex rules create an inflexible catalog. Users' approaches to materials should be anticipated and considered. The author recommends methods of cooperation whereby both departments can improve the usefulness of the catalog to patrons. The importance of an effective catalog cannot be overemphasized.

786.   Lipetz, Ben-Ami. "Catalog Use in a Large Research Library," *Library Quarterly* 42:129-139 (January 1972).

Reported here are the results of a study of the utilization of the main catalog of the Yale University Library. This study was motivated by the question of when and how best to computerize the catalog of a large research library and how to improve the existing conventional catalog. The design of the study provided a representative sample of catalog use.

787.   Lundy, Frank A., Kathryn Renfro, and Esther Schubert. "The Dual Assignment: Cataloging and Reference," *Library Resources and Technical Service* 3:167-188 (Summer 1959).

Divisional library service is considered and related to activities such as book selection. A plan is advanced where both reference and catalog librarians participate in cataloging. A better appreciation of both reference and cataloging is gained as a result. This method was used at the University of Nebraska Library; a case study is given.

788.   Lundy, Frank A. "Reference vs. Catalog: A Basic Dilemma," *Library Journal* 80:19-22 (January 1, 1955).

The conflict between catalogers and reference librarians is destructive of morale and teamwork. The author notes that library schools present cataloging as difficult and esoteric and reference as dignified and "truly professional"; as a result, students prefer reference to cataloging. Students should be educated as librarians instead, and the total library process should be stressed. The author also suggests that in libraries there should be departmental cooperation and interdepartmental assignments. Intensive experience in both reference and cataloging improves the performance of both groups. The author describes the program at the University of Nebraska Libraries.

789.   Lyon, Shirley A. "Assistance for Users of the Catalog in a University Library." Unpublished Master's thesis, University of Chicago, 1963. 59p.

790.   Maxwell, Margaret. "Cataloger vs Reference Librarian. A Cataloger's View,"
        RQ 10:148-149 (Winter 1970).

Discusses the issue of how much information should be supplied on the catalog
card. Reference librarians see the catalog as a reference tool as well as a finding tool
and want the fullest possible information, such as identification of places by geographical area, author dates, etc. The author concludes that the catalog should serve
basically as a finding tool and if it accomplishes this purpose of leading users to
material in the collection, it also serves as a reference tool.

791.   Metcalfe, John. **Alphabetical Subject Indication of Information.** New
        Brunswick, N.J., Rutgers State University, Graduate School of Library
        Service, 1965. 148p. (Rutgers Series on Systems for the Intellectual
        Organization of Information, v.3). 148p.

Discusses conventional subject headings and the problems that arise in practical use
of subject headings, particularly Library of Congress subject headings. Gives an
historical review of the use of subject headings. Also covers cross references, filing,
and searching methods and output.

792.   Mudge, Isadore G. "Present Day Economies in Cataloging." In Rowland,
        Arthur, ed., *Reference Service.* Hamden, Conn., Shoe String, 1964. pp. 214-
        228. (Contributions to Library Literature, No. 5).

Describes nine classes of porposed economies in cataloging. Discusses how readers
use these nine types of information and how in most cases these economies would
constitute a disservice to readers. Stresses that economies in cataloging often result
in transfer of added work to reference staff, increased failures in service, inaccuracies with resultant loss of public respect, and inadequate records which must later
be done over at increased cost.

793.   Palmer, R. P. "User Requirements of a University Library Card Catalog."
        Unpublished Ph.D. dissertation, University of Michigan, 1970. 311p.

794.   Palmer, Richard P. **Computerizing the Card Catalog in the University
        Library.** Littleton, Colo., Libraries Unlimited, 1972. 141p.

The main objective of this study was to determine who used the University of
Michigan General Library Card Catalog during a specified period of time. The
author includes a helpful review of major catalog use studies.

795.   Patterson, Kelly. "Library Think vs. Library User," *RQ* 12:364-365
        (Summer 1973).

Discussed here is the communication gap between the way catalogers and users
think. Library of Congress classification may not seem logical to users who are
not familiar with "library think." Reference librarians must always be aware of
how users will approach subject information and attempt to close the gap between
users and the catalog.

796.   Peele, D. A. "Overdone: Dumping Your Thing and Converting Catalogers into Useful Members of Society in Four Steps," *Wilson Library Bulletin* 48:648-649 (April 1974).

A humorous essay concerning conflict between catalogers and reference librarians. The author takes aim at the misconception often held by catalogers that reference librarians are not needed because the card catalog will answer all reference questions. The author proposes that catalogers take over reference work and a sign be posted that "catalogers will not allow anyone else to interpret the card catalog since only they understand their filing system so all reference questions are referred to them."

797.   Perrine, Richard. "Catalog Use Difficulties," *RQ* 7:169-174 (Summer 1968).

Describes two studies conducted by the Reference Services Division's Catalog Use Committee in university and public libraries across the country. The purpose of these studies was to attempt to diagnose the catalog use difficulties of patrons. Problems reported were those which came to the attention of reference librarians and were reported by them on forms. Filing arrangement, subject headings, cross reference, call numbers, title added entries, bibliographical information are ranked, approximately in that order, as causes of difficulty. Results are discussed in detail for each problem and causes of difficulty are also analyzed. Tables.

798.   Ranganathan, S. R. **Depth Classification and Reference Service and Reference Material**. Delhi, Indian Library Association, 1953. 442p.

Presents 46 papers from the Annual Conference of the Indian Library Association.

799.   Rogers, R. D. "Subject Bibliography Versus Subject Catalog and Periodical Index," *College and Research Libraries* 11:211-214 (July 1950).

Notes that subject bibliography is useful in inverse proportion to the ability of librarians and research workers. This paper "undertakes to demonstrate what good subject bibliography can do which the card catalog and periodical indexes fail to do." It is based on an analysis of book and periodical citations in bibliographies from *Encyclopedias of the Social Sciences*, *Dictionary of American Biography*, *Literary History of the United States*, and *A Shakespeare Bibliography*. Results indicate that 8 percent to 20 percent of material on a given subject can be found by subject bibliographies but not by catalogs and indexes. In certain subjects, 15 percent to 60 percent of material may be found by subject bibliographies, but not by catalogs and indexes. Other conclusions are also presented.

800.   Rugh, Archie. "Catalog, Bibliography, or Index?" *RQ* 13:27-30 (Fall 1973).

The author discusses the lack of accurate subject headings for forms of types of works, particularly indexes, bibliographies, and catalogs. At present, subject cataloging does not accurately distinguish between these types of works. The author suggests Malclès' definition of bibliographies as works which "serve to discover the mere existence of a book" and catalogs which "permit us to locate and procure an existing book." The importance to reference work of resolving this problem is discussed.

801.   Sacco, Concetta. "Book Catalog Use Study," *RQ* 12:259-266 (Spring 1973). The Reference and Adult Services Division's Catalog Use Committee surveyed patrons in one academic and one public library in regard to use of book catalogs that had been in use several years and that had author, title, and subject approaches and reflected the retrospective collection. Interviews and questionnaires were used 20 hours per week during predetermined times. Results indicated that the majority of users had favorable opinions and that there was no noticeable failure due to physical composition.

802.   Seymour, Carol, and J. L. Schofield. "Measuring Reader Failure at the
         Catalog," *Library Resources and Technical Services* 17:6-24 (Winter 1973). The Library Management Research Unit took a survey of four university libraries to determine reader failure at the catalog. The reader was asked to describe items not found, the source of references, and his status. Staff then checked to determine the cause of "failure." Interviews were held with samples of users to determine overall "failure" rate, cooperation rate, and to discover what users intended to do about items not found in the catalog. Results showed failure to be due to incorrect references from teaching staff, books in process or on order, incorrect author's surname, difficulty with subject headings and series, and failure to identify items when found.

803.   Swank, Raynard. "Subject Catalogs, Classification, or Bibliographies? A
         Review of Critical Discussion, 1876-1942," *Library Quarterly* 14:316-
         332 (October 1944).
Reviews the background of the controversy over the relative usefulness of the subject catalog, classified shelf arrangement, and subject bibliography. Considers aspects such as completeness, general versus special classification, amount of analysis, entries for current materials, subject coverage, cost, competence of compilers, accuracy, process of compilation, difficulty of use, amount of use, and the service department.

804.   Tagliacozzo, Renata, and Manfred Kochen. **Information-Seeking Behavior
         of Catalog Users.** Ann Arbor, University of Michigan, Mental Health
         Research Institute, 1970. 38p.
Based on surveys of catalog use at three university and one public library. Both known-item and subject searches are analyzed, along with reasons for failure. Bibliography.

805.   Watkins, David. "Cataloguing Theories Challenged: Reference Maxims
         Ignored," *RQ* 3:3-4, 8 (May 1964).
The author criticizes the article by Paul Dunkin (*RQ*, 3:3-6, March 1963). He points out that abbreviated cataloging may fail to place all the books by an author in the same place, and the greater the physical separation of the reader from the book, such as in cooperative arrangements, the greater the need for detailed bibliographical information. He also notes that the necessary bibliographies often do not exist to supply information formerly available through the catalog. The study of Olivia Faulkner is criticized in that it is done from the cataloger's point of view and is not objective. The author notes that catalogers advocating the abbreviated cataloging

lack experience in helping readers use the catalog and have lost contact with their end product. Reference librarians should make their voices heard in representing the interest of the patron and those of their own profession.

806.　Watson, Eugene F. "The Reference Librarian Looks at the Catalog," *Wilson Library Bulletin* 26:269-270 (November 1951).
Examines catalogs in college, university, special, school, and public libraries in relation to reference use. Describes the differences in the needed depth of cataloging in different types of libraries. Recommendations for improved cataloging are use of realistic subject headings, a shelf list with subject guide cards, liberal cross references and an alphabetical index, and a catalog simple and attractive enough to encourage use.

807.　Winchell, Constance M. "The Reference Librarian and the Catalog." In Rowland, Arthur R., ed. *Reference Services*. Hamden, Conn., Shoe String Press, 1964. pp. 188-200. (Contributions to Library Literature, No. 5).
Discusses the progress of the catalog from its beginnings as a finding tool, its subsequent development into the chief bibliographical tool of the reference librarian, and the present-day swing of the pendulum back toward becoming a finding tool, due to costs and lack of space. Concludes that a simple finding list is not sufficient for a research library and considers the advantages and disadvantages of the following proposed methods of simplifying cataloging: 1) putting less information on cards, 2) doing less research before making cards, and thus eliminating some types of information previously included, 3) simplifying the corporate entry, 4) depending on printed bibliographies and indexes for certain groups of materials.

808.　Winik, Ruth. "Reference Function with an On-Line Catalog," *Special Libraries* 63:217-221 (May-June 1972).
All library processes have a reference function since their ultimate goal is referring the user to information. Automation has emphasized the importance of this philosophy. On-line catalogs are defined and described, particularly with reference to the ELMS (Experimental Library Management System) at the IBM ASDO Library in Los Gatos, California. The usefulness of the on-line catalog to patron and librarian is discussed.

REFERENCE MATERIALS

Reference Collection—Organization and Administration

See also:　Chapter 10, Sources of Information (Reference Materials—Use; Reference Materials—Selection and Evaluation)
　　Chapter 11, Research in Reference (Measurement and Evaluation)

Included here are works that discuss the organization and administration of the reference collection in different types of libraries. Works that consider evaluation of the reference collection are included in the section Reference Materials—Selection and Evaluation, in this chapter.

809.   Bobeen, J. E. "Mutilation of Library Resources: Containing a Study of
       Mutilation of the Reference Collection of the Undergraduate Library,
       Ellis Library, University of Missouri, Columbia." Unpublished Research
       Paper, University of Missouri, 1974. 61p.

810.   Gwinup, Thomas. "A Functional Arrangement of Indexes and Abstracts
       for the Humanities and Social Sciences," *RQ* 13:143-146 (Winter 1973).
Describes the arrangement of humanities and social sciences indexes and abstracts
at the San Francisco State University Library. This arrangement, along with posted
signs, resulted in a significant reduction in directional questions.

811.   Hernon, Peter, and Maureen Pastine. "Faculty Loan Policies for Reference
       Collections," *Pennsylvania Library Association Bulletin* 27:175-183
       (July 1972).
Reports the results of a survey of reference collection loan policies in 60 institut-
tions. Abuse of non-circulating policies is discussed and solutions are considered
such as faculty carrels, and classrooms in the library for use when the professor
wishes to use reference materials. The blacklist system and phone calls are more
effective in general than fines.

812.   "Instant Reference Collection," *ALA Bulletin* 62:789 (July 1968).
The Hamline University Library has acquired, as a gift from Paul Schelling, a
microfilm research center containing 25,000 reels, which represent 100,000 volumes of the New York Public Library's reference collection. Equipment available
in the microfilm research center searches and prints pages at high speed.

813.   Jestes, Edward C. "An Example of Systems Analysis: Locating a Book in
       a Reference Room," *Special Libraries* 59:722-728 (November 1968).
Systems analysis does not necessarily involve mechanization. Librarians can prepare
flow charts outlining step-by-step procedures that will help eliminate bottlenecks
and duplicated effort. The author describes such a systems analysis of the location
of reference books in the reference room of a large university library. Problems
related to the catalog were analyzed and suggestions were made that would save
two minutes in locating a reference book and would cost $152.00 to implement.
It was estimated that $2,000 worth of patrons' time would be saved.

814.   Kuhner, David A. "Some Thoughts on the Arrangement of Reference
       Books," *RQ* 9:146-149 (Winter 1969).
Classification systems often fail to bring closely related materials together. The John
Crerar Library describes its own system of arrangement for reference books, based
on 10 broad categories. This arrangement has been successful in encouraging use of
the reference collection.

815.   Matley, M. B. "A Handiguide: Building Your Phone Book Collection: A
       Gold Mine of Low Cost Information," *Wilson Library Bulletin* 48:318-323
       (December 1973).
Describes the large collection of both white and yellow page directories held by the
San Leonardo Community Library in California, as a valuable information resource.
Suggests compiling a union list of telephone directories over a large area to provide

access to seldom-used materials. Describes the technical details of caring for the collection and points out that such collections can often be obtained free from the telephone company.

816.   Perry, Margaret. "The College Catalog Collection," *RQ* 10:240-247 (Spring 1971).
Discusses college catalogs as sources of reference information. Describes results of a questionnaire sent to small and medium-sized colleges and to large universities concerning the size, nature, acquisition, housing, circulation, and use of college catalogs. Ninety-two percent had such collections, with 65 percent of collections maintained by reference departments. Details are given concerning the technical aspects mentioned above. Reference use was to find 1) comparative curriculum information, 2) information on graduate study programs, 3) information about faculty members, 4) admission and transfer policies, 5) historical information, 6) student activities and sports. It also serves as a browsing collection.

817.   Pipes, Charles D. "Circulating Reference Books," *Library Journal* 87:1551-1552 (April 15, 1962).
Policies and procedures for circulation of reference materials are described as carried out in the Flint, Michigan, Public Library.

818.   Seidell, Atherton. "Microfilms in Relation to Reference Service," *Bulletin of the Medical Library Association* 39:203-205 (July 1951).
Discusses use of microfilms in reference service. Microfilms should be viewed as an extension of reference services as well as a means of sharing resources.

819.   Thurman, William R. "Conservation of Periodical and Reference Volumes," *Library Journal* 66:804 (September 15, 1941).
Discusses the binding of reference books, noting that these should be considered separately from fiction. Suggestions are given in regard to selecting a good binder.

820.   Truelson, Stanley D. "The Totally Organized Reference Collection." In Rowland, Arthur, ed., *Reference Services*. Hamden, Conn., Shoe String, 1964. pp. 97-100. (Contributions to Library Literature, No. 5).
Describes reasons for a central reference collection. Suggests that reference materials be arranged first by form and then by subject. A suggested Reference Collection Form Classification is given, arranged in 20 form categories.

821.   Yenawine, Wayne S. "Wanted: A Functional Reference Room," *Library Journal* 62:237-239 (March 15, 1937).
The real function of the reference room or area is discussed. Needs, such as those for quietness and space, are considered.

Reference Materials—Use

See also: Chapter 3, Teaching of Reference
Chapter 6, Reference Service in Types of Libraries
Chapter 11, Research in Reference (Measurement and Evaluation)

Included here are studies and discussions of the use of reference materials by users in all types of libraries. Also included are studies of the levels of knowledge and skill of library users in working with reference materials.

822.   Allen, T. J., and P. G. Gerstenberger. **Criteria for Selection of an Information Source**. Cambridge, Mass., Massachusetts Institute of Technology, 1967. 26p. (PB-176 899)

Criteria used by engineers in selecting information sources were examined. Results indicated that accessibility of the information source was more important in determining use than technical quality. There was a direct relationship between perceived technical quality and message acceptance.

823.   Bartlett, B. "Study of the Most Frequently Used Reference Sources in a Selected Group of Georgia High School Libraries." Unpublished Master's thesis, Emory University, 1952. 85p.

824.   Chait, W. "Books and Other Sources Used in Adult Reference Service in Branches of the Brooklyn Public Library." Unpublished Master's thesis, Columbia University, 1938. 225p.

825.   Duke, E. C. "Use of the Reference Collection in the Public Library of Norfolk, Virginia." Unpublished Master's thesis, Catholic University of America, 1955. 172p.

826.   Guffy, N. "To What Extent Do High School Freshmen Know and Make Use of Reference Books?" Unpublished Master's thesis, Texas State College for Women, 1954. 60p.

827.   Hannon, Mildred C. "Study of a Selected Group of High School Seniors to Determine to What Extent They Know and Make Use of Reference Tools." Unpublished Master's thesis, Atlanta University, 1952. 43p.

828.   Justis, Lorraine, and Janet Wright. "Who Knows What? What?" *RQ* 12:172-174 (Winter 1972).

The author reports on a survey of graduate students in regard to their knowledge of reference sources. Many students responding to the questionnaire could not list indexes and abstracts in their subject fields.

829.   Reed, Lulu R. "Do Colleges Need Reference Service?" In Rowland, Arthur, ed. *Reference Services*. Hamden, Conn., Shoe String, 1964. pp. 77-89. (Contributions to Library Literature, No. 5).

In assessing the necessity for reference service, the author examines the questions of whether students can use reference resources effectively and whether they need assistance in locating library materials. Describes a study in which some 850 undergraduates took a test of knowledge of reference materials. Discusses in detail the knowledge students have of reference sources and their typical approaches to locating information.

Reference Materials—Selection and Evaluation

See also: Chapter 3, Teaching of Reference (Reference Textbooks and Manuals)
Chapter 5, Reference Service (General Works)
Chapter 10, Sources of Information (Reference Collection—Organization
and Administration; Reference Materials—Use)
Chapter 11, Research in Reference (Measurement and Evaluation)
Chapter 14, Information Retrieval (Applications to Book-Oriented
Data Bases)

Included here are works about the history, definition, preparation, publishing, selection, and evaluation of reference materials. Also included in a separate section are annotated entries for review sources. For computerization and reference materials, see the section, Applications to Book-Oriented Data Bases, in Chapter 14.

Bibliographical coverage is provided by Alma A. Covey, *Reviewing of Reference Books* (Metuchen, N.J., Scarecrow, 1972); Margaret Goggin and Lillian Seaberg, "The Publication and Reviewing of Reference Books," *Library Trends* 12:437-455 (January 1964); Raymond Kilgour, "Reference and Subscription Books Publishing," *Library Trends* 7:139-152 (July 1958); William Katz, *Introduction to Reference Work* (New York, McGraw-Hill, 1974); Frances N. Cheney, *Fundamental Reference Sources* (Chicago, American Library Association, 1971); and Bohdan S. Wynar, *Introduction to Bibliography and Reference Work* (Rochester, N.Y., Libraries Unlimited, 1967).

General Works

830. American Library Association. Reference Services Division. Bibliography
Committee. "Criteria for Evaluating a Bibliography," *RQ* 11:359-360
(Summer 1972).
This outline for evaluating bibliographies covers subject, scope, methodology, organization, cumulation, other aids to use, annotations, bibliographic form, timeliness, accuracy, evaluation of format.

831. Atherton, Pauline A. "Development of Machine-Generated Tools." In
Linderman, W., ed. *The Present Status and Future Prospects of Reference/
Information Service.* Chicago, American Library Association, 1967.
pp. 121-133.
Machine-generated tools include all tools either printed or assembled by any kind of data processing equipment as well as those available in machine-readable form. Basic requirements for reference tools are 1) least effort in use, 2) easy access to information, 3) frequent updating, 4) less duplication among tools. Stresses the need for by-product generation and describes the AIP project where by-products of the central data base will be author and subject indexes, data for abstract journal preparation, citation index data, automatic search files for local information centers, data for annual subject bibliographies, and cumulative indexes. Also

stressed is the need to combine computerized data bases into new reference tools for added flexibility. A comment by Edwin B. Colburn and a discussion follow this article.

832.   Barzun, Jacques. "Bedside Reading: A Reference Book," *Wilson Library Bulletin* 39:246-247 (November 1964).
The author describes the characteristics of a good reference book, considering style, organization, indices, cross references, accuracy, symbols, and abbreviations. The problem of detecting and evaluating bias in reference works is also discussed.

833.   Bauer, Harry. "Mediocrity Better Than Nothing," *RQ* 10:139-142 (Winter 1970).
Reference book reviews serve primarily to call attention to new tools, rather than as selection aids. Reference books are purchased to serve a need, and the first tool that serves that need is bought. Choices are made not of the "best" book of a certain type and subject, but between books in different subject areas, and decisions are made on the basis of which book is most needed and which tools of each kind are already owned. Every reference book contains something useful and will serve until something else comes along. Reviews serve primarily to call attention to reference books, which will then be bought if they are needed, regardless of reviews. Reference book reviewing has little bearing on selection.

834.   Bonk, Wallace. "Articulate Disagreement: What is Basic Reference?" *RQ* 3:5-8 (May 1964).
Describes the results of a study done by the author in 1962, where 1,090 reference librarians in university, public, and school libraries evaluated the usefulness of 352 basic reference sources. This study is compared with the author's earlier study of basic reference sources taught in library schools. The larger the library, the more reference books are ranked as "vital." The author questions whether reference questions of smaller libraries actually differ in quality from those in larger institutions. The implications of this are discussed in terms of whether smaller institutions are providing adequate service and whether regional reference service is needed.

835.   Chen, Ching-Chih, and Thomas Galvin. "Reviewing the Literature of Librarianship: A State of the Art Report." *American Reference Books Annual 1975*. Bohdan Wynar, ed. Littleton, Colo., Libraries Unlimited, 1975. Vol. 6, pp. xxxi-xlv.
Describes the results of a study on the present state of reviewing current English language monographs in the field of library science as reflected in American and Canadian professional journals. Considers review media, duplication of coverage, time lags, length of reviews, and activity and affiliations of reviewers.

836.   Cheney, Frances N. "Gentle Art of Reference Book Reviewing," *Mississippi Library News* 38:215-216 (December 1974).

837.   Cheney, Frances. "New Trends in Reference Books," *South Carolina Librarian* 8:7-8 (March 1964).

838.   Covey, Alma A. **Reviewing of Reference Books**. Metuchen, N.J., Scarecrow, 1972. 112p.

This study considers the adequacy of review and announcement sources for reference materials. One thousand thirty-two U.S. and foreign works with reference interest, published in 1967-1968 and listed in Winchell's *Guide to Reference Books*, 2nd supplement, are traced through announcement and review media. The same books are also traced through indexes to determine access to reviews.

839.   Crane, Kathryn K. "Questions on New Editions: Is This Revision?" *RQ* 9:227-231 (Spring 1970).

The author reports on a comparison of 15 titles on Africa revised between 1961 and 1965. Each new edition was compared with the original edition, and it was found that revisions were frequently of low quality. Good revisions should result in a new book, embodying new research, but based on the fundamental concepts of the original edition.

840.   Dane, Chase. "Evaluating the Reference Collection," *Tennessee Librarian* 17:3-11 (Fall 1964).

In evaluating a reference collection the type of library, the amount of time and money, and the depth of evaluation needed should all be considered. The author lists three methods of evaluation: 1) checklist, 2) a study of unanswered reference questions, 3) a study of the patrons served. Describes the advantages and disadvantages of each method.

841.   Darling, Richard. [Government Publications] "Selection and Reference Use in the School Library," *Library Trends* 15:87-92 (July 1966).

Describes selection and use of documents in the school library and notes that more research is needed in this area. Discusses problems associated with use of documents, such as the fact that school librarians are unaware of much valuable information contained in certain government documents.

842.   Doebler, P. D. "Data Bases in Print Can Compete with Computer Files," *Publishers Weekly* 206:40-41 (September 16, 1974).

Describes those data bases in print in the areas of journalism and current and public affairs. Considers and compares the *National Journal, Facts on File, Keesing's Archives, Deadline Data*, and the *New York Times Index*. Also discusses why print is better for many uses. Describes prospective new markets for new print reference tools derived from computerized bases.

843.   Donahugh, Robert H. **An Evaluation of the Reference Resources in Eight Public Libraries in Four Ohio Counties**. Columbus, Ohio State Library, 1970. 42p. ERIC Document ED046399.

This study was conducted as part of the Appalachia Improved Reference Services Program. Conclusions were that more recent materials, especially science texts and business materials, were needed, and that weeding should be done to remove outdated materials.

844.　Goggin, Margaret Knox, and Lillian Seaberg. "The Publishing and Reviewing of Reference Books," *Library Trends* 12:437-455 (January 1964).
Defines reference works and discusses the ways in which the quality of reference service varies with the quality of available reference tools. Sources that list new reference titles are reviewed and a list is given of those periodicals that feature annual checklists of new reference materials. Various types of publishers of reference materials are considered, and tables are presented for three sources, showing the types and subjects of reference books listed in each. Also covered are sources of book reviews, such as *Technical Book Review Digest*. For effective selection, more critical and current reviews are needed.

845.　Gulick, Melba. "Non-Conventional Data Sources and Reference Tools for Social Sciences and Humanities: A Bibliographical Essay," *College and Research Libraries* 29:224-234 (May 1968).
Considers non-conventional information systems and centers that serve social sciences and humanities in the United States. Covers changing bibliographic and data needs, services offered, coordinating organizations, computer-compiled tools, and other sources of information. A list of publications and articles is included to serve as a directory to these sources.

846.　Harris, Katherine. "Currently Available Tools—Their Adequacy for Today's Needs." In Linderman, W., ed. *The Present Status and Future Prospects of Reference/Information Service*. Chicago, American Library Association, 1967. pp. 103-120.
Discusses the two reference tool systems, that of direct communication through encyclopedias, dictionaries, etc., and the "tracking" system of bibliographies, etc., to record existence of other publications. Raises the question of whether to train users to use tools or adapt the tools to the users. Discusses different types of users of reference materials and their needs. Describes and discusses major bibliographic tools, tools in subject areas, and tools available for selection of reference materials. Considers costs and reference book production. Comments on trends such as paperback reference materials and reprints and considers microfilmed materials as a solution to space problems. Discusses quality of reference sources and concludes that "there is need for tools of greater scope, depth, and currency."

847.　Hernon, Peter. "Municipal Publications: Their Collection and Use in Reference Service," *Special Libraries* 64:29-33 (January 1973).
Municipal publications are valuable in reference service in that they provide statistical data, reports, and information on agencies and functions that are not available elsewhere. Publishing practices, guides available, developments, and major tools are discussed.

848.　Hirshberg, H. S. **Subject Guide to Reference Books**. Chicago, American Library Association, 1942. 260p.
This annotated guide to reference works is arranged alphabetically by subject. Two hundred forty-six subjects, both broad and very specific, are covered. Analytics for specific material in general reference works are frequently provided. For example, under "disasters" are found annotations for general encyclopedias and almanacs containing lists of disasters. Somewhat outdated, but still useful.

849. Johnson, Olive A. "How to Write a Guide to Reference Books," *Library Association Record* 56:394-397 (October 1954).

The author worked on the first supplement to *Guide to Reference Books* by Constance Winchell. She describes the procedures followed, such as "gleaning" of 200 periodicals, watching of "in progress" books, drawing on the resources of other libraries. All books but those in Oriental languages were personally examined, and annotations were compared and criticized. The author goes on to describe the assembling and preparation for publishing, including details of how each step was completed.

850. Kilgour, Raymond. "Reference and Subscription Book Publishing," *Library Trends* 7:139-152 (July 1958).

Reviews the history of reference and subscription book publishing. Discusses some of the major reference sets and reference publishers, especially during the period 1946 to 1957, and notes outstanding new titles and revisions of older sets.

851. Lancaster, F. W. "The Evaluation of Published Indexes and Abstract Journals: Criteria and Possible Procedures," *Bulletin of the Medical Library Association* 59:479-494 (July 1971).

Considers performance criteria for current awareness and retrospective use of published indexes and abstract journals. The criteria are coverage, recall, effort measured by time, and novelty. Optimum ideal and real-life performance must be differentiated. Real-life performance is difficult to assess. Synthetic searches may be used to evaluate the above factors as well as factors contributing to failure. A value for novelty, as well as the above criteria, can be derived from real-life study. Surveys of users and non-users should also be made.

852. Martin, John. "Building a Reference Collection for a New University Library," *Ontario Library Review* 49:68 (May 1965).

Describes how a collection of 1,600 volumes was built up in one year for Trent University. The collection was designed to serve both undergraduates and faculty.

853. Murray, T. B. "Evaluation of the Reference Collections in the Libraries of Seven San Francisco Bay Area Junior Colleges." Unpublished Master's thesis, University of California, 1953. 76p.

854. Nolan, John L. "Reference Books We Need," *Library Journal* 87:1542-1544 (April 15, 1962).

Describes the effort of the Reference Services Division's Committee on New Reference Tools to encourage the publication of needed reference materials.

855. Pritchard, H. C. "Does Continuous Revision Require Continuous Replacement?" *College and Research Libraries* 18:144-146 (March 1957).

Discusses the policy of continuous revision in regard to encyclopedias. Reviews the literature on continuous revision and concludes that the latest revision of an encyclopedia is not always necessary for good reference service. Discusses the ramifications of this problem.

856. "Reference Book Reviewing: Some Other Views," *RQ* 10:138-142 (Winter 1970).

Four brief essays, which are replies and suggestions in reply to a previous article, "Reference Book Reviewing," by Harry Whitmore. Included are "The Pursuit of Mediocrity," by Arthur Young; "Mediocrity Better Than Nothing," by Harry Bauer; "Book Reviewing Indexes," by C. Edward Wall; and "Footnote," by Richard Gercken.

857. Rips, Rae Elizabeth. "The Reference Use of Government Publications," *Drexel Library Quarterly* 1:3-18 (October 1965).

Keys to successful reference use of government publications are 1) knowledge of the government and its agencies, 2) awareness of the vast varieties of types of subjects, 3) proper selection and acquisition, 4) location of documents near the point of use. These points are discussed in detail. Discusses use of 17 types of government publications, including Congressional and legal materials, directories, administrative reports, statistical publications, research reports, semi-popular pamphlets, periodicals, bibliographies, press releases, audiovisual materials, and maps. These materials are discussed in regard to their reference usefulness and the types of questions they will answer. Gives suggestions on ways to make documents more available and useful and also considers selection and acquisition.

858. Scott, J. D. "Ease of Reference," *Spectator* 191:765 (December 25, 1953).

Discusses qualities that make for ease of reference. The reference book "of all books . . . is the least easy to review since its true quality emerges only in a long series of minor crises."

859. Seaholm, F. C. "Comparative Analysis of Three Guides to Reference Sources." Master's thesis, University of Minnesota, 1962. 173p. (ACRL Microcard Series, 158).

860. Seaholm, Frances. "Winchell, Walford, or Malclès?" *College and Research Libraries* 25:21-26, 31 (January 1964).

Three guides to reference materials are compared, and the advantages and disadvantages of each are discussed. Tables are given which compare subject and geographical coverage.

861. Shores, Louis. **Basic Reference Books.** Chicago, American Library Association, 1939. 472p.

Discusses types of reference sources, with mention of specific titles. Consideration is given to historical background and comparative analysis of important tools. A core collection is included in an appendix.

862. Shores, Louis. "Patterns in American Reference Books," *Library Association Record* 54:284-291 (September 1952).

Criteria for evaluating reference materials are discussed. American reference works such as dictionaries, encyclopedias, yearbooks, and geographical and bibliographical sources are reviewed in terms of historical background.

863.   Shores, Louis. "Reference Book Reviewing," *Reference Services Review* 1:3-6 (October-December 1973).
The author describes history and background of reference book reviewing and comments on his own personal experiences. Discusses the following criteria in the context of today's reference book reviewing: authority, scope, treatment, arrangement, and format. The reference book reviewer today must have "sophistication in his literary form certainly on a par with that of the most highly regarded critic of poetry, drama, fiction, essay."

864.   Sims, Edith M. [Government Publications] "Selection and Reference Use in the College Library," *Library Trends* 15:107-116 (July 1966).
Discusses how the size and purpose of the library and whether or not it is a depository influence reference use of documents. Considers problems in documents service such as lack of publicity and accessibility. Describes use of printed bibliographies and indexes and notes that these provide the main approach to the documents collection.

865.   Spargo, John. "Book Selection for Reference Work." In Butler, Pierce, ed. *The Reference Function of the Library*. Chicago, University of Chicago Press, 1943. pp. 267-281.
Reference librarians should not rely on lists but should apply sound individual judgment in selection. The author recommends rigorous graduate training in a subject field. Learn your books thoroughly by using them daily and living with them. An index to the literature on history of reference books is needed and also to the contents of incunabula. Reference librarians need to compile bibliographies drawing together materials from the past. Reference librarians are not publishing material to assist scholars. Instead, they are automatic fact vendors addicted to lists of reference books. Suggests a number of projects in historical scholarship. Librarians must first of all be scholars if they would beget scholarship in others.

866.   Stiffler, Stuart. "A Book Is a Book Is a Reference Book," *RQ* 11:341-343 (Summer 1972).
Describes three approaches to defining reference books—functional, administrative, or attributive. The functional category defines books according to the type of use (specific consultation as opposed to consecutive reading), but some books, such as the Cambridge Histories, are used for both. The attributive category defines by the intrinsic characteristics of the book itself (organizational format and supplementary aides, etc.). Definition by administrative decision consists of an authoritative decision by the reference librarian as to whether a given title shall be "reference." Also, titles are sometimes considered "reference" because they provide basic or definitive treatment or because they provide information important to patrons, but not otherwise available.

867.   Tripp, Edward. "Man Behind the Book, the Reference Editor," *RQ* 4:7-10 (November 1964).
The editor for reference books for the Crowell Company discusses reference book publishing. Some aspects to be considered in the publication of a new reference book are types of readers, reliability of information, scope, significance and balance

of information, clarity of style, objectivity, and accessibility. These points are discussed in more detail.

868.   Wall, C. Edward. "Book Reviewing Indexes," *RQ* 10:140-142 (Winter 1970).
Discusses book review media and suggests a computerized "early reviewing service."

869.   White, Carl M. "How to Avoid Duplicated Information," *RQ* 10:127-137 (Winter 1970).
Reasons for increasing redundancy in reference collections are need for good reference collections, better budgets, increased book production, lucrative seller's market, and book selection by individual titles decreasing. The author feels that duplication is becoming too expensive and extensive and reports on a study of duplication in periodical directories, periodical indexes, dictionaries, information about institutions of higher learning, reviews of current affairs, and general information on activities of government. Considerable duplication was found. The author concludes 1) more control of duplication is needed, 2) better communication about this is needed among librarians, 3) we should study buyer resistance in cases of books that are duplicates, 4) more critical book reviewing is needed. References.

870.   Whitmore, Harry E. "Reference Book Reviewing," *RQ* 9:221-226 (Spring 1970).
Certain major selection tools for reference books are examined. *Saturday Review* (the semiannual "Reference Roundup"), *Library Journal*, *Wilson Library Bulletin*, *Subscription Books Bulletin*, and *Choice* are analyzed and compared. *Choice* is rated as superior to the others. Its reviews are judged "consistently analytical and incisive." The subject competence of its reviewers is noted.

871.   Whittaker, Kenneth. "Basic British," *RQ* 12:49-52 (Fall 1972).
Surveys major British sources of information on reference books. Briefly compares American and British sources of such information. Consider basic sources by Walford—*Guide to Reference Materials* and *Basic Stock for the Reference Library*. Discusses the lack of reviewing journals in Britain and comments on three British review journals—*New Library World*, *School Librarian*, and *British Book News*. Also considers book trade sources, such as *Bookseller* and *Oxford Reference Books*. Concludes by discussing specialized guides, which are considered as sources of information on individual types of reference books or reference books for specific purposes.

872.   Young, Arthur P. "The Pursuit of Mediocrity," *RQ* 10:138-139 (Winter 1970).
The author believes that before conclusions can be drawn about reference book reviewing, we must know more about the use made of reviews, how well they measure up to reviews in scholarly periodicals, and whether there is too much duplication. He agrees with Whitmore's judgment that *Subscription Books Bulletin* reviews are poor, *Library Journal*'s are adequate, and *Choice*'s are best. Reviews should be interpretative and analytical. Problems are lack of competent reviewers

and unwillingness to criticize, perhaps due to respect for books and fear of having their own published works criticized in turn.

Review Sources

873. **Booklist**. Chicago, American Library Association, 1905– . Monthly.
Short annotations of some reference works. Detailed evaluations of certain types of reference works, particularly English language dictionaries, encyclopedias, bibliographies, children's sets of books, and atlases, are done by the Reference and Subscription Books Review Committee of the ALA.

874. Centing, Richard R. "Reference Serials," *Reference Services Review* 2:49-57 (April/June 1974).
This column, discussing types of reference serials, will be continued in future issues of *Reference Services Review*. Types of reference serials and costs are discussed. Sections are included on "serials about serials," book reviews, chemistry, health sciences, journalism, newspaper indexes, nursing, photography, religion and Slavic and East European subjects.

875. **Choice**. Chicago, American Library Association, Association of College and Research Libraries, 1964– . Monthly.
Short reviews of reference titles are given at the beginning of the general reviews section. Bibliographical essays appear occasionally, covering reference materials of different types and in different subject areas. Reviews are not signed.

876. **Library Journal**. New York, Bowker, 1876– . Semi-monthly.
The section titled "Reference Books of _____ (year)" has been compiled since 1958 by a Committee of the ALA Reference Services Division. Now published in the April 15 issue. Annotates some 100 reference titles. The general book review section also covers reference works, as does the section "Professional Reading" and the *School Library Journal* section.

877. **RQ**. Chicago, American Library Association, 1960– . Quarterly.
The section titled "In Review" appears at the end of each issue. Two to five long reviews are followed by shorter annotations for other reference titles. Some 200 reviews are published per year.

878. **Reference Services Review**. Ann Arbor, Mich., Pierian Press, November/ December, 1972– . Quarterly.
Gives book reviews for reference books and other reference materials. Departments include "Recent Reference Books," "Reference Book Review Index," "Government Reference Publications," "Government Serials and Services," "British Reference Books," and "Reference Books in Print."

879. **Saturday Review**. New York, Saturday Review, Inc., 1924– . Weekly.
The section "Reference Roundup" is compiled for the general reader and published twice a year. Brief annotations.

880.   Sheehy, Eugene. "Selected Reference Books," *College and Research Libraries*, 1952– .

This semiannual list covers recent scholarly and foreign works of interest to university reference librarians and is a continuation of the series originally edited by Constance Winchell. It is a project of the Columbia University Libraries. It is not intended to be comprehensive or balanced in coverage. Works are classified under 14 broad subjects and annotations stress scope, arrangement, and usefulness. A substantial number of the works selected for inclusion are bibliographic and source guides. Emphasis is on specialized titles and foreign and scholarly publications. Published in the January and June issues of *College and Research Libraries* since 1952.

881.   Walford, Albert J. **Guide to Reference Material**. 3rd ed. London, The Library Association, 1973– . To be completed in 3 vols.

This work ranks as one of the major comprehensive guides to reference materials. Issued in three volumes as follows: Volume I, Science and Technology; Volume II, Social and Historical Sciences; and Volume III, Generalities, Languages, the Arts, and Literature (not yet published in the third edition). Arranged by broad topic and subdivided by smaller topics. Emphasis is on British materials, but coverage of U.S. materials is almost equally good.

882.   *Wilson Library Bulletin*. New York, H. W. Wilson, 1914– . Monthly.

The section "Current Reference Books" appears in each issue. Reviews, written by Charles Bunge, cover some 20 to 30 significant titles.

883.   Winchell, Constance. **Guide to Reference Books**. 8th ed. Chicago, American Library Association, 1967. 741p. Supplement I, 1965-66. Supplement II, 1967-68. Supplement III, 1969-70.

A bibliography of reference works in all subject areas. Arranged in sections covering bibliography, libraries, societies, encyclopedias, periodicals and newspapers, documents, and dissertations. Other sections cover reference works in humanities, social sciences, and science and technology. Complete bibliographical information and annotations included for each entry. The 9th edition edited by E. P. Sheehy was published in 1976.

884.   Wynar, Bohdan S., ed. **American Reference Books Annual**. Littleton, Colo., Libraries Unlimited, 1970– . Annual.

Designed to provide comprehensive coverage of reference books published in a given year, ARBA reviews some 1,600 to 1,700 titles each year. Includes sections for general reference works, library science, area studies, social sciences, history, humanities, and science and technology. For each title full bibliographical information is given, along with a descriptive and evaluative review; reviews are written by some 250 subject specialists. Reviews in other reviewing media are cited.

CHAPTER 11

RESEARCH IN REFERENCE

GENERAL WORKS

See also: Chapter 2, Theory and Philosophy
Chapter 3, Teaching of Reference
Chapter 5, Reference Service (General Works)
Chapter 9, The Reference Process (Communication and the Reference Interface; Reference Questions; Search Strategy and Reference Technique)
Chapter 10, Sources of Information (The Card Catalog; Reference Materials)
Chapter 13, Information Centers and Services
Chapter 14, Information Retrieval

Included here are works about research in reference in general.

Bibliographical coverage is outlined in the introduction to the section Measurement and Evaluation, in Chapter 11. See also Guy Garrison, "Research in Reference: Is it Possible?," In *Libraries in Transition*, Wisconsin Library Association, 1967; Patrick Penland, *Communication Research for Librarians* (University of Pittsburgh, 1972); and Ruth Rockwood and Louise Shores, "Research in Reader's Services," *Library Trends* 6:160-170 (October 1957).

885.   Bunge, Charles A. "Research in Reference: The Long Look," *RQ* 8:55-56 (Fall 1968).
The first appearance of a column by Charles Bunge, titled "Research in Reference" and intended to become a regular feature. The last column, however, appears in *RQ* in the summer of 1972. This column reports on research of all types related to reference service and the reference process.

886.   Focke, Helen. "The Weinberg Report: Place of the Reference Librarian," *RQ* 4:1-2, 16 (January 1965).
Discusses the Weinberg report on "Science, Government, and Information," and asks where the general reference librarian belongs in the pattern of information flow. Most studies have been done from the viewpoint of specialists and very little research has been done on the accumulated know-how of reference librarians.

887.   Garrison, Guy. "Research in Reference: Is It Possible?" In Schwab,
        Bernard, comp. *Libraries in Transition: Response to Change. Selected
        Papers from the North Central Library Conference, Milwaukee, 1967.*
        Madison, Wisconsin Library Association, 1968. pp. 44-49. ERIC
        Document ED023440.
The author sees reference work in the broader sense as defined by Shera: "an
answering of questions by the accumulation and assimilation of facts which lead to
the formulation of generalizations or universals that extend, correct, or verify knowledge." Surveys of reference resources and reference needs are not research. Critically
analyzes major reference studies and discusses progress in reference research.

888.   Papazian, Pierre. "Librarian, Know Thyself," *RQ* 4:7-8 (July 1965).
Most research has been directed toward machine applications in information service
rather than toward improvement of the human information specialist. We know
next to nothing about the reference process. Studies should be done of both the
practice of information searching and the psychology of information searching.
We cannot improve our performance until we have analyzed it. The author describes
the functions the human mind can perform which the computer cannot. By analytical study of the reference process, we can improve our services and enhance our
professional status.

889.   Penland, Patrick. **Communication Research for Librarians.** Pittsburgh,
        Graduate School of Library Science and Information Sciences, University
        of Pittsburgh, 1972. 132p. (Discourse Units in Human Communication
        for Librarians). ERIC Document ED071729.
Describes research methods in communication in relation to librarianship and
covers proposals, theory, measurement design, observational methods, experimental
control and extrapolation, search and discovery. Includes study questions, sample
proposal outlines and forms, glossary of terms, and bibliography.

890.   Rockwood, Ruth, and Louis Shores. "Research in Reader's Services,"
        Library Trends 6:160-170 (October 1957).
Begins by reviewing research in reader's advisory service from 1926 to the 1950s,
commenting on key findings and trends. Reviews significant studies done on reference service and summarizes and analyzes findings. Concludes with a review of
the literature on trends in reference service, and summarizes the content of these
works and discusses their implications.

MEASUREMENT AND EVALUATION

See also: Chapter 2, Theory and Philosophy
            Chapter 9, The Reference Process (Communication and the Reference
                Interface; Reference Questions; Search Strategy and Reference
                Technique; Users)
            Chapter 10, Sources of Information (The Card Catalog; Reference
                Materials)
            Chapter 11, Research in Reference
            Chapter 14, Information Retrieval

Included here are works about standards, ethics in reference service, and critical works about measurement and evaluation of a variety of aspects of reference service in different types of libraries. Also included are research studies on all aspects of reference service. Research studies on catalog use, classification and analysis of questions, and reference materials as such, however, are included respectively, in the sections The Card Catalog (in Chapter 10), Reference Questions (in Chapter 9), and Reference Materials (in Chapter 10). Also included here are selected works on library standards and measurement and evaluation in general.

Bibliographical coverage is provided in Samuel Rothstein, "The Measurement and Evaluation of Reference Service," *Library Trends* 12:456-472 (January 1964); Terry Weech, "Evaluation of Adult Reference Service," *Library Trends* 22:315-335 (January 1974); Ruth Rockwood and Louis Shores, "Research in Reader's Services," *Library Trends* 6:160-170 (October 1957); and Guy Garrison, "Research in Reference: Is It Possible?," in *Libraries in Transition* (Wisconsin Library Association, 1967); ERIC Document ED023440). Also see S. Ottersen, "Bibliography on Standards for Evaluating Libraries," *College and Research Libraries* 32:127-144 (March 1971) and "Policy Statements, Standards of Service and Memoranda of Evidence Produced by the Library Association from 1942-1972: An Annotated Bibliography," *Library and Information Bulletin* 19:2-18 (1972).

General Works

891. American Library Association. Library Organization and Management Section. Library Administration Division. Committee on Statistics for Reference Service. *Proceedings of the Symposium on Measurement of Reference, July 8, 1974.* Edited by Katherine Emerson. Chicago, American Library Association, 1974. 66p.
Basic concerns of this symposium are whether reference work can and should be measured.

892. Bauer, Harry. "Evaluation of Service in a Technical Library—Library Statistics," *Special Libraries* 30:296-297 (November 1939).
The author bases his comments on the library of the Tennessee Valley Authority. He discusses the basic reasons for evaluation and suggests use of standards already formulated for academic and public libraries. Reference statistics are also discussed.

893. Byron, J. F. W. "Subject Enquiries," *Librarian* 43:1-4 (January 1954).
Discusses the reference inquiry and advocates use of an inquiry form for use by untrained staff or when the request cannot be met from immediate resources. The form described here records patron's purpose, level of material desired, language desired, type of material desired, reference sources tried by searcher, other libraries or persons contacted by searcher, and library materials offered to patron.

894.   Casmir, P. "Reference and Special Libraries, Some Current Problems." In Library Association. Reference and Special Libraries Section Conference, April, 1955, Stockport. *Proceedings*. London, Library Association, 1955. p. 11.

Describes the use of quantitative records of reference service as information resources in British libraries now and in the future.

895.   Childers, Thomas. "Managing the Quality of Reference/Information Service," *Library Quarterly* 42:212-217 (April 1972).

The author begins with a brief review of past developments in measuring the quality of reference service. He stresses the importance of evaluating reference service from the user's point of view and describes his method of "unobtrusive observation." Test questions for use in this method are included, and he describes criteria for judging answers. This method evaluates the entire reference process, including quality of the answer. This method is useful in maintaining quality of service, establishing nationwide goals and standards, assessing reference operations, and improving cooperative reference arrangements.

896.   Cohen, Sidney. "A New Process for Keeping Reference Statistics," *OLA Bulletin* 33:24-25 (January 1963).

Defines reference questions as 1) requests from patrons of a library for information of a definite nature which they expect to be found in printed materials or their like, 2) requests for a certain work or works not readily located in the library. Explains the rationale behind these definitions.

897.   "Editorial Comments," *RQ* 14:101 (Winter 1974).

Brief note of changes in the final draft of "A Commitment to Information Services: Developmental Guidelines," in which extension of the library's information service potential through cooperation with other library or information centers is termed "indirect reference service."

898.   Emerson, Katherine, and others. "Symposium on Measurement of Reference: A Report," *RQ* 14:7-19 (February 1974).

Included here are four papers and a summary from a symposium at the 1974 ALA conference. Both desirability and feasibility of measuring reference service are considered.

899.   Griffin, Agnes, and John Hall. "Social Indicators and Library Change," *Library Journal* 97:3120-3123 (October 1, 1972).

Considered here is the fact that librarians are not able to measure the effectiveness of library service, much less to assess improvements or deteriorations in service. Effectiveness of library service does not come as a result of efficient technical management of the collection. Recommended is an approach that involves developing understanding of social indicators, which indicate whether a problem is getting better or worse. Effectiveness of all aspects and levels of service should be measured, for example, in interpersonal interaction, regional, and national networks.

900.   "Guide to Methods of Library Evaluation," *College and Research Library News* 29:293-299 (October 1968).

This article discusses major areas of evaluation, which include, 1) evidence such as collection, facilities, and staff; 2) secondary evidence—planning documents; and 3) special activities suggesting excellence, such as publications. Suggestions are given on specific points for evaluation in each of these areas and techniques for evaluation.

901.   Halperin, Michael. "Reference Question Sampling," *RQ* 14:20-23 (February 1974).

Described here is a method of reference measurement which involves sampling rather than daily recording. The author presents information on how to determine the number of days on which samples must be taken in order to achieve a given level of precision and confidence in reference statistics. The advantages of this method are that it eliminates day-to-day recording and improves the accuracy and completeness of statistics.

902.   Hawley, M. B. "Reference Statistics: The Numbers Game," *RQ* 10:143-147 (Winter 1970).

The author discusses her attempts to find a satisfactory method of keeping reference statistics. Three suggested forms for recording reference questions from the University of North Carolina and Coe College are reproduced.

903.   Helm, Margie M. "Interpreting Reference Service," *ALA Bulletin* 34:115-116 (February 1940).

There is a need for objective measures of reference to aid in interpreting reference service to laymen and college administrators. This would help to secure recognition and increased budgetary support for reference and bibliographical work. The Library Services Division of the U.S. Office of Education has included questions in regard to reference services in the new statistical forms for college and university libraries. These questions could be adapted to individual libraries. Questions should be stated in ways that give data which are not difficult or expensive to use.

904.   Henry, E. A. "Judging Reference Service," *Library Journal* 64:358-359 (May 1, 1939).

This article, written in a humorous vein, discusses measurement of reference service. Specialized and general service are considered and importance of personal factors is stressed. Suggests that reference librarians should perform scholarly work.

905.   Hirsch, Felix E., ed. "Standards for Libraries," *Library Trends* 21 (October 1972). (Whole Issue)

Thirteen articles written by librarians from different types of libraries on aspects of standardization. University, college, public, state, school, and special libraries are covered. Also covered are standardization in Canadian and British libraries and international standardization. Bibliographies included.

906.   Jackman, Thelma. "Why Measure Reference Work?" *Library Journal*
       84:3826-3827 (December 15, 1959).
Covered here are reasons for measuring reference work, validity of measurement,
and types of reference questions. Discusses ways of counting reference and
directional questions. Gives definition of reference work and describes its functions.

907.   Jestes, Edward. "Why Waste Professional Time on Directional Questions?"
       RQ 14:13-16 (Fall 1974).
Suggests that the nature of reference service makes it difficult to justify. There are
periods of inactivity followed by frantic activity. The role is passive in that staff
wait for questions to be asked. He recommends that research be done to justify the
existence of reference in terms of value to the patron by determining time and
money saved to patrons by reference assistance. Discusses three methods of determining time saved: 1) measure time it takes patrons to find information needed
with and without reference help, 2) librarians could do the same, assuming role
of both types of users, 3) observe users and measure time it takes them to locate
and open a reference book.

908.   Lamble, J. Hoskin. "Statistical Representation of Reference Library
       Use," *Library Association Record* 18:291-292 (September 1951).
Presented here is a graphic method for determining the average number of users
per hour or the number of hours per reader by lines on a graph. All reference and
other inquiries are also recorded on the graph by dots. Thus, statistics can be
obtained on readers using the reference department per hour as related to reference
questions per hour.

909.   Linderman, Winifred. "Introduction." In Linderman, W., ed. *The Present
       Status and Future Prospects of Reference/Information Service*. Chicago,
       American Library Association, 1967. pp. vii-x.
Discusses the urgent need for reference service to adapt to change and the demands
for new forms, and greater depths of service. Describes the planning of the conference and reviews briefly the outcome. Goes on to discuss research needs and
outlines the following areas where research should be done: 1) nature of the reference process, 2) ways reference service is performed, 3) need for greater depth
and extension of services, 4) need to take advantage of new technology and new
techniques, 5) users' needs and characteristics, 6) reference role in networks,
7) possibility that the reference intermediary is unnecessary, 8) implications of
change in reference/information services on library education, 9) library schools'
ability to carry on needed research, 10) possibilities of interdisciplinary research.

910.   Lopez, Manual. "Academic Reference Service," *RQ* 12:234-242
       (Spring 1973).
The reference department comes most often under economic attack for several
reasons. Its contribution is difficult to measure in terms of value and cost effectiveness and it is costly to operate because the staff is predominantly professional and
the collection is expensive to maintain. The following traditional methods of
measurement and evaluation are described: books used by reference staff, number
of questions, difficult questions, and counts of users. The literature is reviewed on

various measurement approaches, such as system analysis, measurement/costs techniques and library cost accounting. The author concludes that effective measurement techniques are available and that, if reference departments do not implement them, inadequate or inappropriate performance measurement techniques may be forced on them.

911. Marshall, Henry. "Reference Libraries and Issues Statistics," *Librarian and Book World* 26:126-127 (January 1937).
The author questions the use of issues statistics without some measure of user time spent in the reference department.

912. Morgan, Candace. "The Reference Librarian's Need for Measures of Reference," *RQ* 14:11-12 (Fall 1974).
A national program is needed for the measurement of reference service to determine how well the library's goals are being fulfilled, to pinpoint where improvement is needed, to assist administrators in planning, and to evaluate interlibrary cooperation. Reference librarians must become involved in planning these standards. Objections raised to quantitative measurement are discussed and suggestions are made. New and improved methods of measurement are needed.

913. Papazian, Pierre, "Librarian, Know Thyself," *RQ* 4:7-8 (July 1965).
Discusses the need for analytical study of the reference process. In order to improve service it is necessary to analyze and evaluate reference procedures in general libraries. " . . . we cannot improve what we do not know."

914. Pings, Vern M. "Development of Quantitative Assessment of Medical Libraries," *College and Research Libraries* 29:373-380 (September 1968).
Suggests such reasons for quantitative measurement as improvement of service, management justification, and budget preparation. The methods of assessment developed by the Institute for the Advancement of Medical Communication are used to evaluate ability to deliver materials to supply simple fact answers, to supply interlibrary loan, and to verify and correct citations.

915. Quinn, Karen T. "Capturing Elusive Statistics," *Special Libraries* 63:404-406 (September 1972).
The author describes a technique developed to collect statistics on reference services and library-staff time utilization. This consists of taking continual inventory of activities and recording them on a specially designed service record card.

916. Rather, J. D. "LAD LOMS Statistics for Reference Services Committee" (Conference, 1974, New York), *Library of Congress Information Bulletin* 33:A182-183 (August 16, 1974).
Describes the meeting of the Library Administration Division, Statistics for Reference Services Committee of the American Library Association in July of 1974, concerning measuring reference service. Reviews the highlights of this meeting, the direction of the discussion, and the comments of speakers.

917.   "Reference Standards," *RQ* 1:1-2 (June 1961).
This news note announces the meeting of the newly formed Committee on Standards
of the Reference Services Division of the American Library Association. This Committee has decided to re-examine the nature of reference work to aid in establishing standards. Included here is a preliminary statement of the "nature and scope of
reference service in the United States and Canada."

918.   Rogers, Rutherford D. "Measurement and Evaluation," *Library Trends*
        3:177-187 (October 1954).
Discusses library service statistics in general and their misuse. The necessity of
statistics is emphasized, but they must be re-evaluated since they are so often mis-
used in library reports. The advantages and disadvantages of using statistics for
reference evaluation are considered.

919.   Rose, Priscilla. "Innovation and Evaluation of Libraries and Library
        Services," *Drexel Library Quarterly* 7:28-41 (January 1971).
More research must be done on innovations in library service. Discussed here are
types of approaches to evaluation, including problems, methods, and techniques.
Also included is a case study.

920.   Roth, Elizabeth. "Can You Measure Reference Costs?" *News Notes of*
        California Libraries 49:303-307 (April 1954).
The author suggests that a continuous record of reference service is better than
making spot checks. A continuous record eliminates the factors of differences in
questions and differences in reference ability and recording of questions. Also
with a larger total number, individual questions assume less importance. Methods
of cost determination are discussed and the value of reference, apart from cost,
is emphasized.

921.   Rothstein, Samuel. "The Measurement and Evaluation of Reference
        Service," *Library Trends* 12:456-472 (January 1964).
The literature on measurement and evaluation of reference service in public and
academic libraries is reviewed. Covered are such aspects as enumeration and classification of questions, clientele, reference collection, reference personnel, and
cost factors. Describes new measurement and evaluation concepts such as Louis
Shores' "service units," the reference scale of the ALA Committee on Standards,
and Goldhor's "case studies." Suggested areas for future development of measurement and evaluation techniques are qualifications of reference librarians, organization and performance of reference service, quality of the collection, patron
attitudes, and the value and impact of reference service.

922.   Runyon, Robert. "The Library Administrator's Need for Measures of
        Reference," *RQ* 14:9-11 (Fall 1974).
Problems in library statistics include terminology, validity, timeliness, and completeness. There is an "utter absence of measures of patron use." Reference statistics
should provide the key to understanding patrons' past usage and future requirements.
Data are needed by the department head for scheduling, manning, and performance
overview, but library administrators need data to assess the total outreach and user
communication program.

923.   Shores, Louis. "Measure of Reference," *Southeastern Librarian* 11:297-302 (Winter 1961).
Based on the work of the ALA Committee on Reference Standards and Statistics, it includes an outline of accepted ALA reference standards and a preliminary check-list of reference activities. A common unit of measurement and evaluation should balance the following factors: educational level of patron, type of question, class of library, and predominant character of library patrons. The importance of measurement is stressed and some quantitative studies are reviewed.

924.   Snowball, George. "Information/Library Statistics as a Management Aid: A Graphic Presentation," *Special Libraries* 63:443-447 (October 1972).
The author proposes three solutions to the problem of treating information/library statistical data graphically. One method is based on the concept of index number and the other two are based on component-bar graphs.

925.   Spicer, Caroline T. "Measuring Reference Service: A Look at the Cornell University Libraries Reference Question Recording System," *Bookmark* (New York) 31:79-81 (January 1972).
This system of recording reference questions was begun in 1948, after which it has been further defined and is now in use in all campus libraries on the Ithaca campus. It provides for tallying questions in five categories of descending complexity: 1) information and directional—does not require library resources to answer; 2) reference—requires use or interpretation of library resources to answer; 3) search—more time consumed—complex—15 minutes to one hour; 4) problem—extensive use of resources beyond reference collection—over one hour; 5) bibliography—original work in compiling bibliographies—over one hour. Applications and problems in interpretation are described.

926.   "A Standard Subject Enquiry Form," *Library Association Record* 74:23-24 (February 1972).
Two standard subject enquiry forms are reproduced. Forms cover amount and level of information, language, progress of work on the enquiry, and how and when the answer is to be communicated.

927.   "Standards for Reference Services in Public Libraries: Approved by the Library Association Council on 7 November, 1969," *Library Association Record* 72:53-57 (February 1970).
These standards for reference service in British public libraries cover needs of various sections of the community, available sources of information, present and proposed standards, salary recommendations, encouragement of library use, and wider areas of service. The appendix includes major reference works needed according to the size of the community.

928.   Stevens, Rolland E. "The Reference Survey as an Administrative Tool," *College and Research Libraries* 8:252-258 (July 1947).
This article discusses measurement and evaluation from the viewpoint of its value to library administration. The types of information most helpful in this context would be information on who receives the benefit of reference service, who receives the

most failures, the cause of these failures, time spent on questions, and weaknesses and strengths of the reference collection.

929.   Stone, Elizabeth. "Methods of Evaluating Reference Service," *Library Journal* 67:296-298 (April 1, 1942).

The following ways of evaluating reference service are discussed: 1) classifying questions, 2) time spent per question, 3) detailed analysis of questions, 4) rating qualities or traits desirable in reference librarians, 5) time studies and analysis of different aspects of reference work, 6) survey of user time spent in the library, 7) number of questions asked, 8) unanswered questions, 9) spot surveys.

930.   Taylor, F. R. "Standards for Reference Services in Public Libraries." In Library Association. Reference, Special and Information Section. *Proceedings of the Annual Conference, 1968.* London, The Association, 1968. pp. 37-45, Appendix.

An interim report on work undertaken several years ago by the Reference Libraries Sub-Committee of the Reference Special and Information Section of the Library Association. As a result of this work, it became apparent that a number of already recognized standards could be incorporated—the Bourdillon Report, the IFLA Standards for Public Library Buildings, and the Library Association Standards. Standards are discussed under four areas: 1) needs of various sections of the community, 2) sources of information available, 3) present standards of reference services, 4) proposed standards for reference service.

931.   Vavrek, Bernard. "Ethics for Reference Librarians," *RQ* 12:56-58 (Fall 1972).

The author notes a lack of interest in professional ethics on the part of reference librarians in the areas of 1) socially sensitive questions, and 2) quality of service, the latter being the most important. He describes how lack of attention to professional ethics in these areas can affect reference service.

932.   Vavrek, B. F. "Sacred Cow No. 4: Implications of the New Information Service Guidelines," *American Libraries* 6:294-295 (May 1975).

Presents his personal views in favor of the new guidelines and comments on important aspects of these guidelines. It is essential to change "reference services" to "information services" in order to indicate that any type of information is available. The term "reference librarian" should be changed to "librarian/information specialist" since this is a function of all librarians, though in a multi-departmental library a special staff is maintained.

933.   Walling, Ruth. "Toward Quantitative Reference Standards for the University Library." In Farber, Evan, and Ruth Walling, eds. *Academic Library: Essays in Honor of Guy R. Lyle*, Metuchen, N.J., Scarecrow, 1974. pp. 61-70.

Discussed here are basic objectives of reference service. Reference service is defined as personal service to users in making materials and information available and education in library use. Discusses factors to be considered in setting standards for staff size, responsibilities, staff activities, hours on duty, and size of the reference collection. Recommends a national survey of reference service in all American university libraries, which should be done before standards are established.

934. Weech, Terry L. "Evaluation of Adult Reference Service," *Library Trends* 22:315-335 (January 1974).

Reviews the literature on evaluation and is intended to supplement Rothstein's article. Covers the literature on evaluation from 1963 on and reviews the following areas: 1) recent trends, 2) enumeration and classification of questions, 3) analysis of reference clientele, 4) study of reference collections, 5) personnel and organization, 6) cost analysis, 7) test questions and unobtrusive measurement, 8) reference evaluation survey. Extensive list of references.

Special Studies

Case Studies

935. Champawat, C. S. "Reference Services in Action: A Case Study," *Herald of Library Science* 12:16-21 (January 1973).

This case study highlights problems in reference service concerning lack of adequate tools, and reference librarians who are overburdened with other assignments. The author advocates development of new reference tools cooperatively by researchers and practitioners.

936. Jestes, Edward C., and David Laird. "A Time Study of General Reference Work in a University Library," *Research in Librarianship* 2:9-16 (January 1968).

Records were kept by two reference staff members at the University of California, Davis Library, from September 1966 to April 1967. Non-reference duties such as interlibrary loan, rare book retrieval, and map and microcopy administration took 6.7 percent of their time. Seven thousand one hundred ninety-seven reference contacts were made, of an average duration of 1.98 minutes. Five thousand three hundred sixty-six lasted less than one minute and, in the author's opinion, needed no professional training to handle. Longer contacts averaged 4.8 minutes and 85 percent required professional knowledge. Twenty-one percent of reference desk time was spent in helping users to find answers to questions and, in the author's opinion, only 39 percent required professional training. The author recommends that technical assistants perform sub-professional tasks.

937. Lawson, Abram Venable. "Reference Service in University Libraries: Two Case Studies." Unpublished Ph.D. dissertation, Columbia University, 1970. 343p.

This study attempted to determine the number and type of activities performed by reference staff in two university libraries and to relate these activities to objectives of the service and determine if these objectives had been fulfilled. In the author's opinion, less than half of the work time required professional competence. Direct reference assistance was used primarily by undergraduates, and the author considered this to be largely instructional and directional.

938.   Wilkinson, B. R. "Reference Services for Undergraduate Students: Four
       Case Studies." Ph.D. dissertation, Columbia University, 1971. 520p.

939.   Wilkinson, Billy R. **Reference Services for Undergraduate Students: Four
       Case Studies.** Metuchen, N.J., Scarecrow, 1972. 421p.
In this study the concept of the separate undergraduate library is examined in regard
to the effectiveness of separate undergraduate reference service. The author presents
case studies of reference service at undergraduate libraries at the University of
Michigan, Cornell, Swarthmore, and Earlham College. Also considered are book use,
seating capacity, hours of service, library instruction programs, and communication
with faculty.

940.   Wilkinson, Billy. "Screaming Success as Study Halls," *Library Journal*
       96:1567-1571 (May 1, 1971).
The separate undergraduate library was evaluated in seven areas, one of which was
reference service. Undergraduate libraries were studied at the University of Michigan,
Cornell, Swarthmore, and Earlham College. Communication with faculty and
reference service were better in the smaller liberal arts colleges. Criticisms of service
at Cornell and Michigan were: no attempt to understand what students were trying
to ask, little dialogue, interaction, involvement, or personal instruction. Earlham
College presented an example of superior service and good methods of library
instruction. The author suggests that the separate undergraduate library should
devote more attention to improving service rather than concentrating solely on
building the collection.

941.   Wilkinson, Billy. **The Undergraduate Library's Public Service Record:
       Reference Services.** San Diego, California University Library, 1970.
       31p. ERIC Document ED042473.
The author discusses the quality of reference services in separate undergraduate
libraries, represented by a study of undergraduate libraries at the University of
Michigan and Cornell. Background and statistical information on these libraries
and their reference service hours is included. The number and types of questions
asked are represented in tables. In regard to quality of service, it was found that
little time was being spent with undergraduate patrons. Out of 96 reference questions at Michigan and 230 at Cornell, it was found that in only 19 and 8 cases,
respectively, was more than five minutes spent with the patron. The author, on
the basis of this study, concludes that undergraduate reference services are of low
caliber and reference assistance is superficial and brief.

Circulation Analysis

942.   Goldhor, Herbert. "Learning from Circulation Analysis: Approach to
       Measuring Reference," *RQ* 3:8, 16 (July 1964).
Discusses circulation surveys done on patrons of public libraries in Evansville,
Indiana, and Champaign, Illinois, Patrons were contacted by telephone in regard
to the book they had borrowed and asked how they had located the book, whether
they had read it, and how satisfied they were with it. It was found that 25 percent

of the patrons chose their books on the recommendation of the librarian, about 50 percent by browsing, and the rest by other means. Analysis showed that those who selected books with the librarian's help read their books and "enjoyed" them more than did other patrons. The author suggests a similar technique for evaluation of reference work in which data could be obtained on the patron's characteristics, his question, his satisfaction, and the length of time and cost required to find the answer.

943.　Kingman, Marion C. "Reference Work in a Branch Library," *ALA Bulletin* 32:834-835 (October 15, 1938).

This article summarizes the results of a survey of one week of reference questions at the Dorchester Branch of the Boston Public Library. A system is described for measuring reference work by classifying it by subject and comparing it to non-fiction circulation. Measurement of reference service is a better measure of educational service in the public library than circulation statistics. This study found that most users of this branch reference service were children and that the questions reflected the educational patterns in local schools.

Unobtrusive Observation

944.　Childers, Thomas. "Telephone Information Service in Public Libraries: A Comparison of Performance and the Descriptive Statistics Collected by the State of New Jersey." Unpublished Ph.D. dissertation, Rutgers University, 1970. 148p.

945.　House, D. E. "Reference Efficiency or Reference Deficiency," *Library Association Record* 76:222-223 (November 1974).

Describes the results of a survey done in Brighton, England, where reference students asked the same question, a request for materials on a little-known illustrator, in 20 different libraries. Describes how the efficiency of the service was affected by available resources, arrangements, personal knowledge, and search strategy and method. Comments on the lack of extended searches. Concludes that variations in quality of answers was due mostly to interest and ability of staff and administrative structure of the library. The lack of a methodological search strategy appeared to affect reference service adversely.

946.　" 'Illinois Snoop Group' Plan Raises Accountability Issue," *Library Journal* 98:2812 (October 1973).

This project was developed by the Suburban Library System to sample the quality of reference service at member libraries. Telephone reference questions were to be called in by unidentified "snoopers." Reference staff opposition to this plan led to the decision to carry out the evaluation only by request from a library.

947. King, Geraldine, and Rachel Berry. **Evaluation of the University of Minnesota Libraries Reference Department Telephone Information Service. Pilot Study.** Minneapolis, University of Minnesota, Library School, 1973. 58p. ERIC Document ED077517.

The purpose of this study was to evaluate the telephone reference service of a university library. Questions were called in by volunteers to different divisions to determine 1) factual accuracy, 2) level of interviewing, 3) attitude of staff. Tables show results by division—Reference, Documents, Newspapers, and Periodicals. Trends were that interviewing was not practiced where it would have been helpful, and the source of an answer was seldom given to the caller. Suggestions for further study and included. Appendix material includes the original proposal, record sheet, sample questions, and an instruction sheet for volunteer callers.

948. "Library Reference Service Found Lacking in Test," *Library Journal* 97:3110 (October 1, 1972).

This brief article describes an unobtrusive test of 30 libraries in the Washington, D.C., Maryland, and Virginia areas. A team telephoned in a number of standard reference questions and discovered that, in general, service was better at smaller libraries than in larger, better staffed ones. Conclusions were that standards are needed for telephone questions. It was also felt that unobtrusive testing is a useful method of evaluation.

949. "Maryland Reference Service Evaluated by Phone," *Library Journal* 99:3166 (December 15, 1974).

Brief note which describes an evaluation of reference service carried out at the Baltimore County's Towson branch, led by Thomas Childers of Drexel University. This study found that area reference librarians answered 60 percent to 70 percent of sample questions phoned in. A reporter for the Maryland Library Association Newsletter, *The Crab*, reported that he was satisfied with only three of the eight libraries surveyed, and that responses ranged from "totally wrong, insufficient, or, at best, noncommital, to the thorough and brightly executed."

950. Nelson Associates, Inc. "Test Reference Questions." In *Public Library Systems in the United States: A Survey of Multi-Jurisdictional Systems.* Chicago, American Library Association, 1969. 368p.

In Appendix T of the survey of libraries in the United States, a list of ten questions is given. These questions were used by a survey team who made visits to six systems. Included are answers and instructions to surveyors.

951. Webb, Barbara. "Childers' Roadshow," *The Crab* 4:2 (October 1974).

Describes experiences at a workshop conducted by Thomas Childers and sponsored by the Division of Library Development of the Maryland State Department of Education. Participants phoned in reference questions to local area libraries to learn more about evaluation of reference service from the patron's point of view.

General Surveys of Reference

More Than One Type of Library

952.   Cole, Dorothy. "Analysis of Adult Reference Work in Libraries." Master's thesis, University of Chicago, 1943. 64p.

953.   Garrison, Guy. **A Statewide Reference Network for Wisconsin Libraries. Prepared for the Wisconsin Free Library Commission.** Urbana, University of Illinois, Graduate School of Library Science, Library Research Center, 1964. 111p.

This survey is organized in sections: 1) background and development, 2) needs for library reference service, 3) reference service in public libraries, 4) reference service in academic and special libraries, 5) the regional reference system—Wausau area, 6) resources of the seven proposed reference regions, 7) conclusions and bibliography. Covered in sections 2, 3, and 4 are content and characteristics of reference work, standards, use and non-use of reference service, users, reference statistics, and policy.

954.   Long, Marie. "Total Resources Survey: Wisconsin Reference Network," *RQ* 3:11-14 (July 1964).

Discusses the Wisconsin Regional Reference System and describes the results of a statewide survey of reference services and resources. Considers the distribution of libraries and resources in the state and notes that state aid is essential in the provision of regional reference services. Results of the study indicate little variation in reference policies. Comparison of questions is meaningless since questions are counted in many different ways. Holdings of major reference titles from Barton's *Reference Books: A Brief Guide* varied from 54 of 64 in large libraries to 12 of 64 in smallest libraries. Bibliographical reference titles from the same source varied from 14 out of 48 in the largest libraries to 2 out of 48 in the smallest ones. Concludes with brief discussion of cooperative reference projects in Wisconsin.

955.   Olle, James G. "Reference Library Statistics," *RQ* 3:3-5 (January 1964).

A summary is given of a four-year study made by the Sub-Committee of the Reference, Special and Information Section of the British Library Association. Covered are reasons for keeping reference statistics; how to record them; interesting, unusual, and unanswered questions; counts of readers; usage of the reference area. A literature review is given. Conclusions are: 1) there is a demand for reference statistics in some libraries, but not in all; 2) we seldom know why this demand exists; 3) librarians have not given thought to what kind of reference statistics are needed; 4) those who do know the kinds of statistics they need cannot find satisfactory methods of measurement. Brief bibliography.

956.   Phipps, Michael, Charles Frieden, and Frederick Wezeman. **Reference/ Information Services in Iowa Libraries.** Iowa City, Iowa, University of Iowa, School of Library Science, 1969. 348p.

This book includes a socioeconomic profile of Iowa and chapters on reference service in public, academic, and special libraries. Conclusions and recommendations are given and tables, maps, and bibliography are included.

957.   Preston, Katherine Harris. **Reference Service to Meet the Community Needs, Survey of the Reference Resources and Services of the Metropolitan Cooperative Library System.** Pasadena, Calif., Metropolitan Cooperative Library System, 1970. 95p. ERIC Document ED046463.
Presents the results of a survey of 17 California libraries in the Metropolitan Cooperative Library System. The survey methods are described. Covered in the survey are collections, periodicals, reference questions, and techniques. Conslusions and recommendations are presented. Maps charts, forms, and lists are included as well as lists of periodical indexes checked for holdings.

958.   Shores, Louis. "The Practice of Reference,"*College and Research Libraries* 3:9-17 (December 1941).
Based on the results of a survey of reference service in public and university libraries, which indicated that subject specialization was considered the most important means to the improvement of reference work.

959.   Sypert, Mary. **An Evaluation of the Colorado Statewide Reference Network.** Denver, University of Denver, 1971. 241p.
Presents results of a statewide study for the purpose of determining who uses the service, what type of requests are being made, how effective the service is, and what its costs are. Many other aspects were studied also, and results are reported in detail. Seventeen recommendations are included at the end of the study. Bibliography.

960.   White, Ruth W. "Measuring the Immeasurable: Reference Standards," *RQ* 11:308-310 (Summer 1972).
Describes how the Department of Library Education at the University of Georgia conducted a study of reference service in the Atlanta area for the Reference Standards Committee of the ALA. The Committee helped to obtain information from this overview to aid them in formulating standards. Results are described here. One hundred and eight libraries of various types and sizes were surveyed. In these libraries heads of reference and 358 users were interviewed. Results of these interviews are discussed here, covering age and occupations of patrons, administration of reference, measurement and evaluation of service, collections, and education in library use.

961.   White, Ruth W., ed. **A Study of Reference Services and Reference Users in the Metropolitan Atlanta Area.** Athens, Georgia University, Department of Library Education, 1971. 83p. ERIC Document ED058912.
This project was commissioned by the Reference Standards Committee of the American Library Association to gather information to use in formulating standards for library reference services. The Atlanta area was used because it offered the entire range of type of institutions providing reference service in a sufficiently large number to be significant. The goals of the study were: 1) to identify current measurement and evaluation techniques, 2) to elicit statements on use of reference statistics, 3) to determine the library interest in standards for reference services, 4) to measure user satisfaction. The following recommendations were made: 1) include minimum quantitative measures of service but emphasize qualitative measures; 2) user needs

should be the most important consideration; 3) standards should initiate a self-evaluation; 4) formulate uniform reference standards for all types of libraries. Summaries of replies to interview questions are appended.

Academic Libraries

962.   Balay, Robert, and Christine Andrew. "Use of the Reference Service in a Large Academic Library," *College and Research Libraries* 36:9-26 (January 1975).

A study of the use of reference service at Sterling Memorial Library of Yale University was conducted for four periods of one to three weeks duration during 1970 and 1971. The purpose was to study patterns of reference use. Reference librarians filled out a checksheet after each inquiry, covering day, time, in person or phone, duration, patron affiliation, type of inquiry, and search locations. Findings in regard to each of these items are discussed. Conclusions are presented in regard to staffing, directory information, catalog problems, bibliographic inquiries, library instruction, outside use, methods, and utilization. Suggests the possibility that due to the large number of directional inquiries (40 percent) an information desk manned by paraprofessionals should be considered.

963.   Burns, Robert W., Jr. **A Survey of User Attitudes toward Selected Services Offered by the Colorado State University Libraries.** Fort Collins, Colorado State University, 1973. 83p. ERIC Document ED086261.

A study was conducted by Colorado State University Libraries to discover needs of students and faculty in regard to library service in general, and services of the science reference desk in particular. Results are presented, along with a literature review of use studies, a bibliography, and a copy of the questionnaire.

964.   Clever, Elaine C. **Faculty Use of University Library Reference Facilities for Citation and Data Information.** Philadelphia, Pa., Temple University, 1970. 10p. ERIC Document ED041613.

A study was done to determine the ratio of citation-bound queries to data-bound queries originated by university faculty and processed through reference department personnel or by independent use of reference material in the university library. Seventy-five percent of the queries are citation-bound. This has important implications for reference service to faculty in that skill is especially necessary to use of citation and journal indexes and other sources of bibliographical information.

965.   Guerrier, Edith. "The Measurement of Reference Service," *Library Journal* 61:529-531 (July 1936).

Reference questions asked in nine libraries for one week were studied and four types of most frequent requests were identified. Two aspects of service—the librarian's ability to answer questions and the ability of the user to receive help—were concluded to be not possible to measure. It was stressed that reference service should be evaluated at intervals.

966.   Guinivan, Ora Jane. "An Analysis of the Reference Service of the Kent
        State University Library." Unpublished Master's thesis, Kent State
        University, 1951. 128p.

967.   Hall, John. "Survey of Information Services in British Libraries," *Journal
        of Librarianship* 7:112-131 (April 1975).
Information services were defined as the direct provision of information through
manual current awareness services, computer-based information services, and
reference services. These services were surveyed in 60 British university libraries.
Detailed findings are given for each of the above areas. In the area of reference
service, for example, respondents provided data on types of service offered—quick
reference, literature searches, and guidance—reference policy, and users of their
respective reference services.

968.   Jones, William G. "How Many Reference Librarians Are Enough?" *RQ*
        14:16-18 (Fall 1974).
Results are given for a survey of reference service in the Northeastern University
Science and Technology Libraries. The following information was recorded for
each question: date, time, duration, mode, class of question, and user type.
Statistics were tabulated and analyzed by computer. Faculty members felt that
reference service was seldom used. Results showed that complex questions were
few, especially during evening hours. Ten percent of significant reference questions
came from the business community. On the basis of these results it was decided
not to increase staff and instead to replace some of the reference service with
other forms of service.

969.   Knight, H. M. "Study of the Reference Collection and Service at the
        Brigham Young University as it Fits the Teaching Program." Unpublished
        Master's thesis, George Peabody College for Teachers, 1951. 70p.

Public Libraries

970.   American Library Association. Reference Services Division. Public
        Libraries Reference Survey Committee. **Reference Service in American
        Public Libraries Serving Populations of 10,000 or More**. Urbana, University
        of Illinois, Graduate School of Library Science, 1961. 22p. (University
        of Illinois Library School Occasional Paper, No. 61).
The goal of this landmark study, done in 1956, was to 1) assist in formulation of
standards, 2) lay groundwork for reinterpretation of reference service, 3) bring
about closer integration of reference with other community services, 4) assess
the effect of newer communication media on reference service. Some areas covered
include holdings of reference materials, type of patrons served, and areas of service.

971. American Library Association. "Reference Work: Public Libraries." In *Survey of Libraries of the United States*. Chicago, American Library Association, 1926-27. Vol. II, pp. 78-149.

This survey found that most libraries preferred a moderate philosophy of reference service. Nearly half of the large public libraries preferred to find the information for the patron. All philosophies—conservative, moderate, and liberal—were practiced by some libraries in the survey.

972. Bishop, Edith P. "Reference Questions—How Well Do We Answer Them?" *Library Journal* 85:3159-3161 (September 15, 1960).

This article is based on a survey of reference service done by the Los Angeles Public Library. The purpose of the survey was to improve the effectiveness of reference service by pinpointing weaknesses in service and also by determining which groups of patrons received the least adequate service.

973. Cheney, Frances N. "Public Library Reference Service in Tennessee—Survey Results," *Tennessee Librarian* 9:5-6 (October 1956).

Discusses a survey done in March 1956 in which 24 Tennessee public libraries participated in a national survey of reference service conducted by the Reference Section of the ALA Public Libraries Division. Though tabulation of findings is not complete, preliminary results indicate that nearly all of the libraries offer some type of reference service to a wide variety of patrons. A wide variation is shown in size of reference collection, level of service, and type of personnel providing reference service.

974. Cheney, Frances N. "Whither the General Reference Librarian?" *Southeastern Librarian* 2:25-34 (Spring 1952).

Reports on a study of reference departments in all Southern college and university libraries holding 100,000 or more volumes. Though some divisional reading rooms were developing, in the main, service was still organized around a general reference department and the general reference librarian did not appear to be on the way out. An important concern is that the general reference librarian not become too involved with clerical tasks better performed by others.

975. Clements, D. W. G. "Public Reference Libraries and Their Use." In Library Association. Reference, Special, and Information Section. *Proceedings of the 15th Annual Conference*, 1967. London, The Association, 1967. pp. 30-37.

This survey of the use of 33 public reference libraries is reported in detail. Two-thirds used the library for study. Of those who utilized library materials, the following was found: 1) 62 percent found all they needed, 14 percent found some; 2) 25 percent asked library staff for help; 3) 10 percent used the card catalog, and abstracts and bibliographies were seldom used; 4) 75 percent of telephone questions were satisfactorily answered; 5) 27 percent used periodicals, 39 percent books, 17 percent directories and yearbooks. Only four libraries satisfied all technical and commercial inquiries. Reference inquiries are grouped into broad subjects and analyzed.

976.   Clements, D. W. G. "Use Made of Public Reference Libraries: A Survey of Personal Users and Telephone, Telex, and Postal Inquiries," *Journal of Documentation* 23:131-145 (June 1967).
Given here are results of a survey of 33 public reference libraries in Great Britain done by OSTI in 1966. Includes statistics on reference use, particularly for technical and commercial information, and also on users.

977.   Conat, Mabel L. "Detroit Public Library Surveys Reference Use," *Library Journal* 72:1569-1572 (November 15, 1947).
Described here is a reference survey carried out by the Detroit Public Library for one month, using the spot check method of evaluation. The purpose was to determine weak areas and needs for improvement and to learn more about patron needs.

978.   Crowley, T. "Effectiveness of Information Service in Medium Sized Public Libraries." Unpublished Ph.D. dissertation, Rutgers University, 1968. 75p.

979.   Darsie, Helen H. "Measuring the Results of Reference Service," *ALA Bulletin* 29:604-605 (September 1935).
This article summarizes a paper given at the Denver ALA Conference. A study was done in three public libraries and four types of questions were identified. Less than half the questions were for locating specific information or for advisory service. Most subjects asked for were of descriptive or non-controversial type. Subjects least frequently asked for are listed, along with the thought that these subjects are probably sufficiently covered in newspapers, thus fewer inquiries are made.

980.   DeProspo, Ernest, and others. **Measurement of Effectiveness of Public Library Service Study. A Report on Phases I and II.** New Brunswick, N.J., Rutgers State University, Bureau of Library and Information Science Research, 1971. 70p.
These two phases are concerned with identifying measurement criteria, developing an operational methodology for collecting, processing, and refining data, demonstrating measurement criteria in a theoretical model. The following were studied: collections, building, usage, circulation, facilities usage, patterns of reference usage, and public service personnel.

981.   Goldhor, Herbert. "Reference Service Analysis," *Illinois Libraries* 42:319-322 (May 1960).
Based on a study of reference service in the Evansville, Indiana, Public Library. Measurements discussed include time per question, number and type of sources used, multiple source questions, personal characteristics of reference librarians, and telephone questions. The results are compared with other studies of this type.

982.   Goldman, S. "Analysis of the Reference Resources and Services in the New Haven Metropolitan Area Public Libraries." Unpublished Master's thesis, Southern Connecticut State College, 1964. 160p.

983.   Haygood, W. C. **Who Uses the Public Library?** Chicago, University of
        Chicago Press, 1938. 137p. (Chicago University Studies in Library Science).
"A survey of the patrons of the Circulation Department and the Reference Department of the New York Public Library" conducted in 1938. Questionnaires were
given to 20,000 adult readers in a week-long investigation. Findings indicated that
patrons of reference were somewhat older than patrons of circulation. Eighty percent were men, the largest group being professional workers. Forty-one percent
were engaged in independent study and 39 percent in study connected with daily
work.

984.   Heneghan, M. A. "Survey of the Reference Services of the Public
        Library of the City of Somerville, Massachusetts." Unpublished Master's
        thesis, Catholic University of America, 1955. 77p.

985.   Hunt, M. Louise, and Marie Newberry. "A Day's Work of the Racine,
        Wisconsin Public Library," *Library Journal* 59:106-110 (February 1934).
A study covering both circulation and information service of the main library and
the six city branch libraries on a Thursday in February 1933. On this day, 2.95
percent of the city's population (excluding illiterates and children under five) used
the library. One hundred forty questions were received by the information service,
mostly from junior high students. Sixty-nine percent of the questions were school
related. Sixty-six percent of the questions in areas of social science and government
were from adults.

986.   Mills, F. L. "Library Use by Adults," *Wisconsin Library Bulletin*
        64:46-48 (January 1968).
Presents results of a study done in the Racine Public Library. Reference requests
were analyzed in regard to volume, time taken, and type of patron. Sixty-six percent of questions were by phone. Twenty-two percent of patrons asking questions
were students and 65 percent housewives and secretaries. In regard to time, 76
percent of questions were answered immediately, 17 percent took up to 10 minutes, and 1 percent took 20 minutes or longer. Types of requests most frequently
made were for addresses, biographical, commercial, geographical, political, and
consumer information.

987.   Mills, Forrest L. "Professional Voices of Wisconsin," *Wisconsin Library
        Bulletin* 64:46-48 (January-February 1968).
This article is based on the annual report of the Racine Public Library and notes
trends and directions in reference service. Statistics were collected on who asked
questions, time taken to answer, number and type of requests. Circulation figures
are also given over a period of years.

988.   "Racine Survey Reveals Service Trends," *Library Journal* 92:2988
        (September 15, 1967).
Brief report on a survey done by the Racine Public Library. Discussed are such
aspects as the number of questions, how this compares to previous years, and
average time required to answer a question. Also considered are types of most
frequently asked questions, sources of answers, and types of persons making
most use of reference service.

989. Rozendal, H. "Study of the Reference Service of the Davenport, Iowa Public Library for the Period from 1925-1934." Unpublished Master's thesis, University of Illinois, 1936. 106p.

990. Van Hoesen, F. R. "Analysis of Adult Reference Work in Public Libraries as an Approach to the Contents of a Reference Course." Unpublished Ph.D. dissertation, University of Chicago, 1948. 219p.

991. Vannorsdall, Mildred. "Reference Survey," *Library Journal* 81:25-28 (January 1, 1956).

A survey taken by the Reference Division of the ALA is reported here. The purpose of the survey was to determine the reference needs of public libraries.

992. Vickers, Mary Lynn. **Regional Reference Survey Report.** North Bradford, Conn., Southern Connecticut Library Council, 1973. 41p. ERIC Document ED088457.

Eighteen public libraries in Southern Connecticut were surveyed by the Southern Connecticut Library Council to determine the pattern of reference use to assist in planning improved services and resources. This report includes an outline, introduction, methods, results, conclusions, and recommendations. Figures and tables are included. It was found that students and teachers comprise 50.8 percent of patrons of reference service and that 76 percent of inquiries were made in person and 23 percent by phone. Monday afternoon was the busiest time in the week, and most inquiries were subject or ready reference questions. Most heavily used materials were the card catalog and the non-fiction circulation collection. The majority of inquiries were subject searches and ready reference questions, and the most popular areas were history and biography. Recommendations include a back-up reference service for busy hours, and compensation for libraries serving a large proportion of nonusers.

School and Special Libraries

993. Carpenter, Helen S. "What Is Back of Efficient Reference Work in an Elementary School Library?" *Wilson Library Bulletin* 10:15-19 (September 1935).

Based on results of a project done with 20 elementary schools in New York City. Analyzes types of reference questions and knowledge needed by librarians and students to obtain answers. Describes most-used sources and stresses the need for a wide variety of reference sources, well-organized libraries, and trained personnel.

994. Colainni, Lois Ann, and Robert F. Lewis. "Reference Services in U.S. Medical School Libraries," *Bulletin of the Medical Library Association* 57:222-274 (July 1969).

This article reports on a survey of 85 medical school libraries concerning reference services. Statistics are given on staff, gradings, hours of service, and preparation of bibliographies.

995. Delius, B. J. "Survey Study of the Catholic Information Center with Particular Emphasis on the Reference Function of the Library," Unpublished Master's thesis, Catholic University of America, 1950. 90p.

996. "LC Reference User Survey Completed," *Library of Congress Information Bulletin* 33:305-306 (June 21, 1974).
Reports on the results of a study of written inquiries sent to the Bibliography and Reference Correspondence Section. This division receives some 1,600 to 1,900 inquiries per month. Describes the policy of answering Congressional and government inquiries first, and declining those that can be answered satisfactorily at another library.

997. Smith, J. M. B. **A Study of Reference Service at the Wayne State University Medical Library, January-June, 1964.** Detroit, Mich., Wayne State University, School of Medicine Library and Biomedical Information Service Center, 1965. 7p. (Report No. 5).
Analyzes 1,600 reference questions at the Medical Library of Wayne State University over a six-month period. Forty percent were for holdings information, 25 percent were for specific information. Findings indicated that requests for specific information required more reference staff time than did requests for holdings information.

998. Stewart, A. W. "Analysis of the Processing of Reference and Information Inquiries by the Legislative Reference Service." Unpublished Master's thesis, University of North Carolina, 1960. 99p.

999. Stookey, M. M. "Study of High School Reference Work." Unpublished Master's thesis, Drexel Institute of Technology, 1950. 39p.

Studies on Various Aspects of Reference Service (Administration, Personal Relationships, Values, Special Services)

1000. Baldwin, Emma, and W. E. Marcus. **Library Costs and Budgets: A Study of Cost Accounting in Public Libraries.** New York, Bowker, 1941. 201p.
Gives statistics on the cost in direct labor of answering a reference question (pp. 130-144). Also gives average time for answering a reference question as 5.4 minutes (p. 144).

1001. Bunge, Charles. **Professional Education and Reference Efficiency.** Springfield, Illinois State Library, 1967. 101p.
Nine matched pairs, each consisting of one professional and one non-professional reference librarian, were selected from 12 medium-sized public libraries, both partners of a pair being from the same library. Pairs were matched as closely as possible in background and experience. Each member of the pair was given a number of factual questions to answer, and search strategy, time taken, and accuracy of answer was studied. Results showed that professionals generally located information faster, but that accuracy did not differ. The parts of the

reference process are discussed, including the following: 1) understanding the question, 2) analysis and formulation of search strategy, 3) translation into sources, 4) strategic decisions, 5) evaluating information. Thirty-two references.

1002.   Critchfield, S. "Information Wanted! Dead or Alive?" *Synergy* No. 41: 10-13 (Summer 1973).
A study was done by the Bay Area Social Responsibilities Roundtable to deter-mine the adequacy of the library as a community information center. Ten San Francisco libraries were surveyed and 14 questions were asked, all of which required referral to some outside agency. The investigation found that only about 50 percent of the questions were given satisfactory referrals. The authors suggest that libraries must improve their knowledge of local agencies and groups if they wish to maintain and operate effective referral services.

1003.   De Hart, Florence."The Application of Special Library Services and Tech-niques to the College Library," *College and Research Libraries* 27:130-133, 152 (March 1966).
A study was done in which advanced services common to special libraries were made available to faculty teaching undergraduate English courses in five colleges. The services included 1) full answers to reference questions rather than guidance, 2) preparation of bibliographies on request, 3) current awareness notification, 4) recommendation of books for purchase. Also tested in a second phase were aid by librarians in compiling course reading lists and provision of a list of useful periodicals for students. Qualitative measurement was done of the use made of certain materials by those faculty receiving special services and those not receiving them. No quantifiable differences were found. Questionnaires were sent to faculty regarding their attitudes toward these services. Reasons why they failed to use these services are discussed.

1004.   Glover, J. "Reference Departments in Large Public Libraries," *Library Journal* 80:50-54 (January 1, 1955).
A survey of the 48 states was made to determine how many public libraries had separate reference departments staffed by one or more full-time reference librarians. Results showed that comparatively few such departments existed at this time, and there were no indications that the number of such departments might be increasing.

1005.   Halldorsson, Egill. "A Study of the Reference Interview and Referral Process." Unpublished Research Paper, Kent State University, 1974. 112p.

1006.   Kramer, Joseph. "How to Survive in Industry: Cost Justifying Library Services," *Special Libraries* 62:487-489 (November 1971).
The Boeing Aerospace Company's Aerospace Group Library evaluated their activities in regard to: 1) literature searches and 2) reference/publication identifying activities. It was estimated that for every hour the librarian spent literature searching, 8.9 man-hours of more highly paid engineering staff were saved. Whereas library staff averaged 12 minutes to answer a reference question or identify a publication, an engineer would have taken 5.42 hours.

1007.   Lopez, Manuel,and Richard Rubacher. "Interpersonal Psychology:
        Librarians and Patrons," *Catholic Library World* 40:483-487 (April 1969).
Reported here are results of a study done to measure the effectiveness of six librarians
in interpersonal relations. Considered were such features as genuineness, empathy,
respect, expression, and the patron's perception. Implications of this study for
reference librarians and reference service are given.

1008.   Murfin, Marjorie E. "A Study of the Reference Process in a University
        Library." Unpublished Master's thesis, Kent State University, 1970. 221p.
This study was designed to determine how satisfactorily requests for information
were answered, in the opinion of both patron and librarian, and to determine the
frequency of poorly phrased and distorted questions. It was found that patron satisfaction was 64 percent and librarian satisfaction was 62 percent. It was also found
that poorly phrased or distorted questions occurred 25 percent of the time. In
addition, descriptive data were obtained on unanswered questions, subject matter
of questions, difficulty level of questions, and graduate and undergraduate requests.
Descriptive data were also obtained on the patrons' class and major and the number
and type of inquiries.

1009.   Murphy, Marcy. **A Regional Survey Helps to Solve the Problem of Identify-
        ing and Comparing Library Service to Users**. Paper presented at the Special
        Library Association Annual Conference, Toronto, Canada, 1974. 38p.
        ERIC Document ED098967.
Describes a survey of reference work by the United States Air Force Academy
Library. Some data come from an earlier user survey. For an in-house survey,
reference staff listed all tasks performed and interviews gave estimates of time
spent on each task on an annual basis. In the external survey, the reference task
list was sent, along with a questionnaire, to the public service head at eight college
libraries in Colorado. Results indicated that the USAFA Library was rich in public
service resources and its higher costs were due to its function as a special library.
Survey results have been used in one- and five-year plans to streamline public
service in that library.

1010.   Nelson, J. A. "Communication Between Reference Librarians and the
        Faculty in Selected California State Colleges." Unpublished Ph.D.
        dissertation, University of California, Berkeley, 1971. 253p.
This survey attempted to determine how well aware faculty were of eleven services
offered by college library reference departments. It was found that, on the average,
faculty were aware of only half of these services. The science faculty was less aware
than those in other disciplines. Factors affecting awareness were rank, library
committee membership, and order of faculty-librarian communication. The author
recommends that reference librarians should have time and opportunity for increased
faculty contact.

1011.   Nelson, J. A. "Faculty Awareness and Attitudes toward Academic Library
        Reference Services: A Measure of Communication," *College and Research
        Libraries* 34:268-275 (September 1973).
A survey of six college faculties was done to determine the level of awareness of
available reference services. The average faculty member was aware of only half

of the services offered by the reference department. Social scientists showed less awareness of services and were more critical of librarian performance than were humanities faculty. It could not be determined whether this was because social scientists had greater needs or because librarian performance was actually less adequate in the social sciences.

1012.   Poundstone, Sally H. "What Records Do You Keep on Reference Work?"
        Library Journal 82:2750-2753 (November 1, 1957).
The Louisville Free Public Library sent questionnaires to various libraries to determine which types of records were kept on reference work. Results are given and prevailing patterns of service are considered. The problem of which types of questions to include is discussed.

1013.   Reed, Sarah Rebecca. "1946-1956 Public Library Reference Services,"
        Library Journal 82:131-137 (January 15, 1957).
This article is based on the results of an ALA survey of public library reference departments in 25 selected libraries. Trends are noted toward increasing subject departmentalization, telephone service, use of audiovisual media, and group work. Reference problems have also increased. The increasing use of a reference coordinator to link the subject departments is also noted.

1014.   Rubenstein, A. H., and others. "Search Versus Experiment: The Role of
        the Research Librarian," *College and Research Libraries* 34:280-286
        (July 1973).
Describes the results of a study of the information-seeking habits of medical doctors in the Chicago area. Both clinicians and researchers are included and their reactions are studied to the introduction of special medical reference service, based at the John Crerar Library. In the course of the study, one doctor replicated an experiment because of reluctance to search the literature. A medical librarian located the same information by verbal contacts in one-half hour while the replication took four hours. The results of the study indicated that in regard to information seeking, most doctors used reference service less than once a month, even though they might use the library frequently. The librarian was not regarded as a valuable colleague. After the new information service was inaugurated, about 40 percent used it, mostly for requests for specific literature.

1015.   Smith, Dorman H. "A Matter of Confidence," *Library Journal* 97:1239-
        1240 (April 1, 1972).
The author reports on a study in which the same indirect and poorly formulated question was asked of 20 librarians in the Boston area. Many librarians responded with a lack of concern and made little attempt to determine the patron's real needs or to develop his confidence in himself or in them. The author emphasizes the importance of showing respect to the patron and discusses the interpersonal atmosphere of the reference interview and the development of confidence.

1016.   Smith, Dorothy J. "The College Reference Librarian and the Faculty,"
        Library Journal 92:1588-1589 (April 15, 1967).
Describes the results of an informal survey made of college reference librarians to
learn their attitudes toward their work and to discover their conception of their
own role. Attitudes toward work and relationships with the college community
were found to be unsettled. The author considers 1) the workload and responsibilities of reference librarians in direct reference service, 2) role of reference librarians
as educators, 3) attitudes of users toward the reference library.

1017.   Swope, Mary Jane, and Jeffrey Katzer. "Silent Majority: Why Don't They
        Ask Questions?" *RQ* 12:161-166 (Fall 1973).
This article is based on the results of a survey taken in 1972 at Syracuse University's
Carnegie Library to determine why some users do not seek help from the library
staff. Results showed that reasons for not seeking help were that they were not
satisfied with help received in a previous encounter, they feel their question is
too simple, or they do not wish to bother the librarian. In order to encourage
patrons who need help to seek it, the reference librarian should be trained in
communication skills, interview techniques and public relations. A user-centered
point of view should be developed.

1018.   "Ten Year Report of the New York Public Library, 1946-1956. Part II,
        Reference Department," *New York Public Library Bulletin* 61:425-449
        (September 1957).
Discusses collection building and gives statistics on reference service. Statistics are
included on readers, materials consulted, telephone and mail inquiries, library use,
and growth and development of the reference collection.

CHAPTER 12

COOPERATIVE REFERENCE SERVICE

See also: Chapter 2, Theory and Philosophy
Chapter 6, Reference Service in Types of Libraries
Chapter 7, Special Types of Reference Service
Chapter 11, Research in Reference (Measurement and Evaluation)
Chapter 13, Information Centers and Services
Chapter 14, Information Retrieval

Included here are works pertaining to reference networks and systems. Research studies of reference networks and systems are included in the section on Measurement and Evaluation, in Chapter 11.

For bibliographical coverage of this area see the works listed at the beginning of this section. Also see Mary Sypert, *Evaluation of the Colorado Statewide Reference Network* (University of Denver, 1971), *Conference on Interlibrary Communications and Information Networks* (Chicago, American Library Association, 1971), and Carl Orgren, "Library Schools and the Network," *RQ* 11:347-351 (Summer 1972).

BIBLIOGRAPHIES

1019.   Huston, Dorothy. "Reference Systems—A Review of the Literature," *Wisconsin Library Bulletin* 57:138-144, 157, 170 (May-June 1961).
The major part of this article consists of a bibliography of materials on reference systems. The possibilities of reference systems in Wisconsin are also discussed.

1020.   Schwartz, Julia. "A Bibliography of Cooperative Reference Service for the U.S. and Canada," *RQ* 6:73-81 (Winter 1966).
A selected bibliography designed to fill an immediate need for information on reference networks. Arranged with categories for general works, works concerning particular states, and works concerning Canada. Entries are annotated.

DIRECTORIES

1021.   Bailey, George M., comp. **Directory of Cooperative Reference Service Programs: A Preliminary Edition**. Chicago, American Library Association, Cooperative Reference Services Committee, 1972. 126p. ERIC Document ED067141.
Arranged by state, this directory lists cooperative library services. Information provided for each program includes name, date established, administrator, participants,

type of agreement, sources, and amount of support, services provided, publications, and where to direct inquiries.

GENERAL WORKS

1022. Aines, Andrew. "The Promise of National Information Systems," *Library Trends* 16:410-418 (January 1968).
It is likely that in the future several national information systems for science and technology will be developed and there will be extensive intercommunication between the systems. Such systems will come about because of the capacity of the computer to store, retrieve, and transmit information, the information explosion, and increased scientific specialization. The "global village" concept of the future will require extensive international and national communication. Projects such as EDUNET linking American universities are being planned. Libraries will play an important role in a possible national information system of the future.

1023. Bunge, Charles A. "Reference Services in the Information Network." In Becker, Joseph, ed. Conference on Interlibrary Communications and Information Networks, Airlie House, Virginia, 1970. *Proceedings*. Chicago, American Library Association, 1971. pp. 109-116.
Reference service is considered in the context of the information network. The following phases of the reference process are discussed: question clarification, question translation, search strategy, search execution, and relevance evaluation. These phases are considered in relation to network development. Problems and solutions are examined and needed research in information and its use is suggested. Information retrieval can support and improve the performance of reference librarians.

1024. Clark, Collin. "Four-Alarm Reference Services," *Library Journal* 93:1594-1595 (April 15, 1968).
Patrons expect that even smaller libraries should have available the materials they need or should be able to obtain them from other libraries. It is now necessary to provide reference service in the same way. Questions could be taken at branches and bookmobiles and transmitted upward when necessary to such sources as universities, special collections, and even specialists. Photocopies and other mechanized equipment could play a role in this service, but computers are not necessary. If it is to be successful, large and small libraries must want to cooperate with each other.

1025. Coenenberg, Richard. "Synergizing Reference Service in the San Francisco Bay Region," *ALA Bulletin* 62:1379-1384 (December 1968).
The Bay Area Reference Center (BARC) is an experimental back-up service serving 17 member libraries in a six-county area. Teletype, facsimile transmission, nationwide TWX, and photocopying equipment are utilized. Seventy to eighty percent of the inquiries are answered within 24 hours. Programs include reference workshops, preparation of bibliographies, exchanges of personnel, and library visits. The Center budget allows for purchase of new and additional reference material for the San Francisco main library.

1026.   Conference on Interlibrary Communications and Information Networks, 1970, Airlie House, Virginia. *Proceedings*. Edited by J. Becker. Chicago, American Library Association, 1971. 347p.

Papers of the Conference are presented based on the Conference theme of networks. These papers explore the implications of establishing a network of libraries and information centers in the United States. The network concept would make possible the goals of 1) removal of geographical barriers to information, 2) equal access for all to the sum total of the nation's knowledge, 3) redirection of the goals of librarianship and information science.

1027.   Connor, Jean L., Warren Boes, and James W. Henderson. "Planning for Cooperative Reference and Research Library Service in New York State," *NYLA Bulletin* 11:5-9 (January 1963).

Emphasizes the need for statewide cooperative reference and research systems. Describes other projects in operation and considers different types of plans. Proposes a pattern of cooperative reference service.

1028.   Connor, J. L. "The Systems Approach to Reference Service." In Texas Library Association. *Reference, Research and Regionalism. Selected Papers from the 53rd Conference, Austin, Texas, 1966*. Austin, Texas, The Association, 1966. pp. 6-12.

Offers a system plan for the improvement of reference service, utilizing experience gained in New York State. Ten guidelines are 1) sound system based in law, 2) competent staff, 3) well-developed central library resources, 4) both state funds and local effort, 5) all types of libraries participating, 6) flexibility, 7) bold planning, 8) strong state library, 9) use of new technology, 10) evaluation.

1029.   Cory, John M. "The Network in a Major Metropolitan Center," *Library Quarterly* 39:90-98 (January 1969).

Describes the New York Metropolitan Reference and Research Agency (METRO), which includes public, university, college and special libraries in the area. The purpose and organization of METRO are described. Services discussed include a Central Advisory and Referral Center (CARES), interlibrary systems design, a Cooperative Acquisitions and Storage Center (CASC), cooperative technical services, related personnel administration activities, in-service training, recruiting and consulting services.

1030.   Costello, Charlyn M. "Reference Contact's Contact," *Illinois Libraries* 55:254-256 (April 1973).

Describes the Illinois North Suburban System (NSLS) reference back-up system. Office space is rented at the Chicago Public Library for three reference librarians. Difficult questions from member libraries are referred to them and questions are researched, using the facilities of the Chicago Public Library. The number of questions has steadily increased.

1031.   Critchfield, S. "Barcs and Bites," *Synergy* 33:11-16 (Summer 1971).
The Bay Area Reference Center (Barc) is described and problems are discussed that
center around the San Francisco Public Library and the system it serves. Problem
areas include conflict of interest between groups of librarians, morale problems,
and lack of communication. The problem of dealing with reference questions by
phone is discussed and suggestions are given. The author sees a necessity for more
communication and cooperation among librarians to give the system maximum
effectiveness.

1032.   "Denver Inaugurates Metropolitan Reference Service Program," *Library
        Journal* 85:3950 (November 1, 1960).
Describes the establishment of a four-county cooperative reference service centered
in the Denver Public Library.

1033.   Duggar, Maryann. "Reference Services Institute," *Arkansas Libraries*
        4:28-29 (Spring 1968).
Concerned here is sharing of resources, equipment, and personnel, with facilities for
communication and delivery. The goal should be to provide free access for users with
total library service for all.

1034.   Gaver, Mary Virginia. "The New Jersey Plan," *ALA Bulletin* 60:1138-1142
        (December 1966).
The New Jersey state plan has as its goals, setting up standards for school, college and
public libraries, and establishing a network of 22 area reference libraries and four
major research libraries. The network of four research libraries has not yet been
completely implemented. Reference service has shown substantial improvement as
a result of the plan. Other projects under this plan have been a survey of medical
literature resources, more depositories for state documents established, library
services for the blind, and a general survey of subject collections. It is estimated
that eight million dollars per year is needed to implement this plan.

1035.   Greenwald, Evelyn. "Southern California Answering Net-Work," *News
        Notes of California Libraries* 65:539-542 (Summer 1970).
Describes the Southern California Answering Net-Work (SCAN) providing reference
referral services to back up local libraries. A special staff of subject specialists use
the resources of the Los Angeles Central Library to answer questions, and two
cooperative library systems are linked by teletype to these specialists.

1036.   Haas, Warren J. "Statewide and Regional Reference Service," *Library
        Trends* 12:405-412 (January 1964).
Considers distinctive features of library networks and discusses different types of
services offered. Some services provide specialized in-depth service in a particular
subject area while others offer comprehensive service over a wide area of subjects.
Lists centers that take part in the Pennsylvania plan for state reference service and
other state and regional systems. Future needs are cost analysis and studies directed
toward increased efficiency.

1037.   Hayes, P. F. "Reference Service: People Plus Resources," *Texas Libraries*
        30:10-13 (Spring 1968).
This article is concerned with quality reference service in relation to the state of
Texas. There is need to interface the many separate systems, networks, and data
banks in the state by relating local centers to regional and national systems.
Problems in accomplishing this relate to structure, functions, and attitudes.

1038.   Josey, E. J. "Systems Development for Reference and Research Library
        Service in New York State: The 3 R's," *BCL Quarterly* 31:3-21 (April
        1968).
The development and background of the 3 R's program are described here. The
program includes 1) reader access to libraries over a wide area, 2) inclusion of
college, university, industrial, and private libraries, 3) development of communication and transport facilities, 4) development of subject specialization, 5) making
available holdings information. Nine systems have been formed, governed by
boards of trustees. In 1968-1969 each system received $35,000. State level proj-
ects include facsimile (FACTS), and an interlibrary loan (NYSILL). A Bureau of
Academic and Research Libraries has been set up to provide consultative service.

1039.   King, Jane. "Information Service Network," *APLA Bulletin* 34:62-67
        (September 1970).
Proposed here is an information network that would make available to users a
librarian who specializes in the user's area of interest. This would utilize special
skills of reference librarians more effectively and provide a more uniform quality
of service throughout the county.

1040.   Klimberger, Joseph. "Cooperative Reference Service," *Library Journal*
        85:1525-1527 (April 15, 1960).
This article reports on the Nassau Library System, Hampstead, New York. The
development of the system is described, along with a description of its cooperative
projects.

1041.   Kochen, Manfred. "Switching Centres for Inquiry Referral." In Becker,
        Joseph, ed. *Proceedings of the Conference on Interlibrary Communications
        and Information Networks*. Chicago, American Library Association, 1971.
        pp. 132-139.
Discusses referential consulting networks where consultants answer questions
through their own expertise, available library resources, and referral to colleagues.
Considers the operational program BUCKPASS, which enables study of turn-around
time and quality of response for such networks.

1042.   Laich, Katherine. "Regional Reference Library Services: An Outline of
        Cooperative Services, Existing or Proposed," *News Notes of California
        Libraries* 56:254-265 (Spring 1961).
Begins with definition and scope, followed by a listing and detailed description of
state plans for Pennsylvania, Maryland, New York State, and Massachusetts.
Metropolitan area plans are described for Toronto, Westchester County, New York,
Denver, San Joaquin Valley (California), North Bay (California), Baltimore County,

and Los Angeles County. City plans are described for New York City, Chicago, Philadelphia, and Los Angeles. Concludes that the common elements in these plans are: 1) cooperative effort and planning; 2) almost all state plans provide local, area, and statewide services; 3) most state or metropolitan plans have been aided by federal funds.

1043.   "Library Cooperation for Reference and Research," *ALA Bulletin* 60:1133-1155 (December 1966).
A series of articles on statewide library services for reference and research. Robert Vosper comments on problems at the state level and the need for increased leadership. E. B. Nyquist discusses the "Three R's in New York." Mary Virginia Gaver describes the New Jersey Plan, James Hunt writes on the "System in Hawaii," and Kenneth Beasley considers "Social and Political Factors."

1044.   Lorenz, John G. "Regional and State Systems." In Linderman, W., ed. *The Present Status and Future Prospects of Reference/Information Service*. Chicago, American Library Association, 1967. pp. 73-82.
Discusses public library regional reference systems and, in particular, considers the following area systems: 1) San Joaquin Valley Information Service; 2) Wausau, Wisconsin Regional Reference System; 3) North Bay Cooperative Library System; 4) Indiana Communication System; 5) Rocky Mountain Bibliographical Center for Research; 6) Connecticut; 7) South Carolina Reference Project. Discusses the New York State Reference and Research Libraries project. Characteristics of successful systems include: 1) coordination of regional and statewide aspects, 2) reciprocal loan, 3) enriched resources, 4) reference centers in large public and academic libraries, 5) quick communication facilities. Most important services are union lists of serials, special collections, finding lists, other union lists, reciprocal stack privileges, bibliographic lists, literature searches, coordinated acquisition, in-service training, and continuing research.

1045.   Markoe, Bonny. "The Cooperative Information Network: A Report," *California Librarian* 35:16-21 (July 1974).
The Cooperative Information Network (CIN) has as its purpose to serve the informational needs of individuals, government units, and businesses in Santa Clara County, California. Three more libraries have recently joined the CIN, and this system could eventually become part of a state network. Libraries are linked by TWX machines and all members agree to respond as quickly as possible to inquiries. Projects include a membership directory listing special resources, workshops, and an intern program for interchange of personnel.

1046.   Mohrhardt, Foster. "The Library Kaleidoscope: National Plans and Planning." In Linderman, W., ed. *The Present Status and Future Prospects of Reference/Information Service*. Chicago, American Library Association, 1967. pp. 87-92.
Reviews the historical background of cooperation on a national level in the United States and mentions accomplishments such as the *National Union Catalog, Union List of Serials*, regional depositories, etc. Due to increased publication, complexity of languages, multiplicity of originating bodies, interdisciplinary needs, and cost

increases, we must have cooperation on a national level. We can simply wait for such a system to come, encourage non-librarians to develop such systems, or work in cooperation with them. The author advocates the third alternative and describes the efforts of COSATI in the "Information transfer chain." Discusses medicine as an example of a developing national system and gives six important features of such a system. Discusses technology that will eventually be used to support such a system and describes the computer as an aid to the reference librarian rather than a replacement.

1047. "National Institute of Information Proposed by Information Industry Association," *Information: News and Sources* 6:225 (October 1974).
Describes a proposal for a National Institute for Information submitted to Congressman William Moorhead by Paul Zurkowski, President of the Information Industry Association. The text of the proposal is given. This institute should be non-governmental, non-subject dominated, and independent of special interest domination.

1048. Norman, R. V. "Mountain-Plains Library Association Information Networks," *Nebraska Library Association Quarterly* 5:6-9 (Fall 1974).
Briefly describes make-up and organization of eight reference networks in the Mountain-Plains areas—Colorado State Wide Reference Network, Kansas Information Circuit, Nebraska Library Telecommunication Network, Nevada Communication Network, North Dakota Network for Knowledge, South Dakota Information Network, Utah Information Network, and the Wyoming Information Network.

1049. Nyren, Karl. "A Reference Roundup," *Library Journal* 92:1582-1585 (April 15, 1967).
A review of reference library activities in the United States. Needs defined are needs for communication, development of cooperative systems, improved financial support, research, and more application of automation. Describes teletype and telefacsimile equipment, and creation of "libraries of last resort." Discusses progress made in cooperative service and federal funds for personnel. Research is briefly surveyed. Financial support is discussed and related to the National Advisory Commission. The role of computers in large systems is also discussed.

1050. Orgren, Carl. "Library Schools and the Network," *RQ* 11:347-351 (Summer 1972).
Describes the University of Iowa School of Library Science reference service by teletype to state, public, and college libraries, manned by students in advanced reference courses. The author begins by reviewing development of interlibrary cooperation and reference service and then describes how the State Traveling Library obtained funds for the teletype to be placed in the School. Students ask for assistance from library science faculty when necessary, and all answers are checked by the course instructor. Library staff do not participate since there are no funds to compensate them for demands on their time.

1051. "Reference Contract Option Chosen by New York Libraries," *Library Journal* 98:1756-1757 (June 1, 1973).
A small library in New York, the Orangetown Public Library, chose to contract for reference services with the library in a neighboring town rather than that in its own

immediate area. The factors behind this decision are examined and services provided by the referral contract are described.

1052.   Reilley, A. "Cooperative Reference Service: A Case Study of the San Joaquin Valley System," *RQ* 6:66-73 (Winter 1966).
Describes the background of this project, along with its goals and objectives. Discusses problems encountered in the development of the project.

1053.   **Specifications of a Mechanized Center for Information Services for a Public Library Reference Center. Final Report in 5 Parts.** Los Angeles, California University, Institute of Library Research, 1968. ERIC Documents ED031276, ED031277, ED031278, ED031279, ED031280.
Part 1 is by Kevin Reilly, "Preliminary Specification: Mechanized Information Service in Public Library Reference Centers"; Part 2, by Kevin Reilly, is "A State Library-Network for Technical Information Service to California Business and Industry"; Part 3, by Nancy Brault, is "Statistics on the Libraries in the State of California"; Part 4, by D. W. Heron, is "The State Library and Public Libraries of California as Centers for Information Services under the State Technical Services Act"; Part 5, by Kevin Reilly, is "Outline for a Simulation of the California State Library Network."

1054.   Spicer, Michael. **A Comparative Analysis of Five Regional Reference and Information Networks.** Columbus, Ohio, The State Library of Ohio, 1972. 36p. ERIC Document ED071667.
The following five regional reference and information networks in Ohio are studied: CAIN, MILO, SWORL, WELD, and AIRS. Compared in the report are services to the patron, time taken to provide services, and cost. Included also are maps, forms, and tables.

1055.   Stanford, Edward B. "MINITEX-Progress Report Covering the Period, January 1-December 31, 1969," *Minnesota Libraries* 22:350-352 (Winter 1969).
Describes the Minnesota Interlibrary Teletype Experiment which, during 1969, handled 84 reference questions of different levels of complexity.

1056.   Stephen, Lorna R. "County Reference Services," *Library World* 71:108-112 (October 1969).
A reference service for Shropshire County in England is described. The union catalogue is held in a Remington Rand Lectriever. Headquarters and six of eight area libraries communicate by telex to answer reference questions. Delivers are made daily to each branch and staff participate in a training program. More publicity is needed to increase reference use by industry.

1057.   Stevenson, Grace T. **A Proposed Plan for Reference Services for San Diego and Imperial Counties.** San Diego, Calif., San Diego Public Library, Serra Regional Library System, 1969. 54p. ERIC Document ED069304.
This study was done to assist in planning improved reference service in San Diego and Imperial Counties. The following recommendations were made: 1) libraries should work more closely with community organizations; 2) objectives and priorities

should be set up; 3) coordination of collection building should be a priority of the Serra Reference Center; 4) cooperation with the Associated Science Library of San Diego should be explored; 5) development of a public information program; 6) use of the latest communications technology; 7) in-service training for non-professionals and continuing education for professionals; 8) develop projects to further objectives of the system; and 9) factors important to establishing area libraries.

1058.　Sypert, Mary. **An Evaluation of the Colorado Statewide Reference Network.**
　　　　Denver, Colo., University of Denver, 1971. 225p. ERIC Document ED05888.
Presents the result of a statewide study for the purpose of determining who uses the service, what types of requests are being made, how effective the service is, and what its costs are. Many other aspects were studied also, and results are reported in detail. Seventeen recommendations are included at the end of the study. Bibliography.

1059.　Toepel, M. G. "Regional Reference Systems: Can We Get There from
　　　　Here?" *Library Journal* 86:1542-1545 (April 15, 1961).
Discusses the expansion of reference services into a statewide network. Considers this in relation to help of governmental agencies and their services.

1060.　Wallis, C. Lamar. "Tennessee Reference Centers," *Southeastern Librarian*
　　　　16:226-230 (Winter 1966).
In 1964, $100,000 was made available by LSCA to establish reference centers in the public libraries of Nashville, Knoxville, Chattanooga, and Memphis. Telephone calls would come in from libraries and business and others and all inquiries would be answered. Interlibrary loan services are described. One hundred seventy-eight questions were received the first year, but 206 have been received during the last three months. A total of 777 requests have been handled. Types of questions are described.

1061.　Wynn, Barbara L. "Information Unlimited: The Story of the San Joaquin
　　　　Valley Information Service . . . A Successful Reference Demonstration," *News
　　　　Notes from California Libraries* 58:315-334 (Summer 1963).
Report of a program begun in 1959 where a group of librarians in this area asked the State Library to establish a demonstration of improved reference service, covering six counties. This cooperative system would serve to meet needs for additional materials and services.

1062.　Wysocki, A., and J. Tocatlian. "A World Science Information System:
　　　　Necessary and Feasible," *Unesco Bulletin for Libraries* 25:62-66
　　　　(March-April 1971).
Describes a four-year joint UNESCO-ICSU feasibility study for the establishment of a World Science Information System (UNISIST). A conference aimed at putting the system into operation will be held in Paris in 1971. Recommendations of the feasibility study are described. Two basic functions of UNISIST are: 1) to stimulate international cooperation between existing information systems, 2) to initiate new projects to improve world information tools and resources. The long-range goal is development of information networks in all subject areas.

CHAPTER 13

INFORMATION CENTERS AND SERVICES

See also: Chapter 2, Theory and Philosophy
Chapter 6, Reference Service in Types of Libraries
Chapter 7, Special Types of Reference Service
Chapter 9, The Reference Process (Users)
Chapter 11, Research in Reference (Measurement and Evaluation)
Chapter 12, Cooperative Reference Service
Chapter 14, Information Retrieval

Included in this section are works on different types of information centers in different types of libraries. Mechanized information centers are included under type of library.

Bibliographical coverage is supplied in H. M. Weisman, *Information Systems, Services and Centers* (New York, Wiley, 1972); Rowena Swanson, *Move the Information* (Arlington, Va., Office of Aerospace Research, 1967); *Bibliography of Research Related to Communication of Scientific and Technical Information* (Rutgers University, 1967); Walter Veazie, *The Marketing of Information Analysis Center Products and Services* (Washington, D.C., Eric Clearinghouse for Library and Information Sciences, 1971).

For bibliographical coverage of information centers in public libraries, see Joseph Donohue, "Planning for a Community Information Center," *Library Journal* 97:3284-3288 (October 15, 1972); Carolyn Forsman, "Resource Guide," *RQ* 12:350-354 (Summer 1973); Carol Kronus and L. Crowe, *Library and Neighborhood Information Centers* (University of Illinois, 1972).

GENERAL WORKS

1063.   Foskett, D. J. **Information Service in Libraries.** London, Crosby Lockwood and Son, 1958. 142p. 2nd ed., 1967. 153p.
Discussed here is the library's role in collecting, presenting, and disseminating information. The development of information services in libraries is reviewed in historical perspective and related to scientific and industrial factors and growth of publication. The most important roles of the library in regard to information are: 1) to organize literature to emphasize its subject value, and 2) to inform users regularly of newly published works in their subject areas. The information officer should have a role in selection and acquisition, arrangement and indexing, dissemination of information and reference service. The educational role involves provision of specialized material for those pursuing courses of instruction. Qualifications and training of information peronnel are considered.

1064.   Hess, Edward. "On-Line Information Retrieval for the Masses?" Paper
         Presented at the American Society for Information Science Mid-Year
         Conference, Johnstown, Pa., May 16-18, 1974. 5p. ERIC Document
         ED092168.
Discusses a coordinated information source of the future based on widespread
development of the interactive communication capability of cable television. Problems of developing such a system include: 1) organizing a vast miscellany of material,
2) determining response forms for various inquiries, 3) developing input documents
for information not published in the usual way.

1065.   Line, M. B. "47th Aslib Annual Conference: Summing Up: The
         Information Service in Practice," *Aslib Proceedings* 26:47-53 (January
         1974).
Important points noted by the author in regard to information services are: 1) the
personal and informal nature of information transfer, 2) integration of information
services in the community, 3) need to reassess the boundaries of library work,
4) need to determine factors in information transfer, 5) utilization of information,
6) image of information services, 7) visibility of information services, 8) balance
between national, group, and individual services, 9) implications of the changing
library world on education, professional education in particular, and professional
organizations, 10) exploration of services to the unserved, 11) packaging and processing of information, 12) the role of Aslib.

1066.   "Mechanized Information Services." In Hayes, Robert M. and Joseph
         Becker. *Handbook of Data Processing for Libraries*. New York, Becker
         and Hayes, 1970. pp. 685-743.
Information retrieval, information analysis, information publication, announcement,
and distribution are discussed. Library information centers are considered in regard
to problems, financial management, selection of data bases, cataloging of data bases
and software for information retrieval systems. Different types of information
centers and addresses are listed.

1067.   Rees, Alan. "Librarians and Information Centers," *College and Research
         Libraries* 25:200-204 (May 1964).
Considers the relationship between librarianship and information retrieval. The
information center represents a serious challenge to librarianship because the
library's functions have failed to keep pace with needs. The increasing acceptance
of information centers indicates that information services far beyond the traditional
concepts of reference are required. The information center differs from the library
in the following ways: 1) degree of delegation on the part of the information
requestor, 2) exercise of judgment functions on the merit of documents, 3) provision
of information and not documents, 4) processing of search out into a variety of
products—state-of-the-art, compacted data, digests, etc. We must change our objective and become concerned with the total information problems.

1068.   Swanson, Rowena W. **Move the Information—A Kind of Missionary Spirit.**
        Arlington, Va., Office of Aerospace Research, 1967. 192p.
Trends in processing information are discussed here and are related to opportunities
for various types of libraries. Appendices contain a summary of activities toward
interagency coordination. Bibliography included.

1069.   Weisman, H. M. **Information Systems, Services and Centers.** New York,
        Wiley, 1972. 265p.
Discusses information needs and uses, definition and scope of information systems
and services, the scientific information system, system design considerations, input,
indexing, information services, management of information services/centers and the
information analysis center.

ACADEMIC AND SPECIAL LIBRARIES

1070.   Adediran, F. "Design and Operation of Reference Systems in Libraries and
        Information Centres: A Comparison," *Nigerian Libraries* 9:51-55 (April-
        August 1973).
The terms "system" and "reference system" are defined and described. The design
of reference systems in libraries and information centers is compared and differences
and similarities noted. The differences between these two types of systems are grad-
ually disappearing, and the author expresses the hope that this will be the trend in
Nigerian academic libraries.

1071.   "Automated Literature Searches Offered at Low Cost," *Library Journal*
        96:2250 (July 1971).
Described here is a plan whereby 33 university libraries offer low-cost automated
searches to students. An arrangement has been made with the North Carolina Science
and Technical Research Center. Access is provided to some 700,000 documents
through the National Aeronautics and Space Administration, the Department of
Defense, the Institute of Textile Technology, and the Educational Resources
Information Center.

1072.   "Computer Reference Service Rated Success at MIT," *Library Journal*
        99:3168 (December 15, 1974).
Describes the MIT service, which includes 15 data bases with eight more soon to be
added and which is funded by the National Science Foundation. There are about 12
patrons per week. The service is not self-supporting and probably never will be.
Charges are based on connect-time, and a surcharge is also made. Resistance to the
concept of paying for library services is waning as users realize the time savings.

1073.   DeBoer, A. H. "Modular Programs for Reference Retrieval from
        Bibliographic Data Bases in a University Research Library." Unpublished
        Master's thesis, University of California at Los Angeles, 1970.

1074.   Hall, J. "Information Services in University Libraries," *Aslib Proceedings* 24:293-302 (May 1972).
This article reviews information services, especially in science and technology, in British universities. Suggests that various services be coordinated on a higher level to avoid duplication. Subject specialists should be hired for bibliographical and current awareness service to faculty. Discusses problems in establishing information services.

1075.   Hall, J. "Survey of Information Services in British Libraries," *Journal of Librarianship* 7:112-131 (April 1975).
Report of a survey undertaken to provide background information for a SCONUL Exchange of Experience Seminar.

1076.   Hayes, R. M. **Mechanized Information Services in the University Library. Introduction and Summary: Planning. Part 1**. Berkeley, University of California, Institute of Library Research, 1967. 25p. ERIC Document ED023412.
Gives an overview and projection of the role that mechanization will play in the university library and the pace at which it will develop in the next 10 to 15 years. Considers issues and policies.

1077.   Hock, Randolph. "Providing Access to Externally Available Bibliographic Data Bases in an Academic Library," *College and Research Libraries* 36:208-215 (May 1975).
Discusses the experiences of the University of Pennsylvania Libraries in providing access to computerized data bases. Describes the approach, questions, and problems encountered, and factors in their resolution. The role of the data base services librarian is discussed, along with costs, philosophies of approach, and the integration of computerized data base services into the reference department.

1078.   Humphrey, Allan J. **Survey of Selected Installations Actively Searching the ERIC Magnetic Tape Data Base in Batch Mode. Final Report**. Berkeley, University of California, Institute of Library Research, 1973. 2v.
Findings of a survey of 29 selected information centers searching ERIC in the batch mode. A table of selected data for all 29 centers is included. Also included in the second volume are printed materials from these centers.

1079.   Institute of Petroleum. **Information and Its Dissemination**. London, England, Institute of Petroleum, 1961. 109p.
Consists of chapters by different individuals covering planning and operating an information service, technical information retrieval, presentation of technical information, internal communications and employee information, and informing the public.

1080.   Jackson, E. B. "Toward Information Centers," *Special Libraries* 62:238-240 (May-June 1971).
Creative librarianship must form a bridge between existing and future information systems. Process involved in this range from utilization of existing systems to

creation of new systems. The new information outlook is discussed, and it is suggested that libraries must change both their physical arrangement and the attitudes of their personnel to become more approachable and reduce barriers between people and information. The future of computerized information services is discussed.

1081.   Jones, E. H. E. "Planning an Information Service." In Wells, M. J., ed. *Information and its Dissemination. Report of the Summer Meeting of the Institute of Petroleum, June, 1961.* London, Institute of Petroleum, 1961. pp. 1-20.
In order to provide an effective information service, cooperation between producers, information specialists, and users is essential. Subjects considered are terminology, user interface, coordination of services, staffing, classification, access to sources, use, equipment, interval records and reports, statistics, and costs.

1082.   Kent, Allen, and John Canter. **Specialized Information Centers.** Washington, D.C., Spartan Books, 1965. 296p.
A questionnaire was sent to 500 specialized information centers in North America. Information centers were defined as "any library or collection of documents which serves more than one or a few people." Case studies, taken from the returned questionnaires, make up the great part of this book.

1083.   Kirkland, Jean. "Reference Service and the Computer: An Experiment at the Georgia Tech Library," *RQ* 14:211-224 (Spring 1975).
Describes how computerized reference service is provided at Georgia Institute of Technology. Reference librarians utilize the computerized services of the Georgia Information Dissemination Center.

1084.   Line, Maurice B. "Information Services in University Libraries," *Journal of Librarianship* 1:211-224 (October 1969).
Developments in reader services, library instruction, and subject specialization are not sufficient to meet the need for information in university libraries. More new and personalized information services should be developed because of the limitations in research use of libraries, user preference for informal communication, increasing time pressure on professors, problems in information retrieval. A special information officer should be created, with functions different from those of the librarian. Costs for information services are heavy, but they can be developed if staff and funds are reallocated for this purpose.

1085.   Marron, Beatrice, and others. **A Study of Six University-Based Information Systems.** Washington, D.C., U.S. National Bureau of Standards, Center for Computer Sciences and Technology, 1973. 96p. ERIC Document ED077527.
Six university-based NSF-supported systems were studied. These centers all operate retail information centers primarily serving campus communities by accessing large commercially available data bases. The systems vary in design, philosophy, mode of user service, transferability characteristics, and operational status. A summary matrix is included.

1086.   **Mechanized Information Services in the University Library. Final Report in 13 Parts.** Springfield, Va., Clearinghouse for Federal Scientific and Technical Information, 1967– .
A study of mechanized information services carried out by the Institute of Library Research at the University of California. Covered are such aspects as discussion of symposia, inventory of available bases, standards of cataloging magnetic tape, nature of typical data bases, evaluation of general file management systems, Marc tapes, and experimental mathematics data bases.

1087.   Morgan, John M. "Information Retrieval Systems for Reference Librarians," *RQ* 9:259-260 (Spring 1970).
A computerized information system for philosophy, called Philosopher's Information Retrieval System (PIRS) is described here. This data base is a product of the computer-produced index published by the Philosophy Documentation Center at Bowling Green State University, titled *The Philosopher's Index: An International Index to Philosophical Periodicals*. This system produces bibliographies and abstracts on subjects in philosophy.

1088.   Rogers, Frank B. "Computerized Bibliographic Retrieval Services," *Library Trends* 23:73-88 (July 1974).
Reviews the history, development, evaluation, and problems of computerized bibliographical retrieval services for biomedical information. The National Library of Medicine and MEDLARS are used as examples.

1089.   Smith, Gerry. "Library-Based Information Services in Higher Education: Towards a Reappraisal," *Aslib Proceedings* 27:239-246 (June 1975).
The author asserts that some British academic libraries are offering information services which are misconceived and/or inappropriate. The author examines reference services and gives reasons against the preparation of bibliographies on demand. He also considers instruction in library use, suggests how this should be done, and comments on library publications. He describes his own experiences with current awareness services, notes that they are an expensive luxury, and suggests alternative approaches. Concludes with a discussion of organization and priorities in information service. Information services should be realistic and "spoonfeeding" of any group avoided.

1090.   Tompkins, Mary L. **Mechanized Information Services in the University Library. Summary of Symposia on Mechanized Information Services in the University Library. Phase I. Planning. Part 2.** 1967. 91p. ERIC Document ED023413.
Summary of the Symposium on Mechanized Information Services in the University Library. Reports on a group of symposia conducted to discuss issues. Specific issues discussed were: 1) viability of information systems, 2) whether a university should provide its own service or use others elsewhere, 3) what types of data bases are needed by faculty and students, 4) whether data bases should be lodged in libraries or computer centers, 5) technical problems.

PUBLIC LIBRARIES

1091.   Asser, Mike. "Information and Advisory Services: The Leicestershire
         Experience," *New Library World* 75:114, 117 (June 1974).
Patterns of cooperation between advisory services, such as the Citizen's Advice
Bureau and the public library, are discussed. The author notes that information
and advisory services can no longer exist in isolation. He concludes that the
library is the best place to locate the information center and gives reasons for
this. The experience of the Leicestershire County Library is discussed. Eventually,
it is anticipated that each of the larger towns in Leicestershire will have one
library/information/advice center to serve all a person's information and advice
needs. Such a complex is already planned for Eastwood in Nottinghamshire.

1092.   Becker, Carol A. **Community Information Service: A Directory of Public
         Library Involvement. Student Contribution Series No. 5.** College Park,
         Md., Maryland University, School of Library and Information Services,
         1974. 92p. ERIC Document ED100325.
An introduction describes the history, concepts, and characteristics of community
information centers. Public libraries with community information centers are
listed by state. Also includes a bibliography on information centers. Appendix
includes a questionnaire, letters, and promotional materials used by public
libraries.

1093.   Berry, John. "A Tip from Detroit," *Library Journal* 100:1287-1290
         (July 1975).
Describes the Conference on Information and Referral Services in Public Libraries
held May 7, 8, 9, 1975, at the Detroit Public Library, sponsored by Neighborhood
Information Centers Project (NIC). Discusses the NIC beginnings, the TIP program
in Detroit (The Information Place), its philosophy, community needs, its beginnings,
outreach, and staff training. Its status is considered along with disappointments,
some unanswered questions and its future prospects.

1094.   "CUIC (Citizen's Urban Information Center) Terminated," *Bookmark*
         34:83 (January 1975).
Gives a brief review of the history of the CUIC and quotes the statement issued by
Kenneth Duchac, Director of the Brooklyn Public Library, when the project was
terminated in January 1975 due to lack of funds. He expresses disappointment and
mentions the need for such centers and the strong public support. The library will
attempt to continue what service they can with their own limited funds.

1095.   Castagna, Edwin. "Pratt's Switching Yard," *Library Journal* 95:2742
         (September 1, 1970).
Described here is a project called the "Public Information Center." This test project
was designed to meet the needs of several dozen Baltimore area health and welfare
agencies. Information files are being organized which can later be adapted to the
computer. The possibility of charging fees is being considered.

1096. Clements, C. Justin, and Sandra L. Kyle. "Can Anybody Out There Help Me?" A Look at I and R Services and Their Relationship to Local Libraries," *RQ* 15:19-24 (Fall 1975).

Describes the functions of non-library information and referral centers and presents some typical questions received. Attributes of such a center are: 1) knowledge of community resources, 2) skill in making referrals, 3) professionalism, 4) accessibility, 5) follow-up and evaluation, 6) pre-service and in-service training, 7) outreach, 8) publicity, 9) free services. Describes problems encountered in each of these areas. Need for such centers is growing due to multiplicity and complexity of helping agencies, and to a desire for speed and efficiency. Discusses ways in which the public library may help and benefits to be derived from joint library I and R efforts.

1097. Croneberger, Robert, and Carolyn Luck. "Defining Information and Referral Services," *Library Journal* 100:1984-1987 (November 1, 1975).

The authors note that "information and referral . . . is the effective communication of information to help people solve problems." The process of linking patrons with information includes locating information in a form useful to the patron and following up to see that the link is made. The information librarian does not provide counseling, but instead a linking function. The librarian's role between patron and agency is one of interpreter rather than antagonist or public defender. The library's function is to help agencies improve services rather than to take a derogatory attitude toward them.

1098. Croneberger, Robert B. "Public Library = Library for the People," *RQ* 12:344-345 (Summer 1973).

Public libraries should establish information and referral centers. Such centers must have effective structural organization, file organization, and referral techniques. The author defines and discusses each of these aspects. Service should be the most important function of the library if it is to be a significant part of today's society.

1099. Donohue, Joseph C. "Planning for a Community Information Center," *Library Journal* 97:3284-3288 (October 15, 1972).

The Enoch Pratt Free Library's new Public Information Center is described in terms of scope, orientation and planning, technical resources, related educational efforts, structure, operation, and implementation. The author also presents his personal concerns and evaluations of the project. Photographs and bibliography.

1100. Donohue, Joseph C. "Some Experiments Fail: The Public Information Center Project at the Enoch Pratt Free Library," *Library Journal* 100:1185-1190 (June 15, 1975).

The author describes the background and formation of the PIC at the Enoch Pratt Free Library and gives the rationale behind its plan. He compares it with the British Citizen's Advisory Bureau. Reasons for the failure of PIC are given as: 1) failure to appoint a full-time professional librarian as head, 2) not providing telephone or branch service, 3) not enough two-way communication with all levels of library staff, 4) failure to publicize.

1101.   Forsman, Carolyn. "Resource Guide," *RQ* 12:350-354 (Summer 1973).
An annotated bibliographic guide to books and other materials on innovative and
non-conventional services. Covers neighborhood information centers, new roles for
the library, "how-to-do-it," NIC projects in public libraries, bibliographies, and
"keeping-up."

1102.   Glaiber, M. "Citizen's Information and Service Program," *RQ* 12:359-360
         (Summer 1973).
Describes the Citizen's Information and Service Program in Dade County, Florida.
Services include social workers for crisis cases, transportation, a suicide hotline,
and cooperation with the local Division of Family Services. One hundred fifty
thousand telephone calls were received in one and one-half years of operation.
Staff training is described. Some accomplishments and activities growing out of
this service have been clearing of vacant lots, restraint of free-running animals,
voter registration drives, and development of bilingual staff to assist community
agencies.

1103.   Glaser, J. "National Standards for Information and Referral," *RQ*
         12:354-356 (Summer 1973).
Describes the development and formulation of information and referral standards
to be presented to the United Way. Discusses purposes of these standards and types
of situations to which they apply. Copies of these standards may be obtained from
the United Way.

1104.   Gonzalez, Mary. "The Community Information Center Project," *RQ*
         12:360-361 (Summer 1973).
Describes a project of the Kansas State Library to establish Community Information
Centers in libraries across the state. The first six months of the project have been
devoted to research and recommendations, including the following objectives:
1) providing information from a single source, 2) coordinating services, 3) collecting
and disseminating information in the CIC Resources Files, 4) training workers,
5) organizing a publicity campaign. Two demonstration pilot projects are planned
in low-income areas.

1105.   Howard, Edward N., ed. "Community Information and the Public
         Library," *RQ* 15:5-7 (Fall 1975).
The author, guest editor for this issue of *RQ* dealing with community information
centers, discusses the central ideas of the six articles in this issue.

1106.   Hug, W. E., ed. **Strategies for Change in Information Programs**. New York,
         Bowker, 1974. 373p.
A group of 24 essays by different contributors. "The opportunity and need exist
in practically every community for a library-media-information program to develop,
coordinate, and articulate the separate information programs—public libraries,
special libraries, schools, organizations, agencies, TV and radio programs. The public
must have access to a program that can quickly assimilate, synthesize, and disperse
information. . . . To realize this goal, changes must be brought about in order for
the library-media-information professions to increase their responding capacities."

Two sections cover "The Subtle and Ubiquitous Nature of Change," and "Alternative Strategies or Ways to Aim at a Moving Target."

1107.   Hughes, Jack. "News and Other Four-Letter Words: Community Information and the Public Library," *RQ* 15:29-31 (Fall 1975).
Defines and discusses the concept of "news" and considers the improvements in library services over the years. Stresses the need for increased hours of service.

1108.   Kennedy, John, and Lynd Mac Gillivary. "Information London," *Canadian Library Journal* 28:432-437 (November-December 1971).
This Center served as a guide to London's agencies, government, social services, and community organizations. It received inquiries which ranged from questions concerning simple facts to those concerning serious personal problems. The first half-year of operation is described, including information collection and updating and publicity. Unfilled areas where community services are needed are discussed. A list of basic reference sources used is included.

1109.   Kronus, Carol, and L. Crowe. **Libraries and Neighborhood Information Centers**. Urbana, University of Illinois, Graduate School of Library Science, 1972. 142p.
The authors suggest that neighborhood information service demands new ways of thinking on the part of librarians. It is difficult to get people in inner cities together with the information they need. A survey in three cities showed that "of 5,000 possible sources of information named by all respondents across problem areas, the library was mentioned once." This system proposes, instead of a traditional reference library, that a national network of units be established, staffed by non-professionals.

1110.   Lacey, S. A. "Queens Borough Public Library's Neighborhood Information Centers," *Bookmark* 34:7-11 (September 1974).
Describes the Neighborhood Information Centers Project (NIC), a five-system consortium with Queens and Detroit joined by Atlanta, Cleveland, and Houston. Considers objectives, staffing, and citizen involvement, inventory of existing neighborhood resources, and implementation.

1111.   "Libraries as Information Centers: Diverse Programs Reported," *Library Journal* 99:3093-3094 (December 1, 1974).
Describes various information center projects, such as that at the Martin Luther King Library in Washington, D.C., the New Orleans Public Library, the Tucson Public Library, the Dallas Public Library, the St. Louis Public Library, the East Central Regional Library in Minnesota, and the Sioux City, Iowa, Public Library.

1112.   Long, Nicholas. "Wisconsin Information Service: An I and R Network," *RQ* 12:356-359 (Summer 1973).
This article reports on the goals, funding, and structure of the Wisconsin Information Service. The program's immediate, intermediate, and long-range goals are discussed at length. Definitions of terms used in the program are also given. This program is administered by the Division on Aging, Wisconsin Department of Health and Social Services.

1113.   Lyman, Helen H. "The Library—A Community Intelligence Center," *Wisconsin Library Bulletin* 57:132-135 (May-June 1961).
Describes the increased need for information and observes that many information seekers do not find the material they need. The answer lies in the community information center, which should have the following characteristics: 1) fit community needs and interests; 2) know the interests, needs, problems, and beliefs; 3) work with institutions and other sources of information; 4) keep up with new developments; 5) select materials to meet needs; 6) be open sufficient, convenient hours; 7) maintain a suitable reference collection; 8) give fast and efficient service; 9) maintain a staff able to locate information and assist and guide readers.

1114.   McReynolds, F. "Reference and Adult Services Division (Conference, 1974, New York)," *Library of Congress Information Bulletin* 33:A 154-156 (August 2, 1974).
Reports on the Reference and Adult Services Meeting at the 93rd Annual Conference of the American Library Association in 1974. Given here are details of the program concerning Community Information Centers. Highlights of programs and progress in this area are presented.

1115.   Mier, Guadalupe. "Houston Coalition of Information and Referral Agencies," *RQ* 12:349-350 (Summer 1973).
Describes the formation of the Coalition of Information and Referral Agencies in which some 35 agencies are represented. Purposes are to develop communication, to coordinate services, to sponsor programs to improve information and referral services, and to work toward filling gaps in community services.

1116.   "Neighborhood Information Centers: Some Answers, New Questions," *Library Journal* 98:3596 (December 15, 1973).
Findings of the report for the first year of the five-city Neighborhood Information Centers Project are summarized by Dorothy Turick. Main points are 1) privacy for clients is important, 2) too much distance between bureaucratic structure and on-line staff, 3) better staff orientation is needed, 4) professional librarians should be included in NIC operation, 5) central libraries should be involved, 6) the library must reshape its organizational and operational patterns. San Diego County is planning to begin such service in its branches. There is need for the experience learned through this project to be disseminated through the professions.

1117.   Ostrom, Kriss. "Public Libraries and Community I and R Agencies: Partners in the Same Business?"*RQ* 15:25-28 (Fall 1975).
The author reports on an investigation of the information and referral network in her own community. Reference librarians in the local public libraries were not familiar with local sources of information nor were they encouraged to be by the library administration. There were 150 agencies in the community which tended to compete for funds and this discouraged cooperation on a central level. Those staffing the centers had little or no interest in the library and did not conceive of it as a partner in handling information referral.

1118.   Schrag, Dale, and Calvin Boyer. "Nonconventional Information Sources
         and Services in the Library: Our Credo," *RQ* 15:8-12 (Fall 1975).
There are countless "new" non-conventional information sources and services which
could greatly enhance the library's worth. Discusses the need for proactive rather
than retroactive information service. Proactive information service seeks to carry
information to the client in anticipation of his needs. Describes some examples of
innovative services and suggests a realignment of priorities so services such as these
can be provided. In proactive information and referral services the librarian must
seek out the information specialists, with perhaps one-third of the librarian's time
being spent outside the library. As a result of these contacts, specialists will begin
directing people to the library and it can become an information clearinghouse for
the community.

1119.   Slanker, Barbara. "Research Needed for a Public Library's Community
         Information Center," *RQ* 15:32-36 (Fall 1975).
Discusses the aspects of community information centers where research is particularly needed. Feasibility studies are needed which relate goals to costs of the
service and available resources. Data need to be collected on the implications of
various roles of such centers. Research is needed in identifying target populations,
inventory of community resources, and in defining information needs. After an
information center is operational, research needs to be conducted to measure its
effectiveness. An integrated research program, incorporating the above elements,
will make the center more responsive to users' needs and improve its quality.

1120.   "Summing Up after Three Years: The Success of Information Referral
         Services in the Five-City Neighborhood Information Centers Project,"
         American Libraries 6:412-413 (July-August 1975).
Describes the Conference on Information and Referral Services in Public Libraries
in Detroit and the TIP program of the Detroit Public Library, which receives some
100,000 questions per year. Gives a typical interview and describes problems such
as staff resistance to "social work," jealousy of other agencies, poor service by
social agencies, etc. Discusses future of the information center concept.

1121.   Turick, Dorothy, ed. "Neighborhood Information Center," *RQ*
         12:341-363 (Summer 1973).
Collected here are 14 essays providing an overview of current developments in
neighborhood information centers, written by project directors, librarians, and
information specialists from all over the United States. The purpose of this
compilation is to review existing services, and their staffing, financial support
and administrative problems, and also to emphasize the need for continuing
research in this area.

1122.   Turick, Dorothy. "Neighborhood Information Centers Project," *RQ*
         12:342-343 (Summer 1973).
Given here is a brief factual description of the development of this national project,
including financial and administrative history. The author is national project officer
for the Neighborhood Information Centers Project at the Cleveland Public Library.

1123. Waters, Richard L. "Community Information Service: Should We? (Yes). How? (Carefully!)," *Texas Library Journal* 51:13-16 (Spring 1975).
Highlights a variety of programs, projects, and services which any or all libraries can implement. Includes an annotated list of nine innovative library-community information services and seven non-library information services. Presents 14 conclusions about how to proceed in developing a community information service. Concludes with a discussion of limitations and gives suggestions as to where the line should be drawn in regard to services provided.

1124. Yin, Robert, and others. **Neighborhood Information and Referral Services in the Urban Library**. Washington, D.C., Rand Corporation, 1974. 62p. ERIC Document ED101735.
Five information and referral centers were examined in this study, four of which were in public libraries. Seven functions were studied, including needs assessment, development of a referral directory, staffing, publicity, accessibility, record keeping, follow-up, and cooperative relationships. Also discussed are state and federal roles in development of such centers.

INFORMATION ANALYSIS CENTERS

1125. Garvin, David. "The Information Analysis Center and the Library," *Special Libraries* 62:17-23 (January 1971).
The function of information analysis centers, under the National Standard Reference Data System of the National Bureau of Standards, is to collect, compile, and evaluate data in a particular field on a regular basis. Research scientists direct these centers and produce and send out bibliographies, tables, and reviews. These same functions can and should be performed by special libraries by collecting their own publications and disseminating them and, if necessary, referring users to appropriate centers.

1126. Sternberg, Virginia A. "Use of Federally Supported Information Analysis Centers by Special Libraries in Large Companies." Ph.D. dissertation, University of Pittsburgh, 1971. 499p.
Results of a survey done to determine the use of federally supported information analysis centers. A questionnaire was sent to around 500 special libraries concerning use and nonuse of the centers and for purposes of evaluation. Conclusions are that the centers are not being used effectively and are not well advertised. Recommendations are given.

1127. Veazie, Walter H., and Thomas F. Connolly. **The Marketing of Information Analysis Center Products and Services**. Washington, D.C., ERIC Clearinghouse and Library and Information Sciences, 1971. 28p. ERIC Document ED050772.
Presented here is the basic philosophy of the information analysis center. Guidelines for marketing products and services are given and service charges are considered. Appendices include a case study of service charges by an information analysis center and another case study of the methods of cost-recovery of a government-sponsored information analysis center. Bibliography.

CHAPTER 14

INFORMATION RETRIEVAL

This section lists works on information retrieval relating most closely to the library setting and to reference work in particular. The listings in this section are highly selective, since materials concerning information retrieval would require a separate comprehensive bibliography.

For comprehensive bibliographical coverage, see the bibliographies and bibliographical sources listed at the beginning of the section Information Science and Information Retrieval. Also see Gertrude Schulze, *Information and Library Science Source Book* (Metuchen, N.J., Scarecrow, 1972); Lynne Tinker, *Annotated Bibliography of Library Automation 1968-1972* (London, Aslib, 1973); and Ronald Havelock, *Bibliography on Knowledge Utilization and Dissemination* (Ann Arbor, University of Michigan, Institute for Social Research, 1972).

For bibliographical coverage of information retrieval and reference service see M. Lorraine Mathies, *Computer-Based Reference Service* (Chicago, American Library Association, 1973). For bibliographical coverage of information retrieval management, see H. B. Landau, "Can the Librarian Become a Data Base Manager?" *Special Libraries* 63:121-124 (March 1971). Coverage of information retrieval and users is provided in Edwin Parker and William Paisley, "Research for Psychologists at the Interface of the Scientist and His Information System," in Tefko Saracevic, ed., *Introduction to Information Science* (New York, Bowker, 1970) and *Annual Review of Information Science and Technology* (1966– ; annual).

Bibliographical coverage of evaluation of information retrieval is provided in B. I. Krevitt and B. C. Griffith, "Evaluation of Information Systems: A Bibliography, 1967-1972," *Information: Part 2,* 2:1-34 (1973); Tefko Saracevic, "The Concept of Relevance in Information Science: An Historical Review," in Tefko Saracevic, ed., *Introduction to Information Science* (New York, Bowker, 1970); and Rudolph Penner, "The Practice of Charging Users for Information Services: A State of the Art Report," *Journal of the American Society for Information Science* 21:67-69 (January-February 1970).

INFORMATION SCIENCE AND INFORMATION RETRIEVAL

Bibliographies

1128. **Annual Review of Information Science and Technology.** Edited by Carlos Cuadra. New York, Interscience, 1966– . Annual.
Covers current developments in information science and technology. Intended to have both current awareness value and reference value. Arranged in areas of planning information systems and services, basic techniques and tools, applications, and the profession. Individual articles on particular topics in these areas give overviews of background and current developments, literature reviews, and extensive bibliographies.

1129. **Bibliography of Research Relating to the Communication of Scientific and Technical Information.** New Brunswick, N.J., Rutgers University, Graduate School of Library Service, Bureau of Information Sciences Research, 1967. 732p.
A bibliography covering 1) information sciences, services, and systems, 2) systems, 3) generation, 4) acquisition, 5) processing, 6) storage, 7) retrieval, 8) use, 9) support. Most sections are divided into a number of sub-sections. Includes 3,698 citations, most of which are annotated. Author and detailed subject index included.

1130. Billingsley, Alice. "Bibliography of Library Automation," *American Libraries* 3:289-312 (March 1972).
Serves to update the following bibliographies: Louis McCune, and Stephen Salmon, "Bibliography of Library Automation," *ALA Bulletin* (June 1967), and Charlene Mason, "Bibliography of Library Automation," *ALA Bulletin* (September 1969). Covers journal articles, books, trade publications, and technical reports. Arranged by subject areas.

1131. Spangler, Marshall. **General Bibliography on Information Storage and Retrieval.** Schenectady, General Electric Computer Department, Technical Information Series, 1962. 390p.
Provides a "comprehensive list of contemporary documentation on information storage and retrieval." Included also are mechanical translation, linguistics, speech analysis and synthesis, artificial intelligence, character and pattern recognition, and self-organizing systems. Arranged alphabetically by author, Includes a KWIC index.

General Works

1132. Artandi, Susan. **An Introduction to Computers in Information Science.** 2nd ed. Metuchen, N.J., Scarecrow, 1972. 190p.
Attempts to provide an introduction to the field, with particular emphasis on document organization. Divided into three parts: 1) an overview of information science and technology, 2) theoretical aspects of document retrieval, 3) basic characteristics of equipment involved in application. Oriented toward general problems rather than particular systems. Discusses current thinking and cites relevant research.

1133.　Becker, Joseph. **First Book of Information Science.** Oak Ridge, Tenn., U.S. Atomic Energy Commission, Office of Information Services, 1973. 86p. ERIC Document ED092136.

Provides basic background for information retrieval. Summarizes history of information from early man to the present technologies. Considers the increasing importance of information as a commodity. Discusses the technology behind computerized information retrieval.

1134.　Doudnikoff, Basil. **Information Retrieval.** Philadelphia, Auerbach Publishing Co., 1973. 113p.

Emphasizes hardware and systems utilized in information retrieval and the functions they can perform. Manual, semi-manual, computer, and electronic systems are discussed, and the pros and cons of each system are considered. Photographs of equipment are included. The possibilities of computer-produced microfilm and data bases on magnetic tape are stressed, and *Chemical Abstracts*, *U.S. Government Research and Development Reports* and *Compendex* are discussed. Case studies are given of how different retrieval systems can be used to meet specific library needs.

1135.　Elias, Arthur. **Key Papers in Information Science.** Philadelphia, Pa., American Society for Information Science, 1971. 223p.

Included here are 19 articles from various sources on information science. Organized in four general categories. The first section, "Background and Philosophy," discusses the relationship of information science and librarianship. The second section, "Information Needs and Systems," describes purposes and functions of information transfer, and the third section, "Organization and Dissemination of Information," considers techniques of organizing and presenting information such as KWIC and SDI. The fourth section covers information storage and retrieval, library automation, and systems analysis.

1136.　Grimes, George. **Information Service: A Survey of the History and Present Status of the Field.** Detroit, Mich., Michigan-Ohio Regional Education Laboratory, 1969. 35p.

Gives a historical overview of library development from ancient times to the present, then presents an overview of the development of documentation, beginning in 1908. Reviews theories of information transfer. Discusses future trends in regard to information networks, information transfer, specialized information centers, mechanization, and the movement away from documentation toward information science.

1137.　Harmon, Glynn. "On the Evolution of Information Science," *Journal of the American Society for Information Science* 22:235-241 (July 1971).

Discusses the expansion of documentation from three divisions to nine and of the similar expansion and development of information science into an interdisciplinary science based on contemporary communication and behavioral science disciplines. Concludes that information science will achieve completeness and maturity as a system by 1990.

1138. Hayes, Robert M. "Information Science in Librarianship," *Libri* 19:216-236 (1969).

Information science is related to librarianship and to the traditional library role of preserving past records. Both theory and practical aspects of information science are discussed, as well as its relationship to library education. Curriculum, course requirements, and sequence are described. Library school students should study data processing in relationship to library principles and goals.

1139. Kent, Allen. **Information Analysis and Retrieval**. New York, Becker and Hayes, 1971. 367p.

This publication has been revised and expanded from the author's earlier *Textbook on Mechanized Information Retrieval*. Designed to teach basics to those who have little previous acquaintance with information retrieval or computers. The logical principles of information retrieval are discussed. Topics covered are hardware, mechanization, analysis and searching, and language.

1140. Kochen, Manfred, ed. **The Growth of Knowledge: Readings on Organization and Retrieval of Information**. New York, Wiley, 1967. 394p.

Based in part on a seminar on information retrieval systems at the University of Michigan. Concerned with ideas of the dynamics of knowledge and the development of information technologies. Divided into three sections. The first deals with goals and directions for information retrieval research, the second with disciplines underlying the sociology of information retrieval systems, and the third covers technological resources for systems construction.

1141. Lancaster, F. W., and E. G. Fayen. **Information Retrieval On-Line**. Los Angeles, Melville, 1973. 597p. (Becker and Hayes Series Book: Information Science Series).

Contains up-to-date detailed information about on-line systems. Discusses advances in areas such as equipment, searching, performance, and evaluation. Future trends are considered.

1142. Lancaster, F. Wilfred. **Information Retrieval Systems: Characteristics, Testing, and Evaluation**. New York, Wiley, 1968. 222p.

Planned to serve as an aid to students and librarians in designing, creating, and evaluating information retrieval systems. Discussed are subject indexing, traditional retrieval tools, vocabulary control, search strategy, current awareness, and mechanized information systems. The requirements of users and their interaction with the system is considered and evaluation of systems is discussed.

1143. Licklider, J. C. R. **Libraries of the Future**. Cambridge, Mass., MIT Press, 1965. 219p.

Considers acquisition of knowledge, uses of knowledge, steps toward precognitive systems, measurement of effectiveness of information retrieval systems, and question-answering systems in libraries.

1144. Meetham, Roger. **Information Retrieval: The Essential Technology.** Garden City, N.Y., Doubleday and Co., 1970. 187p.

Topics covered are communication and memory, storing information, classification and description, on-line, and fact retrieval. Another unit covers the library as a system, discussing information centers and possible future library services. A section on current awareness covers SDI services and evaluation of information retrieval systems.

1145. Norman, Donald. **Mechanized Information Services in the University Library. The Library and Human Memory. Phase 1—Planning. Part 13.** Berkeley, University of California, Institute of Library Research, 1967. 22p. ERIC Document ED024404.

Discusses the differences between the storage problems encountered in a large library and those encountered in the human memory system. Five operations in human information processing are described: 1) sensory transduction, 2) attention and acquisition, 3) short-term memory, 4) long-term memory, 5) retrieval. Describes an effective way in which interaction can occur between users and library.

1146. North, Jeanne B., ed. **Proceedings of the American Society for Information Science.** Vol. 6. Westport, Conn., Greenwood, 1969. 532p.

Contained here are papers accepted for presentation at the ASIS meeting in 1969. Subject areas covered are technical processes, mechanized retrieval systems, indexing, microfilm, information centers, and special libraries, information networks, national and international services, user studies, communication theory, economics, and file management systems.

1147. Pepinsky, Harold B., ed. **People and Information.** New York, Pergamon, 1970. 336p.

This collection includes nine essays. Subjects include methodology, specific attempts to cope with the information problem and a final overview and synthesis of the topic.

1148. Richman, Jon Todd. "Automatic Storage and Retrieval Techniques for Large On-Line Abstract Collections." Unpublished Ph.D. dissertation, Washington State University, 1972. n.p.

1149. Salton, Gerald. **Automatic Information Organization and Retrieval.** New York, McGraw-Hill, 1968. 514p.

Concerned with computer processing of large information files, with emphasis on automatic text handling. Discussed are index and glossary production, citation indexing, SDI, automatic question and answering systems, information search and matching procedures, and methods of user interaction with the mechanized system. On-line information systems and their evaluation are considered. Some basic elements of linguistics, mathematics, and computer programming are included. Major developments in mechanized information processing are discussed.

1150.   Saracevic, Tefko. **Introduction to Information Science.** New York, Bowker, 1970. 751p.
This volume consists of 65 essays, with bibliographies by experts in various areas of information science. It is arranged in chapters covering notions of information, communication process, behavior of information users, concept of relevance, structure of retrieval systems, acquisition, representation of information, organization of information stores, question handling, and search procedures, dissemination, human factors in systems, testing, and economics and growth. Concludes with a chapter on unifying theory.

1151.   Shera, Jesse. **Documentation and the Organization of Knowledge.** Hamden, Conn., Archon Books, 1966. 185p.
Composed of essays concerning the basic techniques of classification and cataloging and new techniques introduced by computers and referred to as "documentation." Also considers other aspects of documentation and effects of documentation on education for librarianship.

1152.   Shera, Jesse H. "Documentation: Its Scope and Limitations," *Library Quarterly* 21:13-26 (January 1951).
Shera discusses general theory of documentation and notes that the modern information center cannot do all the work required of a researcher. Limitations of information retrieval are considered in more detail.

1153.   Shera, Jesse H. "The Sociological Relationships of Information Science," *Journal of the American Society for Information Science* 22:76-80 (March-April 1971).
Based on a talk given by Shera to the 1970 annual ASIS meeting. Discusses the state-of-the-art of information science, including background and present conditions, with emphasis on areas of success and lack of success. Future trends are also considered.

1154.   Vickery, Brian C. **Information Systems.** London, Butterworth, 1973. 350p.
An information system has as its prime function the transferring or transforming of information. This book provides an overview of specialized documentary information systems for librarians and others who wish to learn to analyze and evaluate such systems. Covered are techniques of systems analysis and design, components, search methods, reference retrieval systems, and group dissemination. Practical aspects such as space, staffing, and equipment needed by libraries are also considered. An experimental study of reference retrieval is included. Bibliography.

1155.   Vickery, B. C. **Techniques of Information Retrieval.** Hamden, Conn., Archon, 1970. 262p.
Topics discussed in this book include scientific information problems, traditional reference tools, patterns of retrieval, needs of users, and construction of document profiles. Also covered are bibliographic description, subject indexing, controlled indexing terminology, classification structure, coordination of index terms, files and search strategy, information systems and system evaluation.

1156. Wellisch, Hans. "From Information Science to Informatics: A Terminological Investigation," *Journal of Librarianship* 4:157-187 (July 1972).
The author examines information science in regard to what it is and what it should do. In regard to terminology, he notes that he discovered 39 definitions of "information science" and traces the evolution of the term. He also considers the definition of "information." He concludes that no consensus exists in regard to terminology, common concepts, or central topics of investigation and for this reason information science cannot be called a true science. Includes tables and a bibliography.

1157. Williams, William F. **Principles of Automated Information Retrieval.** Elmhurst, Ill., The Business Press, 1968. 475p.
Intended to serve librarians "as an instructional manual in the design and operation of information retrieval systems." Covers theories of information retrieval, training of information specialists, selection of techniques and equipment, indexing and abstracting, and vocabulary control.

1158. Wilson, T. D., and Esther Herman, eds. **Fundamental of Documentation: Student Papers.** College Park, Md., University of Maryland, School of Library and Information Service, 1973. 220p. (Student Contribution Series, No. 4).
Based on a course in fundamentals of documentation offered at the University of Maryland. This book presents student papers on networks, conferences, directories, user surveys, classification, education, etc. A number of specific subject areas, mostly in science and technology, are represented.

INFORMATION RETRIEVAL AND REFERENCE SERVICE

1159. Becker, Joseph. "The Airlie Conference Plus Five." In Atherton, Pauline, ed. *Libraries and Automation, a Symposium.* Syracuse, N.Y., Syracuse University Press, 1970. pp. 7-14.
New developments in library automation are discussed, including performance of internal library functions, information retrieval, communication with multi-media files, and creation of library networks. The library is viewed as a total system. Research and trends are considered in areas such as machine readable data bases, audio communications, and the answering of reference questions.

1160. Becker, Joseph. "Development of Storage and Retrieval Systems." In Linderman, W., ed. *The Present Status and Future Prospects of Reference/Information Service.* Chicago, American Library Association, 1967. pp. 151-156.
Discusses two problems to be overcome before machines become vital in reference work, one being faster and more accurate input of data, which may be accomplished by optical character recognition. The second problem concerns the need for better concepts for retrieval than subject headings and subject classification. Describes techniques related to this: 1) concordances, 2) automatic indexing, 3) automatic abstracting, 4) automatic dissemination or searching. Discusses machine translation, machine-readable catalog data, facsimile transmission, and on-line systems.

1161.　DeGennaro, Richard. "Providing Bibliographic Services from Machine-Readable Data Bases—The Library's Role," *Journal of Library Automation* 6:215-222 (December 1973).

Discusses whether large research libraries in the future will need to subscribe to the rapidly growing number of machine-readable data bases to provide services for local users. Suggests as less costly that reference specialists serve as brokers between users and regional or other distribution centers. Also covered are costs and allocation of payment.

1162.　DeHart, Florence, and Margaret Stutzman. **Computer-Based Humanities Reference Services and the University Library.** Emporia, Kansas State Teacher's College, Graduate Library School, 1971. 125p.

The purpose of this study was to analyze the responsibilities of the information specialist. Discussed in regard to the information specialist are knowledge, abilities, attitudes, index language and indexing policy, practice in maintaining and updating the file, interaction between the system and users, conceptualization and manipulation of the search, and evaluation in terms of benefits and costs.

1163.　Dillon, Martin. "The Impact of Automation on the Content of Libraries and Information Centers," *College and Research Libraries* 34:418-425 (November 1973).

The author discusses the rapid growth of information needs due to a shift from basic to applied science and to the growing technology of science. Also considered are a documentation component capable of question answering, data bases, and techniques for analysis of literature.

1164.　Finzi, J. C. "Computer-Based Reference Services," *U.S. Library of Congress Information Bulletin* 30:111-114 (July 8, 1971).

A summary is given here of the addresses to the Preconference Institute of the Reference Services Division of the ALA in 1971. The keynote address was given by Margaret Gapgin on "The Role of the Reference Librarian in the Development and Use of Computer-Based Reference Service." Also discussed at the Institute were data bases, the ERIC thesaurus, and the initiating of computerized reference service in a library.

1165.　Graziano, Eugene. "Machine-Men and Librarians, An Essay," *College and Research Libraries* 28:403-406 (November 1967).

Library automation is discussed in regard to a rapidly changing world. Library operations are being defined in terms of process rather than of functions. The systems analyst now has a permanent place in the library world. The author considers the role of the reference librarian in regard to automation and concludes that computerization will not "dehumanize" but will help to provide more personal service. There will always be a place for the generalist reference librarian.

1166.　Heiliger, Edward, and P. B. Henderson. *Library Automation: Experience, Methodology and Technology of the Library as an Information System.* New York, McGraw-Hill, 1971. 333p.

The chapter dealing with applications of the computer to reference work covers computer-produced reference tools, computerized catalogs, SDI systems, and information retrieval.

1167.   Markuson, Barbara. "Automation of Reference and Bibliographic
        Functions." In *Guidelines for Automation: A Handbook for Federal
        and Other Libraries*. Santa Monica, Calif., Systems Development
        Corporation, 1972. pp. 138-145.
Computer applications in reference and bibliographic service are discussed, including
information retrieval, preparation of bibliographies, photoduplication, translation,
special materials, materials handling, abstracting and indexing. In setting up
information retrieval services, available data bases should be considered in
light of cost, ownership, increasing size of file, quality, and staff training. The
author concludes that, for the most part, reference and bibliographic functions
will not be computerized.

1168.   Mathies, M. Lorraine, and Peter G. Watson. **Computer-Based Reference
        Service**. Chicago, American Library Association, 1973. 200p.
This book is based on an annual prepared for the ALA Preconference on Computer-
Based Reference Service in 1971. The first section describes the ERIC System in
detail, the second discusses computer searching in general, dealing with principles
and strategy. The third section covers other machine-readable data bases such as
MARC, U.S. Census materials, and other data bases. Also included are guidelines
for information retrieval and a bibliography.

1169.   Maxwell, Margaret. "The Machine in the Reference Room," *RQ*
        11:23-25 (Fall 1971).
Both traditional reference librarians and information specialists have an important
role in reference service and can gain by working with each other. Reference librarians should help lay the groundwork for information systems by developing effective
means of measurement and evaluation, by analysis of the reference process, and
by a study of functions and duties in relation to computerization. Research in
regard to automation is also needed in areas such as subject headings, abstracting,
and searching.

1170.   Murdock, Lindsay, and Olivia Opello. "Computer Literature Searches in
        the Physical Sciences," *Special Libraries* 64:442-445 (October 1973).
Computerized literature searches are described as a way to provide custom-tailored
service without large increases in staff. Selected current awareness services and
literature searches in the physical sciences are listed here. The author's purpose is
to help librarians become aware of services that are available so they can help
patrons by recommending the data base most suitable for their needs.

1171.   Oboler, Eli M. "Good-Bye Reference Librarians!," *RQ* 4:12-13 (September
        1964).
The question of whether reference librarians will eventually be replaced by automation is discussed here. The author concludes that the type of reasoning and
judgment involved in reference work cannot be duplicated by the computer.

1172.   Park, Margaret R. "Computer-Based Bibliographic Retrieval Services,"
        Special Libraries 64:187-192 (April 1973).
A broad discussion of computer-based information retrieval services. Five to six
years ago the information dissemination center emerged as a retailer of information
interfacing with tape suppliers and users. This interface is discussed in terms of the
nature of the data bases, retrieval results, timliness of service, costs, prices, and
library interests. Also considered are the increasing trend toward licensing and
leasing information services. The author recommends comparison shopping for
information retrieval centers as they often differ substantially in services provided.

1173.   Parker, R. H. "Are Reference Librarians Obsolete?" *RQ* 3:9-10 (July 1964).
Discusses the problems that would come about if reference service was replaced by
computerized bibliographic services. Notes that this would not take care of all the
ordinary day-to-day needs of many students, hobbyists, and amateurs, etc. He also
notes that the cost may be beyond the reach of most people. Manual reference tools
are still cheaper and more efficient for large numbers to use. In regard to microfilm,
if heavily used holdings are converted to microfilm, the space for large numbers of
readers may equal that needed for the same number of books.

1174.   Perrault, Jean M. "Reference and Bibliography." In *Practical Problems of
        Library Automation*. Washington, D.C., Special Libraries Association,
        1967. pp. 23-32.
Reference work is characterized as the manipulation of concepts. Level and degree
of specificity of these concepts are important concerns.

1175.   Prodrick, R. G. "Automation Can Transform Reference Services," *Ontario
        Library Review* 51:145-150 (September 1967).
The author discusses the applications of the computer to university library reference
service and concludes that computerization will not replace reference service but
will, instead, transform it in five areas: library catalogs, production of bibliographies,
interlibrary loan, indexing, and information retrieval. These areas are discussed in
detail. Some examples of the above applications are given.

1176.   Schramm, Jeanne V. "The Great Computer Hoax," *Wilson Library Bulletin*
        49:577-579 (April 1975).
The author, a reference librarian at West Liberty State College, West Virginia,
describes an experiment which she initiated for the purpose of determining patrons'
attitudes toward computerized as opposed to traditional reference service. Patrons
were led to believe that "computerized" reference service was available and if they
submitted topics written on blank punch cards, they would be transcribed and fed
into the "computer," which would then come up with a list of relevant subject
headings and sources. In actuality, this work was done by reference staff. Many
students praised the results obtained by the "computer." Faculty also obtained
"computerized searches." No one detected the hoax until it was revealed.

1177.   Schultz, Claire K. "Automation of Reference Work," *Library Trends*
        12:413-424 (January 1964).
The author reviews the historical development of automated procedures for information retrieval and relates these developments to reference work. Similarities in traditional reference searches and computerized searches are discussed, such as use of
subject heading lists and thesauri, and search strategy. Also covered are input,
computer processing, and output. The MEDLARS system is discussed.

1178.   Shera, Jesse. "Automation and the Reference Librarian," *RQ* 3:3-7
        (July 1964).
This article is written as a rebuttal to an address given by John R. Pierce, Director
of Communications Research at Bell Telephone Laboratories. The author favors
development of information retrieval in reference work and discusses future
advantages and problems. He believes that there will be increasing use of computerized systems and that reference librarians should understand and participate in
information retrieval.

MANAGEMENT OF INFORMATION RETRIEVAL

1179.   Doebler, P. D. "Data Base Publishers Vying for Key Roles as Rapid Growth
        Looms in Business Uses," *Publisher's Weekly* 206:38-40 (September 1974).
In 20 years the data base market could amount to 20 billion dollars annually, according to a vice president of the Chase Manhattan Bank. Discusses the text and statistical
data bases for business use rather than bibliographical data bases. Describes and discusses use of three of these types of business data bases—economic, financial, and
marketing. Also considers econometric techniques for predicting the future.

1180.   Hall, J. "Publicity and Promotion for Information Services in University
        Libraries," *Aslib Proceedings* 26:391-395 (October 1974).
A survey of information service in university libraries obtained details on methods
of publicity. Both active and passive methods were studied, with passive forms
predominating. Active publicity was used most by technological university libraries
and less by civic and new universities.

1181.   Landau, H. B. "Can the Librarian Become a Computer Data Base Manager?"
        Special Libraries 62:121-124 (March 1971).
Librarians must educate themselves to become managers of large machine-readable
data bases. Skills and techniques are discussed and an annotated bibliography is
included.

1182.   Marshall, Doris. "User Criteria for Selection of Commercial On-Line
        Computer-Based Bibliographic Services: An Industrial Practical Case
        Study," *Special Libraries* 66:501-508 (November 1975).
The author describes her own experiences in the Ralston Purina Company Library
in St. Louis, Missouri. Included are a list of criteria covering needs of users, selection
of hardware, mode of transmission, selection of vendors and systems, selection of
data bases, development and testing of search strategy, attitude of management,
and user interaction with the system.

1183.   Sherwood. Peter W. "Information Retrieval Today," *Cost Accountant* 42:404-405 (November 1964).
Considers the economics of information retrieval. Estimates that U.S. expenditures on information retrieval will rise from 20 million dollars in 1963 to 90 million dollars in 1968. The Stanford Research Institute survey of economic parameters for various sytems is discussed, along with the quantitative point below which manual systems are more economical. Currently available systems, both manual and mechanized, are discussed, including FLIP and VERAC. Future developments are discussed and need for research on indexing improvement is considered.

1184.   Stern, L. W., and others. "Promotion of Information Services: An Evaluation of Alternative Approaches," *Journal of the American Society for Information Science* 24:171-179 (May-June 1973).
Three different promotional programs were developed for a batch-processed current awareness service to faculties provided by the Mechanized Information Center at Ohio State University. Programs were: 1) word-of-mouth advertising by opinion leaders, 2) a "blitz" intensive advertising program, 3) person-to-person telephone solicitation. The level of market penetration, user satisfaction, influence of media employed, and cost effectiveness are discussed. The three approaches result in almost equal user satisfaction, but the most efficient methods in regard to costs and market penetration were the blitz and telephone solicitation. Personal interaction was essential for user satisfaction.

DIRECTORIES OF DATA BASES AND INFORMATION SYSTEMS

1185.   Cohan, Leonard, ed. **Directory of Computerized Information in Science and Technology**. New York, Science Associates, 1968– . Looseleaf.
Begins with a permuted index of systems, titles, and key phrases. Directory section is alphabetically arranged by title of system or service. Includes description, dates, hardware, forms of output, availability, contact and reference to publications and reports available concerning each service. Appendices include a state of the art report, bibliography on information retrieval, standards for cataloging magnetic tape material, the library and human memory, and a glossary of documentation terms.

1186.   Fife, Dennis, and others. **A Technical Index of Interactive Information Systems. Final Report**. Washington, D.C., U.S. National Bureau of Standards, 1974. 79p. ERIC Document ED092163.
Interactive information systems are discussed in terms of their technical features and operational status. This state-of-the-art review is designed to assist in system selection. An index includes a list of 46 systems listed by trade name and provides information about over 50 technical features of those systems.

1187.   Kruzas, Anthony, and others. **Encyclopedia of Information Systems and Services**. 2nd int. ed. Ann Arbor, Mich., Edwards Bros., 1974. 1271p.
Includes bibliography of directories and guides to information systems and services. Information systems and services are listed alphabetically by institution or organization, etc. Gives data on sponsors, description of system, scope, subject, input or

data sources, holdings or storage media. Also has the following indexes:
1) geographic, 2) computerized applications and services, 3) commercially available
data bases, 4) micrographic applications and services, 5) library and information
networks, 6) SDI services, 7) consulting and planning services, 8) research and
research projects, 9) data collection and analysis centers, 10) professional associa-
tions, 11) abstracting and indexing services, 12) serial publications.

1188.   Marron, Beatrice, Elizabeth Fong, and Dennis Fife. **A Mechanized Informa-
         tion Services Catalog.** Washington, D.C., U.S. National Bureau of Standards,
         Systems and Software Division, 1974. 59p.
An introduction discusses problems created by the proliferation of data bases,
selection of information sources and services, the prototype system, use of the
catalog, and future plans. Following the introduction are listed some 81 data bases,
including all subject areas, but predominantly scientific and technological. Entries
are alphabetically arranged and include originator, subject, time-span, address,
phone, contact, abstracts, elements, frequency, average number of items included
per year, and purchase or lease cost.

1189.   Organization for Economic Cooperation and Development. **Inventory of
         Major Information Systems and Services in Science and Technology.** Paris,
         The Organization, 1971. 322p. ERIC Document ED051839.
Includes both government and private information systems and services, particularly
mechanized systems. Also includes systems not yet fully developed. Social sciences
are also covered.

1190.   Patrinostro, Frank. **Available Data Banks for Library and Information
         Services.** Tempe, Arizona, Library Automation Research and Consulting
         Association, 1973. 40p. ERIC Document ED076219.
More than 100 data banks are listed, with notes indicating sponsoring agency, type
of material, where available, and the number of references stored annually.

1191.   Schneider, John H., Marvin Gechman, and Steven Furth, eds. **Survey of Com-
         mercially Available Computer-Readable Bibliographic Data Bases.** Washing-
         ton, D.C., American Society for Information Science, 1973. 181p.
This directory, based on the results of a survey conducted by the ASIS Special Interest
Group on Selective Dissemination of Information, discusses 81 machine-readable data
bases. For each is given name, frequency, time plan, source and contact point, subject
matter, scope, derivation of material in the data base, indexing and/or subject analysis
methods, special data elements, tape specification, retrospective and/or SDI, type and
cost of search services, prices and availability of the data base. Data bases not participating in the survey are listed at the end. This directory will be updated by a looseleaf
service, *Computer-Readable Data Bases: A Directory and Sourcebook.* The main volume of this service (1976. 814p.) will be supplemented by looseleaf pages every six
months.

1192.   Sessions, Vivian, ed. **Directory of Data Bases in the Social and Behavioral
         Sciences.** New York, Science Associates/International, 1974. 300p.
This directory is the result of international efforts to list those data bases of value
to the social and behavioral sciences. Arranged alphabetically by institution. Information given for each data base includes addresses, subject fields, storage media,

publications, access, etc. Indexes included are subject/keyword, institution, "personnel," and geographical.

1193.   Steiner, Roberta. "Selected Computerized Search Services in Areas Related to the Behavioral Sciences," *Special Libraries* 65:319-325 (August 1974).
Gives a selected list of some 20 computerized search services in the behavioral sciences. Presented in chart form covering time-span, turn-around time, source, and cost.

1194.   Troutman, Joan. **Mechanized Information Services in the University Library. Inventory of Available Data Bases. Phase I—Planning. Part 1.** Berkeley, University of California, Institute of Library Research, 1967. 57p. ERIC Document ED023414.
A survey of 29 data bases emphasizing reference data bases only. Covers both national projects and those serving particular organizations. Includes address, director, description of contents, file characteristics and size, availability and cost, and references to further documentation.

1195.   U.S. Department of Commerce. National Technical Information Service. **Directory of Computerized Data Files and Related Software Available from Federal Agencies.** Washington, D.C., U.S. Government Printing Office, 1974. 107p. and index.
Arranged under areas of demography, social sciences and government, economics, science, and technology, and then further subdivided into 72 narrower subject fields. Each entry includes description of how data were obtained and relationship of the data to printed sources. Lists printed publications related to the data base. Other basic information is also included. Indexes include generating agency, fine subject index, and number index.

1196.   Williams, Martha, and Alan Stewart. **ASIDIC Survey of Information Center Services.** Chicago, Association of Scientific Information Dissemination Centers, 1972. 127p. ERIC Document ED094722.
A survey made for the Cooperative Data Management Committee (CDMC) of the ASIDIC. Survey results include a list of publicly available data bases, number of times each data base was used for current awareness by a center, a list of internally generated data bases, and data on the amount and kind of service, and equipment used by the centers.

SEARCH STRATEGY
AND THE SUBJECT APPROACH TO INFORMATION

1197.   Boginas, Scott J., and Neil B. Cew. "The Computerized File Management System: A Tool for the Reference Librarian," *Special Libraries* 64:12-17 (January 1973).
A file management system is described here to search technical literature on a subject. The system provides both retrospective and current awareness services and can be utilized either on-line or in the batch mode. Searches can be made by words,

word roots, phrases, or numbers in any part of the entry. Searches can be printed or used to custom-make new machine-readable files. The average batch search requires 11 seconds of CDC 6000 time. This system has been adopted for large machine-readable bibliographic data bases.

1198.   Cooper, William S. "Automatic Fact Retrieval," *Science Journal*
         1:81-86 (June 1965).
The author notes that "reference providing systems" give bibliographical sources while "data providing systems" supply specific facts. The difference between these systems is considered. Most attention has been directed toward reference providing systems. A structured data retrieval system at MIT termed BASEBALL is described. The author discusses how formal logic can be applied to develop fact retrieval systems in which the computer can print out "true" or "false" in response to questions. Such a system at IBM's Research Laboratory in California is described. Difficulties related to logic and descriptive linguistics are discussed. Parameters are given within which an efficient and economical fact retrieval system might be established.

1199.   Foskett, A. C. **The Subject Approach to Information**. Hamden, Conn.,
         Archon, 1969. 310p.
Intended as an introductory text in which cataloging and classification are treated as different aspects of the same problem. The first section deals with theory of information systems covering principles and problems of various cataloging problems. The second section discusses pre-coordinate systems and the third, post-coordinate systems. Part 4 covers classification research and the computer.

1200.   Keen, M. "Search Strategy Evaluation in Manual and Automated Systems,"
         Aslib Proceedings 20:65-81 (January 1968).
Discusses criteria for evaluation of search strategy. Considers new measurement techniques and examines the intellectual process of search strategy decisions. Manual and mechanized search strategies presently being used are compared to the SMART computerized system and results are presented.

1201.   Kerner, C. J., and T. F. Lindsley. "The Value of Abstracts in Normal Text
         Searching." In Schultz, L., ed. *The Information Bazaar.* Philadelphia,
         College of Physicians of Philadelphia, 1969. pp. 437-440.
Test searches were run in which retrieval by search words in abstracts was compared to retrieval by subject terms. Conclusions were drawn that the abstracts were very important search tools and were also valuable to the user in evaluating material retrieved.

1202.   O'Connor, John. "Text Searching Retrieval of Answer-Sentences and
         Other Answering Passages," *Journal of the American Society for
         Information Science* 24:445-460 (November-December 1973).
Describes new text searching retrieval techniques which retrieve sentences and passages from texts. The overall goal of such techniques is to retrieve answers from documents. The relationship of significant words in a sentence can be measured by two new automatic procedures: 1) syntactic joints or prepositions,

punctuation, etc., 2) word proximity. Multi-paragraph answer passages are not usually retrieved by this procedure. This sytem promises greater precision than the SMART system.

1203.   Reilly, Kevin D. **Evaluation of Generalized File Management Systems. Mechanized Information Services in the University Library. Phase I– Planning. Part 4.** Berkeley, University of California, Institute of Library Research, 1967. 46p. ERIC Document ED023417.
Provides a survey of the features of the various aspects of generalized or task-oriented programming systems. Discussed are INFOL, CFSS, MARK IV, GIS, etc.

1204.   Reilly, Kevin. **Nature of Typical Data Bases. Mechanized Information Services in the University Library. Phase I–Planning. Part 5,** 1967. 51p. ERIC Document ED023416.
Treats format and content of major data bases in detail such as MEDLARS, ERIC, etc. Also considers some local data banks. Considers the applicability of generalized or task-oriented programs to these data bases.

1205.   Salton, G. "Search Strategy and the Optimization of Retrieval Effectiveness," In Samuelson, K., ed. *Mechanized Information Storage, Retrieval and Dissemination.* Amsterdam, North-Holland Publishing Co., 1968. pp. 73-107.
A variety of search strategies are described, derived from feed-back from users, and from categories of document requests. These strategies are evaluated by the SMART system and a real-time user search strategy is developed.

1206.   Sparck-Jones, Karen. "Index Term Weighting," *Information Storage and Retrieval* 9:619-633 (November 1973).
Discusses various approaches to term weighting, logic of these approaches, and the effects of these approaches on term retrieval. Results indicate: 1) statistical index term weighting does not degrade performance, 2) variable intrinsic term weighting can be useful, 3) document length weighting is of limited value, 4) collection frequency weighting is usually of value.

1207.   **Subject Retrieval in the Seventies: New Directions. Proceedings of an International Symposium, University of Maryland, May 14-15, 1971.** Edited by H. Wellisch and T. D. Wilson. College Park, Md., Maryland University, School of Library and Information Science, 1972. 185p.
Contains papers from the Conference on the following aspects of subject retrieval: 1) methods, problems, prospects; 2) research trends in retrieval languages; 3) a mode for indexing languages; 4) work of the British classification group; 5) thesaurofacet—a new concept in subject retrieval; 6) precise system for computer-generated indexes; 7) UDC as an international switching language; 8) UDC in mechanized subject information; 9) LC subject headings—review and forecast. Included also are panel discussions, a list of participants and a listing of retrieval systems used by participants.

APPLICATIONS TO BOOK-ORIENTED DATA BASES

1208.   Chen, Ching-Chih. and E. Robert Kingham. "Subject Reference Lists
          Produced by Computer," *Journal of Library Automation* 1:178-197
          (September 1968).
Described here is a system developed at the University of Waterloo in Ontario,
Canada. Since there was no machine-readable approach to the reference collection,
it was decided to prepare a computerized data base consisting of titles of books in
the reference collection according to subject and form. This data base, used to
produce lists of reference materials in 14 subject areas, provides an easy method
of revising, updating, and producing new lists. It can produce lists of reference
material by type, by additions, and for internal or public use. Included are feedback
from users and cost analysis.

1209.   "Computerized Library System to Index Books in Depth," *Library
          Journal* 92:3360-3362 (October 1967).
Reported here is the computerized system for analyzing in detail the subject content of books being developed by the State University of New York at its Upstate
Medical Center in Syracuse. This program, called the SUNY Biomedical Communication Network, is believed to be the first of its kind, linking four medical center
libraries. Each book is computer-indexed by chapter much the same as is done in
a periodical index. Chapters of books can then be retrieved by the subject approach
at an on-line terminal.

1210.   Meredith, Joseph C. "Machine-Assisted Approach to General Reference
          Materials," *Journal of the American Society for Information Science*
          22:176-186 (May-June 1971).
The School of Librarianship at the University of California undertook a research
and development project where the contents of 144 general reference works were
computerized according to 254 different categories of information. Thus, these
works were converted to one "data bank" from which any combination of the 254
categories of information could be retrieved. In response to a reference request
given at an on-line terminal, this sytem, entitled REFSEARCH, submits the names
of those reference works which would contain the desired categories of information.
The background and development of this system are discussed, along with its
potential usefulness in the future.

1211.   Meredith, Joseph C. **Reference Search System (REFSEARCH) User's
          Manual.** Washington, D.C., Office of Education, 1971. 124p.
This work reports on the REFSEARCH research and development project described
above. The project is explained and a manual is provided describing use of the system.

1212.   Morgan, John M. "Machines and the Reference Librarian," *RQ* 9:340-341
          (Summer 1970).
Discussed here is the Ohio Bar Automated Research (OBAR), which is a computerized
information system for Ohio statute and case law. The complete text of reports and
statutes can be searched on all words but articles and connectives. Such a system
would be of value to both academic and public libraries.

1213.   Schwarz, P. J. "Key Word Indexing of Reference Materials," *Mountain Plains Library Quarterly* 18:10-12 (Spring 1973).

1214.   Topper, C. "Retrieving Legal Information," *Data Processing* 8:314-317 (1966).
Described here is retrieval using words from the complete text of law reports. A dictionary is prepared where each word is entered and given a number. This forms a concordance, which is transferred to the tape. Inexperienced users of this system can retrieve information as effectively as experienced lawyers.

1215.   Weil, Cherie. "Automatic Retrieval of Biographical Reference Books," *Journal of Library Automation* 1:239-249 (December 1968).
A description is given here of a program designed at the University of Chicago to locate specific biographical information in biographical reference books. Two hundred thirty-four biographical reference sources in English were indexed by subjects included and contents of entries. The program then was designed to select the five biographical sources that were most likely to contain the specific biographical information desired by the patron. Test results are presented and this sytem is evaluated. It is suggested that similar programs be prepared for bibliographies, dictionaries, and atlases. There is discussion of computerized programs to select reference books which will contain specific information.

1216.   Weil, Cherie. "Classification and Automatic Retrieval of Biographical Reference Books." Master's thesis, University of Chicago, 1967. n.p.

1217.   Yeatts, Wendell, and Kevin Reilly. **Mechanized Information Services in the University Library. Experience with Library of Congress MARC Tapes. Phase 1—Planning. Part 7.** Berkeley, University of California, Institute of Library Research, 1967. 39p. ERIC Document ED023419.
Discusses problems in using MARC information to produce catalog cards and to alphabetize subject lists for use in book selection.

USER INTERACTION

1218.   Artandi, Susan. "The Searchers—Links Between Inquiries and Indexes," *Special Libraries* 57:571-574 (October 1966).
Describes the information specialist as an intermediary between the inquirer and the system. The negotiation process provides him with a description of the searcher's needs and clues to use in search strategy. He then begins the translation process, by which he fits the inquiry into the resources of his library.

1219.   Ladendorf, J. M. "Networks Questioned: Four Misconceptions of Machine Fanatics in Judging Direct Human-Computer Interaction," *Wilson Library Bulletin* 48:561-564 (March 1974).
Describes in humorous fashion the following misconceptions concerning the computer: 1) users need it—in the normal process of literature searching, a computer is rarely able to help; 2) users understand it—a user who cannot confront a card

catalog will not be willing to confront a computer; 3) users are understood—machines cannot yet handle adequately the imprecision of human communication; 4) users are alike—computers cannot interact with the patron and determine the level of information wanted and the purpose of his request which may vary among patrons for the same question.

1220.   Lancaster, F. W. "Interaction Between Requesters and a Large Mechanized Retrieval System," *Information Storage and Retrieval* 4:239-252 (June 1968).

The problems of the user-system interface are discussed. Unsuccessful searches often result from failure in this area. Request statements made by patrons often do not represent the actual information desired. The author suggests ways in which the user-system interface can become more effective.

1221.   Lancaster, Frederick W. "User Education: The Next Major Thrust in Information Science?" *Journal of Education for Librarianship* 11:55-63 (Summer 1970).

The author notes that large segments of the scientific and technical community do not utilize expensive information retrieval services which are now available. Users need to be educated in regard to information services; user orientation programs, such as that at the National Library of Medicine, are described. Library schools should assume responsibility for reaching subject departments and teaching users the potential of information retrieval systems.

1222.   Martin, T. H. "User Interface in Interactive Systems." In *Annual Review of Information Science and Technology, Volume 8*. Washington, D.C., American Society for Information Science, 1973. pp. 203-219.

Describes the state of the art in user interface with the computer. Covers overview, theory, description of interface, user reactions, evaluation, standardization, and integration. Presents conclusions on best methods of training. Suggests 1) on-line newsletters covering pitfalls, 2) colloquia, 3) task-related evaluative indicators, 4) tie-ins to related systems. Extensive bibliography.

1223.   Melnyk, Vera. "1972 Student Paper Award: Man-Machine Interface: Frustration," *Journal of the American Society for Information Science* 23:392-401 (November-December 1972).

Students from the School of Library Science at Syracuse University participated in an experimental reference retrieval system for library literature. A data base was prepared containing library literature citations for 1970. A control group used specified terms while an experimental group could select their terms. Each student then interacted with the terminal to try to obtain citations. Afterward, students were queried as to their attitudes and it was found that 80 percent of the experimental group found the experience "frustrating" while the control group labeled it "interesting" and "favorable." One hundred percent of the controls wished to continue while 79 percent of the experimental group wished to quit.

1224.   Neelameghan, A. "Specification of Subject of Reader's Query: Reader-Computer Dialogue," *Library Science with a Slant to Documentation* 9:636-656 (December 1972).

Concerned with the psychology of the user seeking information. Describes aspects of the inquiry. Stages in specification of subject are: 1) rough enunciation, 2) display classification schedule showing user related subjects, 3) consult alphabetical subject index, 4) user browses in classified section looking at other titles, 5) user narrows down to small number of related entries giving feedback to librarian. Describes two methods of conducting the dialogue between users and the computer.

1225.   Parker, Edwin, and William Paisley. "Research for Psychologists at the Interface of the Scientist and His Information System." In Saracevic, Tefko, ed. *Introduction to Information Science*. New York, Bowker, 1970. pp. 85-94.

Reviews and summarizes findings on scientists' use of information, theory of information use, methods for study of information use, experiments in field settings, laboratory experiments, document analysis, a..d computer-based research in information use. Concludes with discussion of needed psychological research. Bibliography.

1226.   Rosenberg, V. "Technique for Monitoring User Behavior at the Computer Terminal Interface," *Journal of the American Society for Information Science* 24:71 (January-February 1973).

The author describes a technique called "protocol analysis," which can be used to monitor user behavior at the terminal. This method has often been used in experiments on problem-solving behavior. The dialogue is monitored in the usual way, with a printout of user-computer dialogue with time notes in the margin. The user is also asked to think aloud and this is recorded on tape and transcribed with time notations. The tape and the printout are then matched by "timing" marks, and it is possible then to obtain a complete record of the user's thoughts and actions. This gives a useful insight into where the process may be improved. Brief bibliography concerning this technique is included.

1227.   Schultz, Louise. "Breaking the Communication Barrier Between Searcher and Literature File: An Interactive Guide," *Journal of the American Society for Information Science* 25:3-9 (January-February 1974).

The BIOSIS retrospective retrieval service is described. It was necessary to reduce strategy preparation time and to transfer this function directly to the user. Users were given use of a typewriter or video terminal to: 1) learn use of the system, 2) compile and group search terms and interpose logical operators, 3) save the set for later modification and transmit to BIOSIS. Differences between this sytem and that where the user has to prepare a search strategy are described. Includes a sample user session.

EVALUATION

1228.   Bivans, M. M. "Comparison of Manual and Machine Literature Searches,"
        Special Libraries 65:216-222 (May-June 1974).
The Library of the National Oceanic and Atmospheric Administration Environmental Research Laboratory in Boulder, Colorado, compared searches done by man
and machine on the same subject according to scientists' evaluations of their usefulness. (The manual searches and computer searches, however, were done in different
data bases.) Results indicate that both kinds of literature searches were valuable for
background information and planning procedures and should probably be undertaken
for all new projects.

1229.   Byrne, Jerry R. "Relative Effectiveness of Titles, Abstracts, and Subject
        Headings for Machine Retrieval from the Compendex Service," *Journal of
        the American Society for Information Science* 26:223-229 (July-August
        1975).
Describes previous studies and results. Fifty searches of the Compendex data base
were done to determine the relative effectiveness of the above elements in retrieval.
A table shows each search subject and terms used. Results indicate that title words
alone are not satisfactory for efficient retrieval. The combination of titles and
abstracts came closest to 100 percent retrieval, with searching of abstracts alone
doing almost as well. Indexer input, though necessary for retrieval in almost all
cases, was found to be relatively unimportant.

1230.   Chenery, Peter. "Cost of Computer Searching," *RQ* 12:251-258 (Spring
        1973).
Describes operations of the North Carolina Science and Technology Research Center
and gives cost data. Covers data bases available and methods of searching. Describes
publicity, finding customers and marketing services. In regard to costs, a "cost card"
is kept recording time spent on each individual search request. Cards are summarized
and monthly costs reported. By entering these cost cards in a computer file, lists of
costs by file, by size of search output, type of customer, or any other parameter
can be provided. Costs and search prices are then compared and adjusted when
necessary. At this time only direct costs are recovered. Costs of setting up and maintaining files or marketing expenses are not recovered at this time, but may be in the
future as volume increases. Interactive systems will continue in use and become
lower in cost, but for the immediate future batch searching will be cheaper.

1231.   Cleverdon, Cyril. "The Cranfield Hypothesis," *Library Quarterly* 35:121-
        124 (April 1965).
This article answers some of the criticisms made by Don Swanson (*Library Quarterly*,
35:1-20, January 1965). The author draws attention to the following conclusions
omitted by Swanson: 1) the most important factors in information retrieval systems
are recall and precision, 2) physical form of the store does not affect recall and
precision, 3) the main influence on performance is the intellectual stage of concept
indexing, 4) with the same concept indexing two kinds of index languages will give
similar performances, 5) complexity of index language results in greater performance
range, 6) maximum recall depends on exhaustivity of indexing, and maximum

precision on specificity of index language. Maximum intellect applied to indexing language is more important to efficient performance of an information retrieval system than whether that system is conventional or computerized. Applications of intellect to indexing language as opposed to automatic indexing are discussed.

1232.   Cleverdon, C. W. "User Evaluation of Information Retrieval Systems," *Journal of Documentation* 30:170-180 (June 1974).
Recall and precision are discussed in relation to the performance of operational systems. The MEDLARS evaluation system is considered. The limitations within which measures of recall and precision are satisfactory or not are outlined. Evaluation must be user-oriented rather than management-oriented. A hypothesis for user-evaluation and design of such schemes is given. Measures of "search length" and "satisfaction" added to number of relevant citations retrieved are suggested to evaluate performance with regard to user satisfaction.

1233.   Cooper, Michael D. "Evaluation of Information Retrieval Systems: A Simulation and Cost Approach," Unpublished Ph.D. dissertation, University of California, Berkeley, 1971. 209p.

1234.   Cuadra, C. A., and R. V. Katter. "Implications of Relevance Research for Library Operations and Training," *Special Libraries* 59:503-507 (September 1968).
The author examines research studies done on the negotiation process between users and librarians. These studies show that relevance judgment is influenced by the way in which the patron wants to use the information, or "use orientation." Problems arise when this orientation is not explicit. The research reviewed here indicates that relevance is influenced by: 1) skills and attitudes of those making judgments, 2) documents used, 3) stated information requirements, 4) instructions and setting, 5) definitions of relevance, 6) type of rating skills.

1235.   Elman, Stanley A. "Cost Comparison of Manual and On-Line Computerized Literature Searching," *Special Libraries* 66:12-18 (January 1975).
Figures were obtained for the average cost of 48 manual literature searches done from January through August 1973, including $10 per hour as the cost of the professional searcher, $6 for clerical help, $5 per search for reproduction of materials. The average time for a search was 22 hours, with an average search cost of $250. Figures were also obtained for the average cost of 66 computerized searches done on a variety of data bases using the Lockheed DIALOG system, including 41¢ per minute on-line time and other on-line costs; labor, 17¢ per minute; telephone, 25¢ per minute; printer, 17¢ per minute. Labor was calculated only for terminal time. The average cost of the computerized search was $47.

1236.   Foreman, G., and others. "User Study of Manual and MEDLINE Literature Searches in the Hospital Library," *Medical Library Association Bulletin* 62:385-387 (October 1974).
Sixty-six literature searches requested by health practitioners in two hospitals were done both manually and through MEDLINE. The manual search included examination and evaluation of articles with photocopies provided.   The computerized

MEDLINE bibliography was also provided. Sixty-six percent preferred the manual search, but some felt the MEDLINE search would be an "excellent adjunct" to the manual search. Problems with MEDLINE are noted as 1) sometimes earlier literature is needed, 2) too many references without any evaluation of which are most relevant, 3) books or journals not in the MEDLINE data base are sometimes needed. Advantages of MEDLINE are 1) it can find items which would be almost impossible to locate manually, 2) it quickly finds subjects scattered under many headings, 3) in all but two cases it retrieved citations not found manually. The authors conclude that MEDLINE does not replace the manual search, but it is a valuable supplement.

1237.   Kent, Allen, and others. "Relevance Predictability in Information Retrieval Systems," *Methods of Information in Medicine* 6:145-151 (April 1967).
An experiment done at the University of Pittsburgh to study relevance judgments is described here. Motivated users of information retrieval systems judged the relevance of whole documents. The ability of different portions of a document (or the intermediate response product—IRP) to predict the relevance of the whole document was also studied and compared with the relevance judgments of the whole documents. Results indicated 1) little difference between the relevance judgments of the IRP groups and relevance judgments on the whole document, 2) first and last paragraphs predict relevancy at a higher level than any other IRP, 3) abstracts were undistinguished as predictors, 4) citations showed a high predictability rating, but this was not substantive.

1238.   Kiewitt, Eva Lorene. "PROBE: Computer Searches of the ERICTAPES—An Evaluation of a Pilot Study." Unpublished Ph.D. dissertation, Indiana University, 1973. 240p.

1239.   King, Donald W., and Peggy Neel. **Cost Effectiveness of On-Line Retrieval Systems.** Rockville, Md., Westat Research, Inc., 1971. 13p. ERIC Document ED046460.
A recently developed cost-effectiveness model for on-line retrieval systems is discussed. It is flexible in that combinations of alternative systems and subsystems can be compared. The example chosen for discussion gives a cost-effectiveness comparison of on-line index and on-line abstract systems for various levels of demand and recall.

1240.   King, Donald W., and Edward Bryant. **Evaluation of Information Services and Products.** Washington, D.C., Information Resources Press, 1971. 306p.
This text covers information systems design and operation and discusses classification, indexing processes, and screening of documents. Also considered in regard to information are composition, reproduction, acquisition, storage, and preservation. Considers the above subjects in light of quality control and evaluation. Describes different approaches to evaluation and methods and procedures for analyzing findings.

1241.   Krevitt, B.I., and B. C. Griffith. "Evaluation of Information Systems: A Bibliography, 1967-1972," *Information: Part 2* 2:1-34 (1973).
A bibliography limited to literature dealing with the design, testing, and evaluation of information storage and retrieval systems. Consulted were *Research in Education*,

Library Literature, *Information Science Abstracts,* and *Annual Review of Information Science and Technology*. Each citation is listed under only one category. Published monographs have been grouped separately.

1242.   Lancaster, F. W. **Evaluation of the MEDLARS Demand Search Service.**
        Springfield, Va., Clearinghouse for Federal Scientific and Technical
        Information, 1968. 278p. ERIC Document ED022494.
Three hundred actual searches done in 1966 and 1967 were studied. It was found that the system was operating with about 58 percent recall and 50 percent precision.

1243.   McCarthy, S. E., and others. "Evaluation of MEDLINE Service by User
        Survey," *Medical Library Association Bulletin* 62:367-373 (October 1974).
A questionnaire was sent to 250 users of the MEDLINE service at the Calder Memorial Library of the University of Miami School of Medicine. Results indicated that 49 percent used the search prior to preparing a paper or grant proposal and 28 percent used it to solve immediate problems. Broad searches were wanted more often than narrow searches. Most of those who felt they received too few relevant citations ran broad searches. Other findings were that patrons expressed enthusiasm and were willing to pay for searches, but showed a lack of knowledge of MEDLINE. The authors give suggestions and pointers for conducting evaluations, based on their experience in this study.

1244.   Magson, M. S. "Techniques for the Measurement of Cost-Benefit in
        Information Centres," *Aslib Proceedings* 25:164-185 (May 1973).
Modern management techniques are used to evaluate the profitability and value of information services. Program budgeting, taken from management by objectives, is used to prepare cost-activity and cost-function analyses. Alternative costs for maintenance of the program are derived by applying basic critical examination, activity sampling, and work study principles.

1245.   Maier, Joan M. "Scientist Versus Machine Search Services: We Are the
        Missing Link," *Special Libraries* 65:180-188 (April 1974).
Librarians at Boulder Laboratories have campaigned to increase awareness and utilization of computerized data bases by personal interviews, seminars, surveys, and critiques. Describes results of a survey of 101 scientists, including evaluations of manual and machine searches. Concludes in regard to computerized searches that 1) they are best done at the beginning of a project, 2) funds for these searches should be requested as part of the research budget, 3) the degree of satisfaction is directly related to how early the request was submitted, 4) the human interpreter is essential.

1246.   Martyn, John. "Evaluation of Specialized Information Centers," *The
        Information Scientist* 4:123-135 (September 1970).
Four specialized information centers were studied in terms of cost effectiveness and usability. Functions of the centers and methods of evaluation are described, including analysis and cost analysis by means of flow charts and the assignment of values to activities. Difficulties in interpreting routines and systematizing unsystematic procedures are described. The author concludes that a simple and easily applied method of evaluation is still in the future.

1247. Montgomery, K. L. "Factors Affecting Search Time in a Document Retrieval System." Unpublished Ph.D. dissertation, University of Pittsburgh, 1972.

1248. Morikawa, N. "Experimental Study of Relevance Judgments in the Literature Searching Process (resume in English)," *Library and Information Science*, No. 12:259-274 (1974).

Describes studies carried out on librarians, students, and research workers in regard to whether relevance judgments were influenced by subject specialties. Search questions covered both basic and clinical medicine. Results are described which indicate that subject specialty did influence relevance judgments.

1249. Olive, G., and others. "Studies to Compare Retrieval Using Titles with That Using Index Terms: SDI from Nuclear Science Abstracts," *Journal of Documentation* 29:169-191 (June 1973).

This study compares retrieval using titles to that using index terms in an SDI system covering a range of subjects. Results indicated that title searches were almost as effective as searching by subject categories. Recall was higher for subject categories, but each system missed many items found by the others. Recall performance of titles depended on the length of the title. For titles over 100 characters, recall was as good as for subject categories. Reasons for recall failure of the subject category search were: 1) differences between user interests and keyword profiles, 2) differences in specificity between user needs and terms, 3) no terms assigned, 4) profile too narrow, 5) lack of cross references. Failures in title searches were caused by: 1) concepts not in title, 2) non-descriptive title, 3) poor truncation of title, 4) terms too closely linked, 5) concepts not included in profile. Precision failures for subject categories were due to failures in profiling or profiles not explicit. For title words such failures were due to poor truncation, too general a profile, inappropriate terms, and poor communication with user. Failures of precision in both methods were due to the user changing his mind, and to differences in specificity of questions and search terms.

1250. Parry, A. A., R. G. Linford, and Janet Rich. "Computer Literature Searches— A Comparison of the Performance of Two Commercial Systems in an Interdisciplinary Subject," *Information Scientist* 8:179-187 (December 1974).

Searches were done in an interdisciplinary subject in the area of science in two data bases, Chemical Abstracts Condensates, and Automatic Subject Citation Alert based on *Science Citation Index*. Of the retrieved citations considered to be relevant, only 21 percent were retrieved by both systems. The authors discuss the reasons for this and conclude that the two systems are complementary and should be continued for best coverage. They also note that some hand searching and follow-up reference work must be done to obtain full coverage.

1251. Penner, Rudolf J. "The Practice of Charging Users for Information Services: A State of the Art Report," *Journal of the American Society for Information Science* 21:67-69 (January-February 1970).

At this time, charging for searches is not common and data for specific costs are difficult to compare in a meaningful way. The literature on billing and cost-accounting systems is discussed. A chart is included giving unit costs for each segment of the retrieval process such as indexing, structuring and analyzing a search, etc., and the source study and date for each unit cost are given. Costs of computerized versus manual searches are included. The author notes that libraries either do not do cost accounting or do not wish figures released. One authority suggests that librarians are frightened of the costs of automation and they do not know or want to know the cost of their present systems. Extensive bibliography.

1252. Rees, A. H. "The Relevance of Relevance to the Testing and Evaluation of Document Retrieval Systems," *Aslib Proceedings* 18:316-324 (November 1966).

This article is concerned with research done at Case Western Reserve University on relevance judgment. Information retrieval systems are based on the concept of relevance, but little experimental observation has been done. Studies of user behavior are necessary to design systems that can determine which information is significant and provide it in concentrated form. The author discusses the studies done at Case Western Reserve on patterns, variability, and basis of relevance judgments and, on the basis of this, advances a theory of relevance.

1253. Salton, Gerald. **Information Storage and Retrieval, Reports on Evaluation, Clustering and Feedback.** Springfield, Va., Clearinghouse for Federal Scientific and Technical Information, 1967. 346p. ERIC Document ED020748.

The first section, on evaluation, summarizes retrieval results from 60 different text analysis experiments. The second and third parts are devoted to experiments where the user participated in the retrieval process. Feedback information is used to improve subsequent searches.

1254. Saracevic, T. "Comparative Effects of Titles, Abstracts, and Full Texts on Relevance Judgments." In *American Society for Information Science, Proceedings, Volume 6.* pp. 293-299.

Describes results of a study in which 99 questions were searched by information retrieval systems for 22 users and 1,086 documents retrieved. These documents were presented to users in three different forms—titles, abstracts, and full texts—to see how well users could judge relevance from shorter forms. Results show that of 207 documents judged relevant from the full text, 131 were so judged from titles, and 160 from abstracts.

1255. Saracevic, Tefko. "The Concept of Relevance in Information Science: An Historical Review." In Saracevic, Tefko, ed. *Introduction to Information Science*, New York, Bowker, 1970. pp. 111-151.

A detailed study covering operation of information retrieval systems and relevance, theories, system performance and relevance, definitions and hypotheses, experiments, synthesis, and relevance-related distributions. Includes bibliography.

1256. Scott, E. J., H. M. Townley, and B. T. Stern. "A Technique for the Evaluation of a Commercial Information Service," *Information Storage and Retrieval* 7:147-165 (November 1971).

Discusses an evaluation of the DRUGDOC service. Timeliness, selectivity, and indexing were evaluated by comparing journal articles chosen by an organization as relevant with those found by the DRUGDOC service. Citations appeared in DRUGDOC after 11 weeks of receipt of the issue. The average number of descriptors per article was 8.1. Pilot studies on SDI profiles produced 192 hits from 2,302 items with only six relevant items missed.

1257.　Vickers, P. H. "Cost Survey of Mechanized Information Systems," *Journal of Documentation* 29:258-280 (September 1973).
Covers a cost survey of 18 operational computer-based information systems in Europe and the USA, using a structured cost analysis scheme. These systems include data base producers and self-contained systems that create their own data bases. Unit costs have been computed for most operations, and these are discussed. Results show that costs are affected more significantly by system management, salary variations, and productivity of staff than by such factors as depth of indexing, data preparation methods, or computer programming. Total operating budgets and patterns of cost distribution, including overhead, are discussed.

1258.　Standera, O. R. "Costs and Effectiveness in the Evolution of an Information System: A Case Study," *Journal of the American Society for Information Science* 25:203-207 (May 1974).
A case study is used to illustrate how cost and effectiveness studies are related and how they should be developed and carried out. These procedures should be developed with the system and should be an integral part of the system. Cost-effectiveness can be measured by cost per relevant hit and cost per question (or user). This allows comparisons to be made among individual services and months and also provides planning and budgeting data.

AUTHOR INDEX

TITLE INDEX

273